# COSMIC ACCOUNTING:
## A JOURNEY TO ENLIGHTENMENT

"Shanti Paradise - Peaceful Ways"
Sedona, Arizona, the first day of spring 2008

*"Life was given that we might find the eternal life.
Peace was given that we might find the eternal peace."*
*--Paramhansa Yogananda--*

Copyright © 2012 T. Indeara Hanoomansingh

All rights reserved. No part of this book may be used or reproduced by any means, graphic, electronic, or mechanical, including photocopying, recording, taping or by any information storage retrieval system without the written permission of the publisher except in the case of brief quotations embodied in critical articles and reviews.

Balboa Press books may be ordered through booksellers or by contacting:

Balboa Press
A Division of Hay House
1663 Liberty Drive
Bloomington, IN 47403
www.balboapress.com
1-(877) 407-4847

ISBN: 978-1-4525-4340-6 (sc)
ISBN: 978-1-4525-4341-3 (hc)
ISBN: 978-1-4525-4339-0 (e)

Library of Congress Control Number: 2011961495

Because of the dynamic nature of the Internet, any web addresses or links contained in this book may have changed since publication and may no longer be valid. The views expressed in this work are solely those of the author and do not necessarily reflect the views of the publisher, and the publisher hereby disclaims any responsibility for them.

The author of this book does not dispense medical advice or prescribe the use of any technique as a form of treatment for physical, emotional, or medical problems without the advice of a physician, either directly or indirectly. The intent of the author is only to offer information of a general nature to help you in your quest for emotional and spiritual well-being. In the event you use any of the information in this book for yourself, which is your constitutional right, the author and the publisher assume no responsibility for your actions.

Any people depicted in stock imagery provided by Thinkstock are models, and such images are being used for illustrative purposes only.
Certain stock imagery © Thinkstock.

Printed in the United States of America

Balboa Press rev. date: 04/13/2012

# COSMIC ACCOUNTING:
## A JOURNEY TO ENLIGHTENMENT

*Nine Keys for a Life in Balance*

Indeara Hanoomansingh, Author
Jonathan Eastman, Editor

# DEDICATION

Firstly I would like to offer praises to the Great Masters. My love for them is beyond measure, and this book would not be possible without their guidance. To the Divine Mother who sustains all life in the universe. She fills all of creation with her unconditional love as the Goddess who heals our hearts. To the Sages, Great Saints, and Masters from all walks of life, I bow to their lotus feet for their divine teachings in the spirit of this work. This one lifetime of mine is not enough to repay their kindness.

To my mother Moonwattie Surujnarine, who passed away on June 16, 1982, she is the poet in my heart. She whispered her last words in my father's ear on the eve of her death, and her dream was for us to live in a sacred world. Mom was like a Moon Goddess whose cosmic beams shone through my soul. It was not her presence alone that graced me, but her absence which shaped my destiny, and the story in this book.

I follow in the footsteps of the great teachers who expanded our spiritual awareness. I dedicate my heartfelt gratitude to Lao Tzu, Paramhansa Yogananda, Krishnamurti, Dr. Wayne Dyer, Dr. David R. Hawkins, M.D., Ph.D., John Gray, Ph.D., Jack Canfield, Hale Dwoskin, Catherine Ponder, Dr. Deepak Chopra, Caroline Myss, Don Miguel Ruiz, Eckhart Tolle, and countless others who led the way in new thinking. I build upon their wisdom to integrate spiritual ideals, and how they relate to our collective consciousness, so that we can achieve a balanced lifestyle.

# ACKNOWLEDGEMENTS

Special thanks to the entire Balboa Press Hay House team, and my Publishing Consultant Joan Schaublin for getting this book to you. They were a tremendous help for me as a first time author. My sincere gratitude goes out to my beloved, Jonathan, for his patience, diligence, love, support, and the years of sacrifices that we made to make this dream come true. I hope the blessings return to him a thousand times.

To our family, circle of friends, and clients who supported us, I hope each and every word that flows through these pages will enrich their lives. I would like to thank my dad, Pertab Baba, for teaching me discipline, hard work, and dedication to achieving my dreams. To my sisters Donna, Sasha, and Anna, my brother Sunny, and brothers-in-law, Wasir and Krishna, I feel blessed to be part of our family, thank you for allowing me to fly free. To my nieces and nephews: Nadia, Brianna, Justin, Brian, Christopher, and Kevin, they are a most special part of my heart. I hope that their futures will be sprinkled with eternal joy.

To my relatives, especially my cousins, I love and miss them very much. To my uncle Chaitram and his wife Ahilia, thank you for the invaluable suggestions and feedback. Special thanks to Greg and Gigi Alexander, David Cutler, Audrey Stephens, Lori Stevenson, Carter Young, and Luci Gaudreau for their input. I am ever grateful to all of my Professors at the City University of New York, Queens College for their knowledge, wisdom, diligence, and how much they taught me about the world of accounting.

For you the reader, it is my wish that you will get to explore, and soar into the higher realms of enlightenment within these pages. I wish you a miraculous search for your true *Self*, and the rediscovery of your divine purpose. It is my wish that you cherish this spiritual gem as much as I loved writing it, and gift this message to those whom you love. Together with the highest and best good for all, we can co-create a most beautiful, enlightened, and peaceful world.

# CONTENTS

**Dedication** .................................................................................. vi

**Acknowledgements**................................................................... vii

**Foreword** ................................................................................... xii

**Introduction** .............................................................................. xv

**Chapter by Chapter Description**........................................... xxiii

**Chapter 1   Our First Destination** ....................................... 1

Accounting for Life – My Journey Begins

**Chapter 2   Our Second Destination**................................... 24

Find Your Infinite True *Self* with A Personal Inventory

**Chapter 3   Our Third Destination** .................................... 44

Ancient Native Voices – A World Out of Balance
Wisdom for a Life in Balance

**Chapter 4   Our Fourth Destination** ................................... 61

Reclaiming Your Divine *Self* – Realizing Enlightenment
Spiritual Accountability
Our Nature As Beings of Light

**Chapter 5   Our Fifth Destination**....................................... 87

Ancient *Vedic* Wisdom – Moving Beyond Enlightenment
The Cosmic Plan – Key to Wealth

**Chapter 6   Our Sixth Destination** .................................... 117

Make Empowered Decisions – Uncover the Power of Personal Choice
Magical Miracles in Accountability

**Chapter 7    Our Seventh Destination**..................................................137

Accrual Accounting – Synchronizing Universal Laws with Profits
Consistently Walk on the Pathway of Peace

**Chapter 8    Our Eighth Destination** ..................................................160

Principles to Stand in Your Integrity
Bringing it all Together for Success

**Chapter 9    Our Ninth Destination**....................................................171

The Life Balance Process for Inner Transformation
The 9 Keys for a Life in Balance

# LIST OF ILLUSTRATIONS

1. Shanti Paradise–Peaceful Ways
2. Time for Reflection–Red Robin
3. Lotus–Transcendence
4. Ceremonial Fire–Letting Go
5. Immortality–Light of Consciousness
6. Lord Nataraja–Cosmic Dancer–A Metaphysical Reality
7. Thrilled–Expression of Gratitude
8. Synchronicity–A Divine Transmission
9. Delicate Blossoms–Perfect Symphony of Souls
10. Holy Sage–Altar Piece

# LIST OF TABLES

1. Sacred Messages in Numbers
2. The Four Pillars of *Vedic* Wisdom: Divine Purpose, Pursuit of Wealth, Enjoyment of Wealth, Spiritual Freedom
3. The Decision Making Flow Chart
4. The Feng Shui Nine Trigrams

# FOREWORD

It is my honor to write the foreword to such a special book, and I will forever be grateful. It took some time to think of the best way to word an introduction for someone who means so much to me. Indeara has been a guide, friend, and partner since April 2002. We met at the Grand Canyon at sunset after some amazing synchronicities. After the powerful experiences that I had within hours of meeting her, I came to the realization that this was no ordinary "chance encounter."

I soon figured out that Indeara was not just an ordinary person. She was already teaching me how to feel the energies of the Grand Canyon, as we were staring at the sun going down near Bright Angel's Peak; and I didn't immediately know what she was talking about, but since then she has shown me many of the inexplicable things about our reality. Most of us can't see with our regular eyes what Indeara can see with her spiritual sight and enlightened awareness. We have been on this journey together ever since.

I had a scientific outlook on the world, and I was skeptical about many things, especially the things I could not see. Indeara has helped me realize the true nature of our reality, which is constantly affected by our thoughts and emotions. When I projected skepticism, I would experience a reality that proved exactly what I was thinking, and I would shoot down positive and miraculous occurrences, before truly understanding what they meant. I was usually right to be skeptical, as many of the things that I once questioned surfaced with truth, and crumbled to reveal the façade in society some years later. Despite my difficulties warming up to new and exciting ideas, there is an honesty and genuineness that she emits that I couldn't deny.

The unconquerable will of such a pure soul touched my heart, and helped me feel free once again. After almost a decade of witnessing many healings, stunningly accurate predictions, transformations, and energetic shifts in people's lives, I am more of a believer in her gifts than anyone can be. I invite you to listen to what she has to say in *Cosmic Accounting: A Journey to Enlightenment*. It's well worth its weight in gold, and the teachings are invaluable. If you can be open to the harmonious energy and intentions put forth in it, then I assure you that it will have a profound effect on changing your life for the better. Read this book with the understanding that Indeara sees the world, both past and future, in a way that few people alive today can. She has an ageless wisdom about her.

Throughout the years that I have known her, I have come to witness countless amazing occurrences with her connection to the Great Masters, and some can only be deemed miracles. *Cosmic Accounting: A Journey to Enlightenment* is a culmination of her experiences with them. *The 9 Keys for a Life in Balance* can help you when you follow the simple and divinely inspired steps. I found it intriguing that so many different types of information have been synthesized into just one book.

It is best to give you a little background about Indeara as a teacher. In her *Meditation Classes* and *Peace Paradise Wellness Retreats*, I have seen her use her gifts to transform people's lives. She has also been a friend to thousands of people on their spiritual journey. These lessons and insights into spiritual wisdom do not come without tests. Throughout the years, every day through numerous experiences, many have come to witness what I have seen. Many people have been truly grateful for their experiences with her. Yet, Indeara does not like to take credit for any of these transformational healings. In fact, she says if their Higher *Self* speaks to her, she is not afraid to use her gifts to help others. It takes real courage and strength to speak the truth from the Divine Beings, and pass on their messages to empower us.

This wonderful work, *Cosmic Accounting: A Journey to Enlightenment* weaves together Eastern and Western philosophies. These principles and *Nine Keys*, when practiced, can lead us to an enlightened, prosperous, and purposeful society. I really enjoy Indeara's sense of humor, and I am entertained by her words; it is a lot of fun to read about her journey. It is refreshing because she is so genuine that it can be hilarious. I learned that enlightenment and spirituality can surely have some great humor. It's like a stage show and a game in the end, so we can have fun.

*Cosmic Accounting: A Journey to Enlightenment* sheds light on some of the darkness that has created an imbalance in our world. It expresses a unique twist on ancient and modern wisdom. The universality of this book encourages everyone to stay on their chosen spiritual paths, unlike many organizations that believe enlightenment and spiritual advancement is only through their chosen way. Indeara has been loyal and devoted, and she has had to overcome many challenges, but she has shown a lot of courage in not selling her soul. Many believe that they don't have any other option but to settle for less than they deserve. With these teachings, I have been able to overcome my fears, and finally step into my power.

*Cosmic Accounting: A Journey to Enlightenment* can give you hope to overcome many challenges and difficulties in this world. Many people are getting out of balance, and the imbalances are affecting the environment as well. Indeara shares that we as humanity have to understand that there are many Angelic Beings we cannot see, and they are connected to us. These benevolent beings are holding our delicate world together, and they are gifts to humanity. Hope is not lost for the world of existence. Enjoy the cosmic journey.

Jonathan Eastman

# INTRODUCTION

As we embark on this cosmic journey of transformation together, I hope that you will find the experiences along the way fascinating. Meaningful coincidences occur because everything in the cosmos operates in divine timing. I encourage you to take a moment out of your normal routine, and welcome the divine flow of synchronicities into your life. Make room for the profound messages within these pages which can lead you to enlightenment. This timely book is like an oracle that not only poses the questions and provides the answers that you may be seeking, it also gives you a chance to transform your life by understanding a cosmic, higher perspective.

More than theoretical presumptions, these principles are based on my personal journey as an accountant, timeless truths of enlightenment, and ancient wisdom. If these universal principles have transformed my life, they certainly can help you to do the same. It is said, if we pose the questions, the answers already exist. I questioned whether there could be a global prosperity movement, and a *"Global Enlightened Business Network."*

Were there permanent solutions to economic, political, societal, environmental, and corporate problems? Were we suffering unnecessarily? Did our environment and how we treat each other have anything to do with the difficulties that we were facing? What role did accounting play? How would we go about resolving the problem of poverty? What would be a fair and new medium of exchange with the monetary system? Was there anything that individuals could do to contribute to resolving those problems? How could we as individuals live a harmonious, prosperous, and balanced lifestyle?

I once thought that accounting was only a way to look at financial reports, but I heard the same "accountability" word everywhere. Corporate accountability, financial accountability, spiritual accountability, personal accountability, environmental accountability, and political accountability were at the forefront. It dawned on me that we were dealing with a Universal Cosmic Law, and I termed it "The Law of Accountability."

Why is it that we usually seek to understand the great mystery of life when tragedy occurs? Is it the pain which prompts us to look beyond the ordinary into the world of extraordinary reality? I was once no exception to this fact. However, I am now able to transcend into the world of Angelic Beings and Ascended Masters, and would love to show you how you can do the same. My journey to enlightenment began with excruciating pain that brought me to my knees after the tragic events of September 11, 2001, and the murder of my beloved sister, Staff Sergeant Nalini D. Singh.

On that cold October night in 2002, the news of her death shook me to my core, and I thought I would be numb in pain forever. It was almost as if the neurons in my brain and hands refused to communicate with each other. Her death triggered the pain of losing my mother many years earlier. Nalini was just twenty-eight years old. How could she have passed away from this world so quickly?

I stared at the computer screen at work, trying to cope in disbelief. Unable to cope, and in search of anyone or anything to stop the pain, I moved away from the big city life in New York. I wanted answers. Leaving behind everyone and everything, I did some soul searching and embarked on a spiritual journey into the mysterious metaphysical world to conquer my pain and suffering.

Many years later, I realized that her death served as a catalyst for my spiritual awakening. The challenges of our lives are like pillars of truth which plant the seeds for our ultimate freedom from the bondage of this physical reality. I dived into the unknown, and explored the mystical realms, which eventually served as a way for me to regain happiness and a connection to my true *Self*. I invite you to join me on this quest for eternal bliss, and our immortal nature as beings of light.

In the words of the Great Master, Paramhansa Yogananda, if it were not for pain, would you want to seek your real purpose to find your eternal divine *Self*? On this cosmic journey, you and I will explore the nature of our higher *Self*. Throughout this book I use words such as cosmic creator, source, higher power, divine consciousness, and higher *Self* to explain a spiritual energy beyond words. Also, whenever I use capitalized letters to refer to the Angelic Beings, Great Masters, Eastern Mystics, Yogis, Angel of Peace, Angel of Transformation, and Angel of Wealth, I am referring to specific beings that I have met and worked with. *Self* is the common thread in all of existence; it encompasses all that was, is, and ever will be. It is that Supreme Being which allows for all life in the entire cosmos to function in such grandeur.

My hope is that my story will move you to begin the search for that part of you which is the everlasting permanence of spirit, unlike the physical body which is impermanent in nature. This cosmic journey will take you beyond the world of mundane activities, stress, and concerns, to the realm of miracles and enlightenment. I will not ask you to forsake your path of spirituality either. It is my belief that everyone is free to learn from the divine teachings of any saint or sage who has graced our planet. It is not necessary for you to give up your business, career, family, relationships, home, or living a normal life to reach the epitome of your true *Self*. The path to enlightenment is no longer restricted to the isolated forests. The modern day yogi or yogini may have given up the loin cloth as an ascetic to wear a leopard print skirt or pants, and walk around in the jungles of city life.

Even though the world has changed, the process to experience enlightenment has not. It still requires strong faith in the higher spiritual laws, some dedication, and a little bit of sacrifice. This amazing journey of cosmic consciousness will show you that freedom was inside all along. The messages of the Great Sages will transform your life. This story is based on my personal experiences, and knowledge of peace, faith, and a higher power. Since I have been able to achieve a life in balance and happiness, I believe anyone can. It is my sincere wish that you will be able to take comfort in challenging times knowing that a divine helping hand is ever close by, and always within reach.

This fascinating journey is set in the sacred and mystical lands of Sedona, Arizona. On this divine quest you will rediscover an inner wisdom and power residing within you. It will leave you with a feeling of confidence, and the realization that thoughts are real, and indeed manifest to prove our reality. In 1997, when I was a sophomore in college, I had an intense burning desire to become an enlightened person. More than anything else, I wondered what it would be like to be infused with the divine consciousness of golden light. For most of my life, since early childhood, I was fascinated by Angels, the Hindu Deities, and the teachings of Jesus Christ. I sought a deep sense of connection with the cosmos and all that exists. On the full moon in July of 2008, my desire for the experience of becoming enlightened was fulfilled.

Beginning on the 4$^{th}$ of July, 2007, I spent about fifteen to seventeen hours in daily meditation. About a year later, I received an email regarding a celebration in India called *Guru Purnima*. The email stated that on the full moon in July, many of the sages who once graced our planet would come back to the earth plane and bless humanity. *Guru* is a Sanskrit word which means teacher, and the one who removes ignorance and darkness from our lives. *Purnima* means the full moon. *Guru Purnima*, the full moon of the Guru, occurs once every year, and honors all teachers who give humanity the light of wisdom and knowledge.

In a moment of humility, sincerity, and a bit of skepticism, I looked up at the beautiful golden full moon above the Sedona red rocks in awe, and said, "Flying Gurus on the earth plane, and the veil is thin, yeah right!" I remember humbly asking that if there were indeed beings of light and such a thing as enlightenment, that I should receive a divine sign. What happened next is the subject of chapters 4, 5, and 6. I entered a cosmic stream of intelligent light which can be described like being in heaven, and communicated with heavenly beings that were pure translucent light, and that one moment changed my perspective on life forever. I felt bliss beyond words, and experienced unity with all of existence. I vanished from my physical body, and became immersed into a world of divine consciousness, and I called it the *"inner world."*

As I reentered my physical body, the *prana*, which is a Sanskrit word for vital life, I experienced it as an intelligent light, communicated that I should bring back a piece of that experience to share with humanity. In my Peace Paradise Wellness Retreats, and Meditation Classes, I share that experience so that many can feel that divine energy. After answering the questions in these chapters, you can begin to learn techniques that move the *inner world* of consciousness to help you create the things you want in your life, and eliminate the things that you don't want.

I realized much suffering in our lives is due to the fact that we perceive our bodies as our existence. Yet, the nature of the human body is death, disease, and old age. What would happen if we lived our lives as if we were already immortal? Why fear death, and wait until it arrives to experience eternal peace? Dying is only the doorway to immortality, and in every ending there is always a new beginning. Since the fact remains that all of us will one day exit the physical body, we are pleasantly reminded that our journey through life is what makes living worthwhile. Why fear the end, when we can remember enlightenment which gives us the freedom to live our lives to the fullest now?

Once we step out of the consciousness of the body, which is based in matter, we can experience untold amounts of joy, inner peace, and bliss, which come from our immortal bodies of light. That immortal essence of the soul, whose nationality is spirit, and country is all pervading consciousness, cannot be confined. We are connected to everything and everyone in the entire universe. Anyone who sincerely meditates toward the goal of enlightenment will surely reach their destination. I encountered the beings of light in the quest to find my divine purpose, and discovered my true *Self*.

Join me on this cosmic journey where you can discover your true *Self* in the process. This *Self* is distinguished from the individual logical little self because *Self* is the higher nature of our being; immeasurable and boundless is this great spirit of life. *Self* is governed by the creative, and defies all logic. There are no words to describe it. In order for you to connect with your true *Self*, you must have a firsthand experience of the *inner world* consciousness of divinity. Once you are able to connect with the boundless part of yourself, you can persevere through life, no matter how challenging it may seem.

It is said that establishing a connection to the great masters is not a difficult task. A connection can be made through thought energies, which function very much like a wireless cell phone. To feel a master's presence, you can get an image of your favorite master, and simply focus your love, devotion, and attention on their eyes, then humbly request their guidance.

I pleaded with the Great Master, Yogananda, after a tragic incident around the 4th of July, 2007. My cries for help were heard. It was almost as if Yogananda invisibly guided me to recovery. His saving grace came when I walked into Barnes & Noble in Flagstaff, Arizona, and found his book *Autobiography of a Yogi*. The book was sitting on a table, far from its designated section, and seemed as if it was conveniently left where I could see it. I bought it, and read it for almost three days without stopping. It was my first glimpse at the world of mystery, magic, and miracles of the saints of India. I made photocopies of the Masters from the book *Autobiography of a Yogi*, and simply stared into their eyes out of curiosity. I was able to connect with Yogananda by simply concentrating on his image. Many centers and spiritual schools around the world still honor the Great Master's teachings to this day.

In *Autobiography of a Yogi*, Yogananda introduced Mahavatar Babaji as the Yogi-Christ of India. Babaji is an Immortal Master of light who sincerely cares for humanity and our suffering. Yogananda described that, a long time ago, *kriya yoga* was reserved only for hermits who lived in the forest. At that time, Lahiri Mahasaya requested that Mahavatar Babaji relax the rules of *kriya yoga* to include householders. Mahavatar Babaji agreed, and he assigned Master Lahiri Mahasaya the task of teaching *kriya yoga* to householders.

Master Mahasaya then taught his disciple Swami Sri Yukteswar, who in turn became Yogananda's teacher. Sri Yukteswar wrote *The Holy Science*. With great foresight, he saw the psychological, physical, and spiritual suffering of modern man. Swami Sri Yukteswar wanted to bring universality and spiritual harmony to all nations. Ever concerned for the well-being of humanity, Sri Yukteswar showed us that the teachings of Christ and Krishna shared a common message.

Our prayers do not go unheard in the great cosmic skies. Ever present, the masters guide our destinies. I found that it was easy to connect with Master Lahiri Mahasaya in the same way that I connected with Yogananda, by meditating on his image. Lahiri and I shared a few things in common. Like me, Master Mahasaya was an accountant until the age of thirty-three when he met the great Mahavatar Babaji.

Lahiri Mahasaya said if one utters the name "Babaji" with devotion, they will attract a spiritual blessing immediately. These great beings want to alleviate our suffering. By fusing together Eastern and Western disciplines, their intention was to combine the best of both worlds, where the Easterners could learn from the materialism of the West, and the Westerners could learn from the spirituality of the East. Paramhansa Yogananda came to America in 1920 to share this important message from Babaji with us.

In Babaji's philosophy, it was better to earn one's living than to depend on charity. Although I did not recognize who he was at the time, a vision of Mahavatar Babaji came to me in a dream. I saw a youthful masculine figure whose eyes were filled with the energy of mesmerizing beautiful lights, and as he looked at me, they dazzled like rainbows of golden hue. I was awestruck with feelings of intense unconditional love that were so magical that they transformed me, and I felt instantaneous bliss.

With his divine inspiration, I felt compelled to facilitate the process of enlightenment for those who were ready. I pleaded with Babaji that times were difficult for many people, and extreme measures were being taken. I felt that since Master Mahasaya could plea with Mahavatar Babaji to relax the *kriya yoga* rules for householders, maybe, I could make a similar plea on behalf of humanity.

I felt that working men and women deserved enlightenment simply for working, because they were already disciplined like yogis. They already possessed all the qualities required for enlightenment, such as self control, discipline, and sacrificing for the greater good. I thought that the everyday working person should be graced with inner peace, and the knowledge of enlightenment to help ease their burdens and stress. My dream is to create a *Global Enlightened Business Network*, in service to the Great Masters, where we can connect with our soul's divine purpose. Amazingly, the Great Masters must have had compassion for us, because *Cosmic Accounting: A Journey to Enlightenment* serves as an instrument for their sacred message.

During the initial years of writing this book, I meditated almost daily on the Great Immortal Master of Light, Mahavatar Babaji. Fortunately, it must have been divine timing to share this message. There is indeed an interconnectedness of *Spirit-Wealth-Empowerment*™. The divine qualities required for one can be attributed to the accomplishment of all three, where money and enlightenment are part of the same cosmic energy source.

During the editing phase I repeatedly heard the name "Master Kuthumi." I purchased an image of him and meditated on it. He touched my heart during the final phase of this book. Master Kuthumi's energy was much closer to our earth plane than Yogananda's. Master Kuthumi truly cares for the world's finances. I hope that I am forever humbled by his invisible presence. I felt blessed to work with Master Kuthumi, and I look forward to learning about many more teachers, and ascended masters to share their amazing energies and messages with you. In the end, I realized the Great Masters are all part of the one essence of cosmic energy, regardless of the individual names that I called them.

It feels wonderful to have the words that I wrote remain pure and true to the Great Masters. Sometimes their words were magical, yet, at other times they were direct and truthful. I meditated on Master Lahiri Mahasaya's image, and I asked the Great Merciful Master what to name the book. As I stared at the twinkle in his eyes, he bestowed the title with so much love. I heard the title of the book *"Cosmic Accounting"* resounding in my ears.

A few years passed as I wrote on and off, and I continued my day job as an accountant. The completion of this book was put on hold for many years, but with divine timing, the rest of the title appeared effortlessly. Several years later the full title, *Cosmic Accounting: A Journey to Enlightenment*, came in synchronicity with my meditations, and inspirations from the Great Masters. I hope that you will enjoy reading it as much as I loved writing it, and share their sacred message with many others, so that we can all live in an enlightened world.

## How You Can Get the Most Out of Cosmic Accounting: A Journey to Enlightenment

Although you can read this book any which way you would like to, I recommend reading it from cover to cover, because it is best if you follow the divine principles, one step at a time. It's like no other book you've read because it holds the keys to enlightenment through everyday work. Give yourself a moment to just be you because for the most part, our society teaches us that we are not good enough. As you become more spiritually awakened and conscious of how your thoughts create your reality, you will be able to harness the power of thought to change circumstances that prevent you from living the life of your dreams.

Rather than waiting for the right moment, I encourage you to take baby steps towards your dreams. Little things done consistently, make a big difference, because our habits shape our destiny. I am writing my story so that you may take courage and strength from it. It may take some time and planning to eventually achieve success and your dreams, but never give up. I've heard many people say they put off their heart's deepest desires due to financial or other reasons. If you have a great idea that you have been putting off for a long time, think about how much more beautiful our world would be with your visions and dreams. One little step taken towards your dream each day brings you hundreds of steps closer to its manifestation and therefore, making your dreams become reality.

Be sure to keep an open mind as you read, and surrender all of your thoughts, this way you will be able to grasp new ideas, concepts, and divine messages more easily. Your inner guidance will be like a lighthouse on the dark seas of life. You will have to follow your heart as you enter the divine path. When you take the time to know your heart, your soul's destination is revealed to show you an enlightened perspective. Remember, all that matters is your train of thought. It does not matter if you are sitting in a coffee shop, in your living room, in an office, at a train station, meditating on a mountain, or on a retreat, you will be able to connect with your true *Self*.

If you can, allow yourself to relax with soothing sounds of relaxing, classical, or sacred music. Next, clear your thoughts, and empty your mind by using your breath. You can release tension and connect to the intelligent life force within you. Breathe deeply to awaken your super-conscious state of mind. Our breath is our connection to our heart because it brings oxygen to fuel the pump which works tirelessly, twenty-four hours a day, seven days a week to keep us alive. Our heartbeat is the connection to the entire universe and the heartbeat of Mother Earth. After that, you can then begin a silent meditation for a few minutes to clear your mind of chatter, and this will help you to connect to the Great Masters. Sip a warm cup of herbal tea or your favorite drink, and allow these words to permeate and digest in your consciousness to soothe you.

Even though *Cosmic Accounting: A Journey to Enlightenment* is filled with the enchantment of synchronicity, it is not a magic pill. The real magic of divinity is hidden inside of you like a treasure, and it convinces you to uncover the keys to your higher *Self* within "*yourself*." By following the 9 simple keys, you can begin to live your life in balance.

# Chapter by Chapter Description
## A Modern Yogini's Journey

Chapter 1: On our first destination, I embark on a trip down memory lane and travel back in time. You can explore a glimpse of my personal life journey. I show you my background with a chronology of events that led me to the present moment. I share a fascinating journey from the tropical lands of South America, to New York City, and then to the sacred, mystical lands of Sedona.

Chapter 2: On the second destination, I go on an inward journey to meet the Eastern Mystics and Yogis. Here, you can explore the inward journey where the tree of knowledge blossoms. When we take the time for contemplation, it bears the fruits of wisdom. I explain a basic and concise definition of many of the accounting terms used throughout the book. Together, we delve within ourselves with an understanding of the perpetual and periodic inventory systems. We track our soul's progress as individuals interconnected to the larger system by using questions and self inquiry, which is one of the most effective tools for discovering our true *Self*.

Chapter 3: On the third destination, I take a journey to the American Southwest to visit the Hopis. You will get a chance to explore the values of these ancient people who understood the cosmic nature of our being. They share the importance of balance and the Law of Accountability from a galactic perspective. I give a comparison to the Dogons of Mali. Together, we get a magical glimpse of the world as we look through the visionary eyes of a Great Native American Chief. We look at the future costs of natural disasters, such as the oil spill, and do a cosmic accounting, and a balance sheet of the planet Earth. Our journey takes a turn with synchronicity to meet Chief Oren Lyons of the Iroquois Confederacy. We begin to understand the Cosmic Law of Accountability from an environmental and future generation's perspective.

Chapter 4: On the fourth destination, I am introduced to the enlightened Master Kuthumi while driving on Highway 89A. You can explore the journey when I get to visit with my family in New York and Massachusetts, and I make a connection to my ancestors from India. Together we understand karma and its connection to the cosmic accounting of life. We apply the realization principle of accounting, and show how it relates to the realization of enlightenment. We begin to understand the Cosmic Law of Accountability from a spiritual perspective.

Chapter 5: On the fifth destination, we move beyond enlightenment into the cosmic plan. Explore with me, humanity through ancient yogic goggles, to get a better understanding of our true *Self.* We delve further into the Yogis' ancient wisdom to conquer death with the *Vedic* Four Pillars, which are: our divine purpose, the pursuit of wealth, the enjoyment of wealth, and spiritual liberation. We see that debt is like enslavement which shackles us to work the karmic wheel, life after life. Our journey continues to show us how to bring our true *Self* into our work. We learn how to set ourselves free with an enlightened awareness.

Chapter 6: On the sixth destination, we uncover magical miracles with accountability. You can explore the world from the level of electrons, and get to experience bliss beyond words. The magical experience of enlightenment leads us to *Make Empowered Decisions*™. The journey moves us with the Law of Accountability to the level of spiritual and personal accountability. A great message empowers you to remember that you can change anything with just a thought. We enter into a higher awareness to greet the Angels of Peace and Transformation, and the Goddess of Wealth, who is called Divine Mother, *Lakshmi,* in Sanskrit.

Chapter 7: On the seventh destination, we continue on our cosmic journey to a thousand acre ranch in Texas. You can explore as we learn the importance of cooperation and networking, as we enter into an enlightened, cosmic consciousness. We compare the accounting principle of consistency, and learn to make paradigm shifts in our reality with habits that lead us to success. Our journey takes us to the magic which awaits us with the understanding of accrual accounting. Explore with me as we move into a meditation on the future of money, and feel the shift in consciousness of money as a medium of exchange. We learn how to make a direct link to the Divine Mother of Wealth and Abundance. The Law of Accountability shows us the correlation of net worth, and self worth from a spiritual perspective.

Chapter 8: On the eighth destination, I bring all the concepts together. You can explore and learn how to put the enlightened knowledge into practice. We relate to many people around the world, and understand our connection to the energy of life. You can learn how to live in harmony, *har-money,* with this one source of cosmic, intelligent energy, and our collective divine consciousness.

Chapter 9: On the ninth destination, *The Life Balance Process for Inner Transformation*™ is composed of nine keys; it is a step by step approach for inner peace, abundance, and a connection to your higher *Self.* The process can transform your life by showing you the nine areas that are needed for balance spiritually, emotionally, and physically. The process stimulates your mind to find answers from within. You can awaken spiritually, and open your eyes to view the world, like you've never seen it before, no matter how challenging it may be. You can achieve your dreams, and live life to its fullest potential, one choice at a time. Each moment of your life can help you reap the rewards of a bountiful harvest of fulfillment. When you practice the principles in this book, you will be able to achieve inner peace, joy, and happiness.

# CHAPTER 1
## *Accounting for Life – My Journey Begins*

"Time for Reflection – Red Robin"

My amazing journey of transformation began in April 2002, when I took a vacation to the Grand Canyon. Even though each and every day poses new questions for growth and learning, I feel like a caterpillar that emerged from the cocoon, and unfolded its wings as a butterfly. The great mysteries of my life unfolded until I reached the epitome of experiencing enlightenment. I discovered my true *Self*, similar to the stages of metamorphosis, and it was like a larva leaving the chrysalis, which changes its entire genetic structure from a caterpillar to a butterfly. Layer after layer of energy were transformed for me to earn my wings. My life's difficulties can be compared to the struggles within the cocoon. I found that life was like a great adventure which leads to the final stages of becoming one with all of existence, and eventually allows us to fly free.

When I was a child, more than anything else, I wanted to find where my mother went when she passed away. My grandmother told me that Mom was with the Divine, so I searched everywhere to find the Divine. I thought I could make a plea bargain with him or her, to return my mother to me. I felt lost without her love. Like a game of hide and seek, I climbed up trees and searched in the water where the tadpoles and frogs lived. I went to our little farm yard, and chased the chickens, gobbled with the turkeys, quacked and clucked with the ducks, but I didn't find her anywhere.

I then turned my attention to reading stories that comforted and distracted me from the pain and sorrow of missing her. By the time I was eleven, I read many books including *My Book of Bible Stories*, *The Bhagavad Gita*, and *Darwin's Theory of Evolution.* I came to the conclusion that the theory of evolution, and humanity's emergence from apes, was somewhat misguided. I could not find mother there either, and my quest continued. I closed the book on Darwin's theory, and wondered how mother could have come from an earth worm. As I grew up, I understood that mother would not return, and I became determined to find something greater. It was this spiritual quest for my mother which led to my connection with the Divine from a young age.

As a child, discipline, hard work, and practical business application were part of my upbringing. When most of my friends were learning how to count, my dad was teaching me how to do the inventory for our little family restaurant in South America. Mom went to the culinary arts school and she became a Master Chef. She made the most delicious pineapple tarts, pies, and cakes. Mother made good use of the water from the pond in our backyard by planting many exotic fruit trees, such as mango, guava, papaya, coconut, golden apple, grapefruit, orange, lemon, and cassava which were in full bloom. Each day when I woke up, my siblings and I would race around our pond to gather ripe and delicious mangoes to eat.

When I was a baby, my mother gave me quarters to play with from our restaurant's pool table earnings. I had fun playing with those coins, and I thought money was a toy. My favorite treat was vanilla ice cream, and I had many friends because Mom would buy a big one gallon size for all of us. Once we heard the ice cream truck, I would scream in excitement, "Mom, the ice cream truck is coming." The music from the truck would get my friends running out of their houses like mad, ding-ding-ting-dong-ding-dong-ding.

My fondest memories as a child were on the banks of the Atlantic Ocean where the water was once sparkling clear, unlike it is now. The ocean was once tame, and I loved its sandy beaches. Family time was on Sundays at the beach. I would love running along the shoreline, jumping the waves, and chasing the wind. I made mud baths, collected as many sea shells as I could find, and with my bag full of seashells, I skipped along the water's edge. Mother's gaze was always close by, and I loved her so much.

Once every year, on the beach, we celebrated a holiday for charity called *Teerat*. The day was honored because it was told that many of the great saints and sages were disguised as beggars to test our true divinity, and charitable giving nature. On that day there were hundreds of beggars lined up with their arms outstretched. They were asking for donations of money, clothing, or food. Each year up to the age of six, my mother took me with her to give charity. As mom's little helper, my job was to hand out quarters from the one gallon ice cream dish which I cherished, while her job was handing out dollar bills to the outstretched hands.

Those charitable days ended when Mother died. I was devastated, and my life was never going to be the same ever again. Mom had it right with being charitable, because there was always an abundance of food, friends, and relatives around the house. It seemed as if when mother died, she took the magic with her, and the hundreds of people dwindled. Business had taken a bad turn. I learned early on that giving, and being charitable, activates the Law of Reciprocity for us to receive abundance, because when we give, we get back in return.

After Mom passed away, I had my fair share of cleaning up in Skylab's Restaurant, which went on for a few years. When I was nine, I got a break to escape from the difficult work cleaning up the glasses and dishes from the restaurant. The Head Master at my school, No. 59 Primary School in Corentyne, Berbice, gave me an assignment. I was assigned the role of the little banker. Each week, I collected money from the kids and took their deposits to the bank. It was a fun job because I got to take long trips away from home.

Life fast forwarded to when I arrived at JFK International Airport in November 1987. My new life in America began in Queens, New York at the elementary school PS 54Q in the sixth grade. My teenage years and puberty were tough, and I was relieved when it ended. In 1994, I graduated high school and went on to college in the fall. In 1995, I took a part-time job with Citibank as an assistant to a Tax Accountant. I worked for a few Vice Presidents in Citibank's corporate financial control department at 850 Third Avenue in Manhattan. I learned a lot about complex loans and cross border transactions in the Asia Pacific region.

Even though it was a tough and nerve wracking job, it was wonderful to have been of service to the people that I worked with. I found that it was interesting to have a Revenue Officer in our department at Citibank; his job was to help us stay in compliance with the IRS. I worked two jobs part-time and went to school at night. It was very tiring, and that situation lasted for years. At the time, I was a sophomore in college and had no clue what my major would be. I tried my hand at computer science and pre-med classes to no avail.

Then one day Dr. Erlach, who was a Professor of Accounting, gave a lecture at the City University of New York (CUNY), Queens College. I decided to take an entry level accounting class, and it was fun because I remembered some of the business terminology that my dad had taught me as a child. I loved my first accounting class, and did not struggle like I had in pre-med and computer science classes. I was getting A's effortlessly, so naturally, accounting became my major, and I was passionate about it.

Time went on and it was August 1998. I took a job as a Junior Accountant with the New York Board of Rabbis on 10 East 73$^{rd}$ Street in Manhattan. I reported my work to Bob and Jay, who were accountants at an Upper East Side CPA Firm. They were a tremendous help for me as a young accountant. It was a beautiful place to work with Central Park, and the Madison Avenue retail shops across the street. I loved to walk by the designer boutiques that were in Vogue Magazine. Fashion was the "in thing" growing up in New York City. The world of textbook theoretical accounting was not difficult, but it was not fun either. It was a lot of work, but counting the price tags at Vera Wang as I was window shopping and looking at pretty dresses made accounting easier to understand.

Back then I saw accounting as black and white. It was kind of like a journal article dominated by my logical mind. I had no idea that there was such a thing as the creative mind. The only thing that I knew from my pre-med classes, about the creative world of spirit, was that my brain had a right hemisphere and left hemisphere, that is, a left side and right side. The closest that I ever came to understanding the creative mind was when I saw the music and art students from time to time on campus, carrying their sketch pads and guitars.

In June 2001, I graduated with Honors in Accounting, and I was excited when PriceWaterhouseCoopers recruited me to work as an Auditor. I loved auditing and the people at PWC. That was a great job and I received a lot of support from the Partners and Senior Management. I traveled the East Coast from Rochester to Stamford, Connecticut, and it was fun to stay at the Marriott and other beautiful hotels. It was during my job at PriceWaterhouseCoopers that *Cosmic Accounting: A Journey to Enlightenment* took on a life of its own, and began to reveal itself. I had been commuting and working about twenty-two hours per day with only Sunday to rest. Mostly I was too overworked and burnt-out, so I took a much needed vacation to Sedona and the Grand Canyon in April 2002.

The trip changed my destiny, and when I got back to work, I constantly had the urge to write. Even though I was always psychic as a child, it caught my heart by surprise, and the voice of the words in this book changed to wisdom. It was then that the magic of my dreams and intuition began. With time no longer being linear, I was able to see into the future and the past at the same time. Simultaneously, the years began to switch back and forth. The rest of this book is a flow of the magical intuitive world, and how it communicated with me.

## Prophetic Dream of 9/11

I had a dream that warned me not to be in Manhattan on that terrible day of September 11, 2001. The first hint of something going wrong came while I was in my studio apartment in Bayside, New York, where I lived at the time. The night before, on September 10, 2001, I was asleep. As I woke up, I sat on my bed and cried from a nightmare that felt so real. It was the first dream that I would ever write down in minute details.

In my dream, I looked up and saw two crafts that were like UFOs hit a tall building which looked like a skyscraper hotel in Manhattan. I said to myself, "Funny, these are not the same UFOs as the ones from outer space." In my dream state, the pilots of the craft were not aliens. They were humans who wore white space suits like astronauts, and I thought to myself, "These aliens look like government workers." Reality hit the next day when I saw the same images on TV, when the World Trade Center was demolished. A few days later, I saw the same astronaut clothing from my dream. It was the protective white clothing worn by the military and government workers during the anthrax scare.

## My First Encounter with an Angel

The dream continued, and I was looking for a hotel room to sleep. I was led by an invisible being who was giving me a tour of Manhattan hotels. At first, I could hear her, but I could not see what she looked like. As she was taking me from room to room, I saw many people stuck on stair cases, and they were trying to get down. When I got to the stairway I felt so afraid, and I was in a state of pure terror and thought I would die. It was in that moment that the Angel appeared. This Angelic Being was very tall, and seemed to stretch as high as the entire staircase of the World Trade Center.

I became mesmerized by her golden hair which was like translucent, shimmering particles of light that draped her shoulders, and streamed down to her waist. The beautiful Angel was dressed in a long white flowing gown made of transparent, white light. Her presence was real, but she did not have a physical body. She gracefully stood at the top of the staircase, and looked straight into my eyes while she communicated with me telepathically, without moving her lips. She reassured me as she said, "Everything is going to be alright, and many lives will be saved."

To this day I contemplate the meaning of the Angel's words. Afterwards, since that dream proved to be significant, I became open to receiving messages from my dreams. We should keep in mind that our dreams are personal, and are subject to each dreamer's own interpretation. The symbols and experiences are unique to each person's subconscious connection to their own conscious wakeful state. For me personally, the message from the Angelic Being of golden light meant that there was much more to September 11th than was revealed on television.

Deep down inside to the very core of my being, September 11th shook me up. I was never going to be the same because something inside of me changed on that day. Commuting for my job became extremely difficult, and I had to travel for three hours to get to work. One thing led to another, and I no longer worked for PriceWaterhouseCoopers. In 2002, I landed a job working at a smaller CPA Firm in Brooklyn. I owe my most sincere gratitude to a man of high intelligence, Mr. Shah, who was the Audit Director that trained me.

**Tragedy Strikes Again and This Time It Hits Home**

On the morning of October 30, 2002, I sat at my desk in Brooklyn, New York. I clicked away at a calculator, and stared at a blank wall into the distance, almost as if the wall wasn't there. My fingers were moving, but I was seeing a movie on the white wall in front of me. It was as if someone stood behind me with a movie projector. In the beam of light in front of me, I was watching a movie of my childhood. In the movie, I was with my sister, Nalini. We were picking mangoes, chasing each other around when we were kids, and playing dress up, wearing Mom's shoes and clothes that were too big for us. It startled me when my boss came by and asked me something. I saw his lips moving, but could not hear a word that he said. I snapped out of my daydreaming when I heard him say, "Some people take their job for granted."

I received a phone call that night from my other sister, and she said, "Nalini's dead!" All I remember is screaming at the top of my lungs, "No-no-no-no!" and I collapsed to the floor. My cousin ran from his room, and my aunt and uncle ran into the house from the road as they heard my outcry. They helped me stand up. I was in disbelief, and I could not bear the pain. My stomach went up in knots as if the very life was taken from my body. My family and I mourned my sister's death with a wake that was highly unusual. It lasted for twenty-five days, because her body was military property, and they did not immediately release her body to us. After the funeral, I was completely out of it, and unable to concentrate at work. My sister's death brought our family closer together, and I spent a lot of time with my father and sisters.

## Journey to Arizona in 2004

For about eight months, I was telling my sisters that I would be moving. It got to the point where one of my sisters said, "If you don't go away, how are we going to miss you?" Naturally, they did not believe me when I said I was moving away for sure. Jonathan and I decided to move to Arizona where we had met each other in April 2002. Reality sank in for my family when we generously gave away all of our possessions, except for a few boxes of books. We packed the car with a few things, and moved away from New York City. My father made sure to warn me to be careful, and he said "Stay away from the high crime areas." Jonathan and I drove to Massachusetts where we spent three weeks with his parents. Tears welled up in my eyes when we departed his parents' home. Snow began falling, and we were letting go of everyone and everything we ever knew, for an unknown destination in a far away state.

The adventure ahead left us feeling ambivalent with high spirits and sadness at the same time. We had no choice but to trust the uncertainty of the road ahead. We drove over three thousand miles from the East Coast to the West Coast. We did the amazing journey in just a few days. We ate a lot of Subway sandwiches in the car on the way. We stopped in Maryland and I saw my uncle, while Jonathan went to Virginia to visit his relatives. We stopped in Tennessee, and I thought of Elvis at the Heartbreak Hotel, and I loved it there. We kept on driving along the road, and once in Oklahoma, we visited the Cherokee Trading Post which was nice.

The next day, we continued on I-40 to Texas where I waved to the people in Amarillo. The drive seemed to last forever, compared to the smaller states. As we crossed the border into New Mexico, we saw green and purple flashes of dry lightning for the first time. We pulled over to rest at a truck stop, but it was too creepy at night. I was sure I saw the ghost of a young girl telling us, "Get out of here." We high-tailed it out of there and stayed at a local hotel instead. The next day we finally saw the sign for our destination, welcoming us to Arizona.

We arrived in Flagstaff and saw the snow capped mountains of the San Francisco Peaks, home of the Hopi Kachinas. Our first stop was to eat at a local Denny's diner. After we ate, we drove from north to south on Highway 89A. In about an hour we experienced different weather patterns from hail and sleet, to hot and sunny. We thought, "Wow, Arizona has pine trees and snow too." I always envisioned everywhere in Arizona to be a scorching hot desert. We drove to Sedona down Scenic Route 89A, and it was oh so beautiful! The serenity of the megalithic red rocks entranced me, and took my breath away. The landscape and picturesque scenery of Sedona made the long drive worthwhile.

We drove through Sedona to Cottonwood. We went to see Glen, who was about ninety years old. He was renting a place that we wanted to take a look at. Many years before, in the 1950s and 1960s, he won the money to pay for his house in a Las Vegas Casino. In those days, it seemed, Las Vegas gave plenty of money away. Glen told us the tale of how he was wooed with chips to stay in Vegas. Electronic shufflers sure took the fun out of counting cards. Glen reminisced about his wife, and his days living next to the Playboy Mansion. We initially thought we would go to dinner with him, but when he said, "Didn't know whether to fire'em or shoot'em," about someone he had working for him, we had a change of heart. When Jonathan went to the bathroom he said, "You're purty." We ran away as fast as we could, but we ran into many other scammers and swindlers. The "Wild Wild West" was still going strong.

We drove to another place that was for rent in Sedona. There, we met a man, who we nicknamed Bobo the Clown. He demonstrated a striking resemblance to a clown with his hair parted in the middle. He proceeded to tell us that we cannot smoke, while he puffed a cigarette in front of us. Jonathan made strange sounds like, "aaaaahhhh" and "ooooouch." I looked at him, and he was in real pain. I said, "What's the matter?" He said, "My teeth, they are aaaaaa-hhh-ooooouuuuuuchch killing me." So we ran as fast as we could from Bobo the clown. That was it for the toothache. It subsided when we left the house of Bobo. We were relieved to leave Bobo, but left Sedona broken hearted.

We ran into people who claimed to have all the answers, and some who said they were "Jesus Christ" or "God." Despite a small internal economy and a few scammers, our experience in Sedona proved to be of pure magic, and quite phenomenal. We entered Highway 89A driving north again to Flagstaff. In a sudden flash, we met a man who pulled over in a dash. His motorcycle spun around and pulled up in front of the Red Rock Lodge. The nice man, whose name was Pat Farley said, "Looking for me?" We joked to ourselves, "Mr. Farley on his Harley," yes of course we were looking for him. He was the Innkeeper. We stayed there for a few nights, and then drove up north. We got close to Kayenta and stopped at a gas station, with no clue of our destination once again.

We just had to ask the universe, and the synchronicities showed up; without saying anything to them, two women came out of their car, and they told us to go to Monument Valley. It is known as the Valley of the Gods. They were raving about their trip, and shared their joy with us. We visited the Navajo Nation, and there we met two really nice Native Americans selling their jewelry. We made friends with Kalvin and his cousin Ronsin. We purchased a stone carved Kachina Doll of a dancing flute player named Kokopelli. Kalvin worked by candle light because he did not have electricity or cell phone reception where he lived. Kalvin loved beer, and he asked us to get a four pack for him. We stayed at the Anasazi Inn for a few days. We then went to Canyon de Chelly, and it was as beautiful as Sedona, yet untouched by modern developments. It was peaceful there.

**Twin Rainbows Led Us to Sedona to Live**

We then drove back from Northern Arizona to Sedona, to say our goodbyes. We were heading to the Silicon Valley in California to find jobs. As we were leaving, a rainbow came out of nowhere, and the further we drove, the bigger the rainbow got. Rain droplets were beating on the windshield. I looked to my right, on the other side of the road, and there was no rain. The other half of the road was sunny. It was raining only on our car, and I thought it was weird. The rainbows stretched for miles from Sedona to Cottonwood with a small rain cloud hovering over us. Suddenly, another rainbow appeared. The twin rainbows seemed to touch my lap. It felt like the rainbows had long magnetic hands on the car. I had such a powerful feeling of connection to the rainbow that it brought tears to my eyes. We pulled over on the highway, and several other cars stopped in the breakdown lane as well. We were all looking at the magnificent light show in the sky. We felt compelled to turn the car around, so we headed back to Sedona.

We met Bob, our landlord who was a nice guy. He lived in the Village of Oak Creek. Bob told us that years ago they called the Village, Sedona, to sell real estate. The cost of living in Sedona was expensive. I was lucky that I landed a job at the Enchantment Resort which made it easier. However, the commute was forty minutes each way, so I applied for a job at the Sedona Hilton Resort which was within walking distance. On the day I was supposed to start the new accounting position, the Hilton's management claimed that I was not a US Citizen. My US Citizen Passport meant nothing to them. Several trips to the Social Security Administration were a waste of my time. I could not bargain for my job. Little did I know, the Hilton would outlaw a little brown person like me, based on what management called their "Pilot Program."

I settled for working three jobs, seven days a week, to keep up with the cost of living. Overworking made me get sick, and it took three weeks to recover. I was prompted to start a private accounting practice. I drew from the experience working for Mr. Shah, who signed off on my CPA work experience requirement for New York State. Performing accounting duties in Sedona was unusual, and unlike any other place. One of my clients purchased several properties on a ten acre ranch, located on the unpaved areas of Dry Creek Road. The area was famed for "Men in Black and UFO activities," as written about by Tom Dongo and Linda Bradshaw in their book *Merging Dimensions*.

One night on his way home, my client said several vehicles pulled up, and blocked his way to get home. Being a former bombs specialist from New York and a tough guy, he decided to get out of his truck and fight back. He said several men in black pulled out guns, and told him, "Get back in your truck!" Staring down the barrel of a gun can be very convincing. He was, after all, in the "Wild Wild West." He was forced to abandon his route home that night.

Sedona attracts many tourists for its beauty, spiritual healing energy, and vortexes. These power places on earth were revered by Native Americans for thousands of years. After all, that was one of my reasons for being attracted to Sedona. Yet, on some levels, I felt that Sedona proclaimed a false sense of security and reality. Away from home and family, I was seeking solace outside of myself. It left me feeling even more hurt and taken advantage of because in that state of mourning, I was still vulnerable.

We tried to live normally among the residents for a few years, then our neighbor rented to some druggies, and after their violent outbursts, we had to move. Many people that we met there were unwilling to walk the path of truth, self responsibility, and discipline. They believed that a marijuana high, or a tattoo of a Deity was good enough for them to get to the path of enlightenment. I came to the realization that life will be life, with its ups and downs, no matter where we live. Planet Earth by its very nature is dualistic with light and dark, day and night, yin and yang, tall and short, good and evil.

After many years of searching, I understood a valuable lesson about the world of spirit by delving into the depths of my true *Self*. It was the only place that I found peace. Even though others might be able to point the direction, no one can embark on the journey of inner peace for us. For the truth seeker, the answers can only come from within.

### Balancing the Spiritual and Mundane

I had completed a very busy tax season preparing tax returns, and I was happy to get back to writing. The creative process had a life of its own, and it was like a wild stallion, untamed and free spirited. It felt like the book inside would drive me bonkers if I did not write. The editing process can be grounding, yet at times it was difficult. As the sun flickered on my computer monitor, I picked up the manuscript and began writing again. It was not easy for me to balance being an accountant and spiritual simultaneously. There were many times when I felt torn between my responsibilities of being a professional, being in a relationship, and being a modern day yogini. That process continued for almost a decade. Nevertheless, I managed to balance my work life, family life, and spiritual life.

It was now April 2009, and I started my day walking outside. The spring day was warm with a cool breeze, and the Easter sky was magnificent. The red mountains in the backdrop were shimmering in the twilight hours of dawn. The humming birds in the distance were whispering sweet sounds as they darted across the sky, and were scattering their love and nectar on the soft petals of the peach tree. They left me captivated by their speed. They are so special, those little birds. Tiny and beautiful, they travel over long distances, and like ballerinas they whirl around the nectar of life from flower to flower. My greatest wish is to be one with nature every day.

On that morning, magic filled the air. The little field mouse, as it heard me walk to the door, ran away in the shrubs with the rustling sounds of leaves. It was a special creature, and it has its place among creation. It looked like the angels of spring were making their beds on the yellow and purple tulips. Later that evening, I fell asleep and had a dream of a Native American Chief with long feathers, riding on a white horse. He had a staff in his hand and piercing eyes that gazed at me, almost looking through me. I woke up and was drawn to the Barnes & Noble bookstore like bees to the peach flowers.

## Our Cosmic Journey Begins: Galactic Travel
## We Are All Made Up of Stardust

I was itching to travel, so the next day we took a long car ride. I felt a sense of wonder as we were driving along the highway. The Natives refer to highways as "rivers of stone," due to the heat from the sun's reflection on the concrete, which creates a watery mirage effect on the road ahead. We were headed to see the Hopis. They are Native Americans that have been living in Northern Arizona for over ten thousand years in the same village, Old Oraibi. To the untrained spiritual eye, the Hopi reservation looked like an impoverished place. Like most ancient cultures, they are adept in spiritual knowledge. They are connected to the star nations, and all life, through their sacred ceremonies and dances.

Our planet Earth is one of the fastest moving vehicles, carrying all of us simultaneously. Our magnificent planet, with 8,400,000 life forms, rotates on its axis once every day. It also revolves around the sun once every year, yet we don't feel it moving. All of us are travelers through space on this journey in the cosmos. The misconception that space is something "out there," makes no sense. We are part of space. We can feel it and breathe it. The microcosm is related to the macrocosm through the body's energy centers. The ancient yogis called these energy centers in our bodies, *chakras*. When we understand more about ourselves, and our connection with the cosmos, we do not have to look far for the clues as to who we are.

The understanding of reality first begins with inner consciousness, and then extends to the outer world at the cosmic level. Our bodies are composed of the same elements that the universe is made up of. In essence, on a microcosmic level, we are the universe. We are indeed made in the image of the cosmos. Our Sun is made up of hydrogen. It is a star that gives life to everyone in our solar system. It takes two hydrogen molecules and one oxygen molecule to make water. Seventy to ninety percent of our body is composed of water. Clouds are mainly water. The process of evaporation and condensation is similar to, perspiration and respiration in a human body. Scientifically, we are composed of the same hydrogen molecules as the sun and clouds. We are made up of stardust!

Many indigenous cultures say that their ancestors came from the stars. Hydrogen molecules prove what the ancients knew a long time ago. The same solar power that can heat up a home, can certainly give us the energy we need for sustenance. I was able to live on sunlight for about three months, with a very light diet that consisted of only fruits and vegetables.

## *STRATEGY FOR ENLIGHTENMENT*

**The ancient cultures around the world worshipped the sun. Today, many health practitioners, doctors, and nutritionists are recommending that we add more fruits and vegetables to our diet. The ancient masters and yogis would make the same recommendation because on a spiritual level, to become "enlightened," we should eat more foods that are filled with sunshine and direct sunlight. The yogis said that meat darkens our aura. Hence, a diet that is "light," with fruits and vegetables, facilitates the process for us to become more enlightened.**

We went to a lecture in Sedona and learned that like the Hopis, the Dogons are another ancient culture. They are a tribe from Mali in Africa who claim that they were visited by beings called the *"Nommos,"* who came from the Sirius Star System. The Dogons' history was passed orally from generation to generation. Their fascinating story has been passed down for thousands of years. Two French Anthropologists, Marcel Griaule and Germain Dieterlen apprenticed with the tribe for many years in the early and mid 1900s.

Astronomers knew about Sirius A, and thought it had a companion star. However, they were not certain of the fact because the telescope was not as advanced as it is today. Prior to Galileo's use of the telescope, the Dogon Priests revealed secrets about the Sirius Star system by honoring it with sacred ceremonies. They say that Sirius B is the heaviest star, and white in color. *Po Tolo* is the Dogon name for Sirius B. In their language, *Tolo* means star, and *Po* means smallest seed, which refers to creation. How could ancient cultures have names for an invisible star, thousands of years before it was confirmed by modern science? The Hopi name for Sirius is Blue Star Kachina.

Many years later, astronomers confirmed the characteristics of Sirius B as a white dwarf. The Dogons claimed that there is a Sirius C named *Emme Ya*, which means, "Sun of Women." They say it has a moon called "Star of Women." They describe its density as being four times as light as Sirius B, and the home of the *Nommos*. Interestingly, this fact that Sirius had a third star was proven only recently in 1995, by modern French astronomers Daniel Benest and J.L. Duvent, who discovered Sirius C. There findings that it is a small red dwarf star, were published in the *Journal of Astronomy and Astrophysics*. Could our modern astronomers one day discover the "Star of Women," or the *Nommos*?

Sedona is famous for its dark skies, and it is heaven for sky watchers. I have had several otherworldly experiences in Sedona. Many times, I have looked up in the sky and seen glowing orbs of golden, yellow light. Many nights they were watching over us as they hovered above the trees. I am now able to communicate with these guardians of light, yet their nature is still mysterious to me. My thoughts began to take the shape of local residents. I was no longer a skeptic. Something about the beautiful red rocks exposed truth beyond words. What seemed unreal became reality. I had newfound respect for the psychics and mystics on the metaphysical path, and our nature as beings of light.

## Everybody, and *"Every" "Body"* Is Family
## We Are All Composed of Water "$H_2O$"

On this journey of life, we all have our own trails to walk. The magic happens when we can accept and show consideration for each other's journey along the way. I started to see everyone as family. In the end, we were all brothers and sisters in the cosmic dance. Our mind is a veil which convinces us of a certain reality. To go beyond that limited reality is like a never-ending well, and the more I went within its depths, the more I knew about the expansive inner light.

I began questioning economic and financial principles. I tried to comprehend the ever-changing infinite mind. In essence, we experience life as a separate existence, but to understand infinity is to know that we are indeed part of the whole universe. Even though we may not be able to experience it from a logical perspective, we are indeed a strand in the web, and not the entire web of life in the cosmos. Scientifically, it would be embarrassing to compare the size of planet Earth to the countless millions, billions, or trillions of planets in the Universe. Earthlings would not measure up.

Our entire planet, with six billion people, would be just a speck of dust in the grand halls of infinity. Similarly, if we were to view ourselves from an airplane, we would not be able to locate any one person from great heights. It is the logical mind or ego which thinks itself to be in control of everything. To establish a relationship outside of the logical mind, we have to bring our hearts and spirits together.

**Mountains – A Place Where Heaven and Earth Merge**

Let's take a seat five thousand feet above sea level, where the peaks of the mountains and the sky connect. Mountains are considered sacred in many ancient cultures. It is a place where the energies of the heavens are more easily felt. There is an invisible stream of light that can be seen by enlightened beings, which connects everything and everyone in the universe. I was once immersed in this intelligent light, and I realized that the entire universe is alive. Each and every molecule is in constant motion. It was like looking at life through an electron microscope. Heaven is a state of mind and so is hell. We create our own purgatory, or gateway to the angels. There is no invisible hand responsible for our happiness or suffering. The journey through life is like a ride, and the ride through life does not have to be painful. Our mind drifts emotion by emotion, and sadness and happiness are like fleeting clouds.

You can step away for a moment from the emotional rollercoaster of life to breathe in this experience with me. Imagine a cool springtime breeze flowing around you. Feel the warmth of the sun as the clouds above float like cotton balls in the sky. They are almost within reach and slowly changing shape. The sun shines with reflections like golden tinsel hung over city streets during the holiday season. The clear turquoise blue sky envelopes the glistening landscape. Our thoughts are changing as the clouds drift along the horizon. Emotions transition into mere nothingness once they have been experienced, yet we hold on to a memory. We replay them in our mind over and over, trying to recreate the past. If we can let them go, we will be free to experience emotions in the now.

Allow yourself to feel the captivating energy of the brick red-orange majestic mountains. More gorgeous than any natural wonder you've seen before, these megalithic monuments capture your heart, and unseen tears of joy and gratitude flow. Our gestures are softening as the doors to our hearts open. Allow yourself to enjoy this cosmic journey with an open mind and heart. Dr. Wayne Dyer said:

> "A mind that is open to everything means being peaceful, radiating love, practicing forgiveness, being generous, respecting all life, and most important, visualizing yourself as capable of doing anything that you can conceive of in your mind and heart."

Our journey continues. It is like taking a vacation with many destinations. On the mountain far above, you can forget about the concerns of the mundane world. The morning dew and droplets of water are stilled by the fresh scent of evergreens and pine trees, which fills the air. The morning mist upon the mountains helps awaken your consciousness to your divine *Self*. Dawn is stirred by the movement of the speeding cars on the winding highway below. We awaken to a new day. Allow yourself to explore your life like an observer.

As we sit on the summit of one of the most beautiful mountains, we become engulfed in a mesmerizing tale. In the distance, a jet black raven appears amidst the clouds high above. The bird looks at you and almost through you. It soars round and round as it locks eyes with you, and shows you a grand view of your true *Self*. You can feel the magnificence of the royal spirit inside. Many images of your life are now flashing in front of you. In the accounting of your life, you will be able to take a step back and contemplate its meaning.

## An Accounting for Life Now Begins

From this level of vision, we can take into consideration the cosmic view of life. We do not have to wait to get a life review. You can pause for a moment in silence, and listen as your soul calls out, "Is this for real?" You don't have to wait until you meet the Angel of Death to do an accounting of your life. We can begin now. So where does the accounting of your life begin? It begins like all things on earth, with a thought and a decision to know more about it.

We are going to do an accounting for your life with pictures, where your life is revealed to you image by image, like photographs in an album. You will need to take a look at a picture of yourself, and a few pictures are needed. It does not matter if it is a recent or past photo. Even a digital picture taken in the moment will do fine. Several pictures, even if they were taken five minutes apart, will reveal how quickly your life is changing; or if you have pictures from when you were younger, your changes and growth would be much more noticeable.

All that matters is that you raise your consciousness, and unconditionally love the person in the picture. There should be no judgments about your image or experiences in the photo. You can use the following techniques with the Law of Allowance, to shift your consciousness, accept all the positives and negatives of your image. Allow yourself to feel these experiences fully, cherish them, then breathe and let them go. To connect to your innermost being, self love is very important.

Let go of things that you normally think about. For this moment, release everything, such as concerns about your bills, house, apartment, car, job, business, family, or relationships. Meditate on your innermost self. Imagine each day of life as a new beginning on the journey. When we hold on to yesterday, it stops the flow of the joy in this moment. Begin by looking at the image of yourself. Stare into your eyes, and answer the following questions:

1. What do you see? Make a note of it mentally or write it down.

2. What do you feel when you look at yourself?

3. What kind of thoughts come up when you're looking into your own eyes?

4. Who am I?

5. In the end, what is life?


Isn't our life a composition of shadow and light, like pictures in an album? If we can get an album of our great grandparents, and look at their pictures, we would understand that they too were here for some time. Now their lives are just images, and memories left for us to cherish. The same way, our children and grandchildren will look at the photo imagery we leave behind when we are gone.

Scientists say that matter is neither created nor destroyed because it is just energy which changes its state from solid, liquid, or gas. The same way, all of our experiences are just that, an experience. There is no need to connect all the good and bad experiences, and lump them into one. It is best to let bygones be bygones. Our fears from past experiences do not have to be carried into the future days of our lives. We can rest at night by letting go of each day's experiences.

## STRATEGY FOR ENLIGHTENMENT

**An enlightened being arises each day, renewed in the spirit of forgiveness. To experience enlightenment, and to feel "lighter," we must forgive everyone and everything that has hurt us, whether it was intentional or unintentional.**

As we enter the golden age of enlightenment, we must be able to define ourselves and our values. Regardless of who you are, you have to do something with your time on earth.

1. What can you do that will give you money, joy, and happiness at the same time?

2. What is the ultimate goal of life?

3. Is lasting inner peace attainable?

No matter who we are, regardless of age, race, affluence or non affluence thereof, isn't it reasonable to say we are all seeking happiness? Isn't contentment and being happy the point of our lives? It is the reason why we are motivated to do the things we do. Would you like to know a little secret? When we share in the spirit of service, our life becomes joyous. Our true *Self* is nourished by our hearts; it is the organ that fuels our being, and our breath is its nourishment. So when we open our hearts, we allow for more life energy to flow in and out of us. When you are aware of who you really are, you can begin to love yourself infinitely.

As you begin to see a bigger picture of your life, you can begin to evaluate your true *Self.* Now close your eyes for just a second, and let your mind hear itself speak. The logical mind may sound ridiculous, but the true *Self* always reveals "truth." Think about the following questions:

1. Are there two sides of me?

2. Is there a part of me that I let everyone see, and is there another part that is secret, that only I know of?

3. Am I being true to myself?

4. Is there a secret side to my life?

5. Have I ever heard my heart speaking to me?

6. Did I follow that heartfelt intuition or did I ignore it out of fear, only to regret it later?

7. Is love something that I give to others?

8. What is self love?

## *STRATEGY FOR ENLIGHTENMENT*

**Loving one's self is just as important as loving others. To get a glimpse of the eternal part of your being, you have to live your life with all the love that you can muster. Love is the opposite of fear. It is expansive in spirit, whereas fear constricts.**

We can feel the power of self love if we take the time to move into our higher *Self*. Self love leads us to a happy life because it is not identified with objects, but rather with intangible situations. Happiness can become fleeting because situations in our lives are always changing. When we know our true *Self*, we are in touch with a higher power, and that brings us happiness. We can then transcend the physical level into the metaphysical. *Metaphysical* can be translated from the Greek prefix to mean "beyond the physical."

### An Antiquated Education System for the Modern World

In our early years, we had no choice about what decisions to make for ourselves. They were made for us by our parents and society. If you are an adult, that may no longer be the case. As adults, we can choose to make the right decisions for our lives based on truths in our hearts, but sometimes we don't listen to our hearts because of fear.

Most of us learned that, to be a good student, we needed to get an "A" in class. We had to compete ruthlessly with the other students to get an "A." The rest of the students would fall under the standard norm curve. There was room for only a few students at the top of the class. There was the one kid who always seemed destined to be the valedictorian. The pressures that are put on a young person's mind to do well in school are enormous. The school system is based on fear. Teachers are doing their best to follow a school system that is inadequate for the vastness of the human spirit. Cooperation and collaboration should be encouraged if we would like to see a better society.

Are you a parent who would like to see your child do great in school? Have you considered what your child is learning in their classes? Do they receive the life skills necessary to face the challenges of this world, or are they learning a mechanical career or trade? Are you a college graduate who can't find a job? I was conditioned that with good grades, and upon high school graduation, I stood a chance of going to college and getting a degree to land a good job. To make it in the world, we had to get a bachelor's or master's degree.

After the world financial crisis in November 2008, that system fell apart because there were not enough jobs for college graduates. The formula to do well seems to have been great for the classroom, but in the school of life, an "A" did not hold up. I found myself lost at times, because more than eighteen years of education did not teach me about valuable life skills. It is almost as if someone teaches us for eighteen years of our lives to be one way, then as soon as "real life" sets in, all the rules change. My accounting and economic classes did not inspire my entrepreneurial skills; those were acquired from my parents. A college degree does not ensure success in business. It is only a stepping stone.

**Society vs. the Heart – An Organ of Truth**

Many of society's problems come from the fact that young people are unprepared to deal with their problems. Their only means of coping are drinking and socializing. There is one problem with this situation because most people blame themselves for all their problems. People turn to alcoholism, suicide, or various other narcotic substances as outlets to numb the pain. Their life becomes like a maze. They become defensive, fearful, and angry on the inside, and their fears wreak havoc in their lives. According to the Youth Suicide Prevention Program, many teenagers die by suicide each year, about one dies every two hours.

Fear leads to physical constriction on the heart muscles. How many people die from heart attacks? Heart attacks rank high in the killers of Americans. How could the heart, a vehicle of truth, go against itself? We can analyze the available statistics. Researching the facts will show some studies conducted prove that most heart attacks were reported in hospitals on Monday mornings. Would you like to guess the exact time? between 9:00 AM and 10:00 AM.

The stressful way of life hardly seems appealing, unless the financial rewards are worth the price we pay for them. Even in the middle of Monday morning rush hour traffic, we can learn how to release stress. We do not have to quit our jobs. The merciful masters left a blueprint for us to find happiness. Even in the most difficult situations, we can transform our lives by using the power of our thoughts. All we have to do is learn to release stress and cultivate inner peace. Meditation is the key.

## The Never-Ending Karmic Wheel of Existence
## Is the Grass Always Greener on the Other Side?

In this accounting for life, death is its opposite, and we do not have to fear it. When we live our life without spirituality, our efforts become futile. It is like a hamster running on a never-ending wheel, scurrying for a piece of food. Is that piece of food worthwhile? Or was that the societal brand of conditioning? We have been conditioned to think the grass is greener on the other side, and so we sacrifice our families, our health, and our spiritual life, for the mundane.

We forget the cost of the greener pastures. If we get to the greener pastures, we might have to mow a bigger lawn, and there are much more responsibilities. Is the greener grass worth the extra effort? We can choose if we want the grass to always be greener on the other side. It may be convincing that the grass is not always greener on the other side, a Chinese proverb states, "The same amount of happiness that can be contained in a big house, can be contained in a smaller house."

Does everyone have to keep up with the Joneses? During the recession which has lasted from November 2008, and has continued into 2012, many people could no longer afford the utilities in their five thousand square foot homes. With overspending on second mortgages, and lines of credit taken out on their homes, many lost a place to live. Luxury is not inexpensive.

Eating on silverware and fine china made of pure silver and gold is not necessary so long as we can afford the silverware that we're eating on. What is important is that we do have silverware and plates. Investing in the greener pastures of your higher *Self* yields the golden energy of enlightenment. This does not yield a big profit, but then again it is free, and its results are a permanent escape from suffering. To obtain inner peace and contentment in this moment now, all that is required is your diligence and time.

The simple life is not at all a bad thing, so long as we have adequate food, clothing, shelter, and love. We do not have to remain with the teachings from the classroom, and the things that we learned when we were children, and compete with the imaginary "Joneses." The Joneses are not real, and if we constantly pursue objects of material desire, we could find ourselves caught in the web of illusion that material possessions bring us happiness, when in fact, they only bring a temporary feeling which passes with the fads. What is important for us to remember is a balance with the material and the spiritual.

Remember, our upbringing and society had a lot to do with who we are. We competed with each other in the classroom. We were conditioned to do everything perfectly, all by ourselves, and if somehow we didn't, then we were considered a failure, and received a grade of "F" on the report card. If we are to succeed in "real life" then we must change our attitude, and remember, we do not have to do it all by ourselves. We have access to spiritual beings who can assist us in our daily lives.

**Fear Hinders the Growth of Success**

According to Yogananda, it is better to have failed living our dreams than to succeed in the pursuit of someone else's. A Chinese proverb states, "Failure is not falling, but the refusal to get up." Never let fears and doubts hold you back from living the life of your dreams. We shouldn't fear for tomorrow because fears do not exist in the present moment. Fears are concerns about tomorrow or worries about the past. We should not allow doubts about the future to enter our minds, nor should we allow our minds to wander and worry about the past.

Our thoughts attract our fears, and bring them into our reality in order for us to face and overcome them. The only way to do this is for us to understand our fears, and not try to escape from them. We must not blame ourselves for the difficulties we face, and realize that they came from our early childhood and upbringing. Any situation can change. Our society was designed for us since kindergarten, but not with our highest and best good in mind. The reasons for the complexities in the fabric that intertwines society are beyond the scope of my first book.

Our young people today are faced with more challenges than ever, and fewer resources available for their resolution. What seemed to have worked in the past is no longer relevant in the age of social media such as Twitter, Facebook, and Blogging. The culture has rapidly changed. In honor of my parents' generation, I learned that independence is very important. In today's socialite culture, the concepts of interdependence and interconnectedness have been added to our lexicon for common usage.

Many students from colleges such as Berkeley and Harvard, along with millions of other people throughout the world, decided to stand up in a peaceful protest, called "The Occupy Wall Street Movement." The global movement against the one percent of the global elite, corporations, and banks who control over ninety percent of the wealth on the planet, began in September 2011. "The Occupiers" called themselves "the ninety-nine percent."

Remember, our thoughts create our reality. Even though we may not be physically present, and part of the protests, our vote for prosperity, peace, and abundance counts in the *inner world*. It is not necessary for us to get a beating with a baton, physically, because our thoughts and decisions can change anything. If we firmly believe that there is an injustice on the planet with the monetary system, the education system, the political system, the economic and financial system, the environmental treatment of our planet, and many other systems with inequalities, we can change them with our thoughts; and therefore we can change our world. The Angelic Beings taught me to share a powerful message with humanity on how we can *Make Empowered Decisions*, which is explained in later chapters.

Krishnamurti, who was an inspirational speaker and writer, said, without freedom from the past, there is no freedom at all, because the mind is never new, fresh, and innocent. Krishnamurti went on to say the following on the importance of living without fear in his book *Meeting Life* (HarperCollins Publishers, 1991, Page 187):

> "So how does one see the totality of fear? To see something totally, or to listen to something completely, there must be freedom, freedom from prejudice, freedom from your conclusions, from your wanting to be free of fear; freedom from the rationalization of fear, freedom from the desire to control it."

## *STRATEGY FOR ENLIGHTENMENT*

### Meditation Releases Stress and Fear

**We can see through the façade, and break free from the chains of fear by understanding that we are already enlightened beings. It is time**

to remember who we truly are, and breathing deeply awakens our true *Self*. When we meditate, it allows us to overcome our fears, and let go of tension and stress. You can begin a simple meditation by allowing your breath to flow in and out with ease. Sit upright, so that your spine and back are straight, and take a few deep breaths in and out.

**Breathe my friends, breathe.** Take a deep breath and visualize white-golden, translucent, liquid light flowing into your body, then release it. Breathe in, and feel your breath as it carries the vital air to your lungs, and energizes all of your cells. Release your breath now, and let go of all the tension or darkness that you may be feeling.

You can access a *free meditation video* on our website, www.indeara.com. Also, the "Resources" page at the back of this book provides a link to another meditation class, *Chakra Meditation and Balancing*.

# CHAPTER 2
## *Find Your Infinite True Self with A Personal Inventory*

"Lotus – Transcendence"

**Meditation Unlocks the Mysteries of the Higher Mind**

On our first destination, we learned about meditation. It is the first key, and it opens the doorway to inner peace. It is a tool that gives us access to the higher mind, and the workings of the metaphysical and spiritual world. It allows the mind to empty, and it creates a peaceful and blissful experience. It allows us to detach from the drama of life, and create more harmony, *har-money*, and inner peace. We can accomplish anything great, and surely our heart's desires, and highest potential can be achieved with a solid plan. If we take action for a few minutes each day, consistently in alignment with our plan, ultimately it leads us to our goal.

On this step of the cosmic journey, you'll get to know more about yourself by taking a personal inventory, and you can make note of your qualities as a divine being. In the translation of the *"Tao Teh Ching"* (St. John's University Press, 1961, Page 67) by John C. H. Wu, *Verse 33*, Lao Tzu said:

> "He who knows men is clever;
> He who knows himself has insight.
> He who conquers men has force;
> He who conquers himself is truly strong."

We continue our journey now, from a cosmic perspective, with the realization that we are all travelers on this ride through life. As we pack for the second destination, we are allowed to bring only one carry-on suitcase. In our baggage, we must be sure to bring along a handful of compassion, and a few notes of forgiveness. Bear in mind that a belief in a higher power is necessary. This may seem like a lot to pack, but trust me, it's worth it. This is the trip of our lives.

## Cosmic Consciousness – True Value Is More than Physical Reality

We will need to discuss the Law of Accountability before we can understand a personal inventory for our lives. In the accounting for our life, the Universal Law of Accountability is to simply understand that we are more than the physical senses. Our true *Self* accounts for the physical, emotional, and spiritual aspects of our being, and the connection of the body, mind, and spirit. The spiritual state governs the entirety of our being. Our thoughts and will govern our physical body. The Law of Accountability is to accept responsibility for all the choices that we make along the road of life. Something that happens to one person halfway across the world, impacts everyone's consciousness. This powerful universal force connected through our thoughts is commonly known as the butterfly effect.

The Law of Accountability is about accepting responsibility for one's life. In truth, it is not the same as saying "it is my fault, his fault, or their fault." There is no blame game. This can change if we practice the teachings of the great masters. According to the masters, this life was conveniently designed for our suffering, and we must endure it. We were conditioned to view spirit and matter as separate, meanwhile, the Yogis explain that they are one energy. Cosmic consciousness is not an easy concept to express in words. It is something that must be experienced, and it takes time to be understood.

I would like to explain *cosmic consciousness*, as energy vibrating at different frequencies. For example, water is denser than air, so swimming is slower than flying. Water can become frozen solid as ice or evaporate as steam. Water is composed of oxygen, and so is air, but with additional elements, air is a different energy, vibrating at a different molecular rate than water. The same hydro, electric, solar, magnetic, and nuclear power of the universe is in every cell in our bodies. Our physical, emotional, and spiritual nature are one in the same, but vibrating through different densities and frequencies of light and sound.

In an accounting of our lives, our physical body is sustained by food and water. Our emotional body is sustained by positive and soothing emotions, whereas it is destroyed by negativity. Our spiritual body is sustained by light. Humanity cannot live without sunlight. We ingest and breathe in oxygen in the form of light to survive. Our bones are composed of calcium, and they seem heavy for our skeletal structure, and therefore, we can understand why our medical doctors speak of bone density. If we were to look at a single calcium molecule, versus a single oxygen molecule, they would be vibrating at different frequencies.

In chemistry, the periodic table of elements measures the atomic number of the living molecules. If we were to fill up our lungs with calcium, then we would die. If we were to fill up our bones with oxygen, we would not have much of a skeletal structure. On a microscopic level, calcium molecules are vibrating at a certain frequency, and are magnetized by the electromagnetic currents in our spiritual bodies, to keep our bones from rattling off into outer space.

The same way, our spiritual bodies sustain our physical bodies, and vice versa, the physical body is a home to our spiritual body. Therefore, spirit and matter are not separate. They are one energy vibrating, and even in our bodies, we can see that correlation. We can begin to see that certainly, there is more to us than just the physical aspects of our being. This is when we begin to understand our true *Self*. In the accounting of our lives, our thoughts are like an electric motor which generates current through the blood stream, and brings energy throughout the human body. And like the flow of our blood, cash flows in society through the currency system, and in accounting, cash is known as the "life-blood" of a business. In accounting, we find tangible and intangible assets, that is, the physical and the unseen.

Finding truth in the stoic world of accounting, and bean counting, was the last place that I thought I could find my true *Self*. In the traditional sense, accounting generally looks at price and dollar amounts. A person's skills, abilities, talents, and the quality of products or service are not easily measured, but they are factored into intangible assets such as Goodwill. Over the years, I came to see that numbers tell a story of a business or person's life. On this cosmic journey, I share the interpretation and value of the intangibles, which cannot be measured objectively. Intangibles are like electricity, their power exists, however, we cannot see it, but if we were to stick our finger in an electric outlet, we would definitely feel its power.

From a visionary perspective, I saw accounting as a universal principle called *The Law of Accountability*; it is a universal spiritual law, but it is not easy to measure spiritual laws. The only way we can measure a spiritual law is by an outcome, and how it affects our lives. When we live in harmony with it, we see beneficial results, or when we go against its principles, we suffer negative consequences in our lives from the transgression of universal laws.

Some things can be looked at from the obvious, meanwhile intangibles are more subjective. The Universal Law of Accountability factors in the unseen, and the intangibles; that is, how much something costs in energy and peace of mind. It is also about our values and principles, which are incalculable and invaluable. Part of the Law of Accountability is taking into account how our thoughts, deeds, and actions affect each other and the planet. Our success depends on how well we can keep track of the intrinsic value of what we do to each other and our planet.

**What Is Accounting?**

The double entry system of bookkeeping and accounting began with Pacioli in 1492. Today we will talk about the golden rule of accounting known as debits and credits. Just kidding! An introductory college accounting course would be the best way to get started if you would like to know more about complex accounting theories. Rather, I will be sharing the mystical side of the Law of Accountability with you, by explaining the balance between the logical and the creative mind, and how this system of balance can best serve us with a personal inventory of our lives.

Accounting is a system of recording transactions into a book or ledger. Today this can be done with software such as MYOB, Peachtree, and QuickBooks. Accounting began with merchants in ancient Egypt to account for livestock and grains. The commodities markets today are remnants of that system. Accounting was created to keep track of the merchants' grains, and to collect taxes for the government. Accounting is known as the language of business. It records, keeps track of, or "counts" things by using numbers or currency, and it is a value based system. An account of something is simply a listing of transactions. Some examples of accounts include: a bank account, credit card account, car payments, mortgage payments, student loans, donations, or a tab at the bar.

Someone cannot just purchase accounting software and call themselves an accountant. Accounting is a profession, and it requires a formal college education with an accounting degree. Accountants are crucial to the success of any business. Certified Public Accountants are distinguished from accountants because they sit for a very rigorous and extensive accounting exam. It also requires work experience, and then someone can call themselves a CPA. I met the requirements for the education and work experience. However, I need to take the exam to become a CPA.

It took me years of practice with thousands of little steps along the way to fully understand accounting, and yet, there are many areas of accounting to be developed and implemented. It is my hope and sincere dream that the areas of environmental accountability, and spiritual accountability will evolve and become mainstream in our society. I have been working on these for some time. There is so much more to share, but my research is too elaborate to fit in just one book. I can see myself writing about spiritual accountability until the end of my days without scratching the surface.

## Accounting Principles Add Value to Our Lives

Financial statements like the balance sheet and income statement, can be interpreted with an underlying spiritual principle. The Law of Accountability can be understood with a simple story that my grandmother shared with me when my mother passed away. At the time, trying to make sense of a world without Mother's love was not easy. My grandmother used an analogy from the ancient *Vedas* to comfort me. She said there are two birds sitting on a tree in my heart, where the eternal soul resides. One bird sits there silently watching over the other. In the movie *"What the Bleep do we Know?"* quantum physicists described it as the observer. One bird represents my life now, and the other bird represents the supreme soul which never dies. Ever present, the supreme over-soul would look over the other soul with unconditional love for as long as I live. What Grandma was explaining was that the *Self*, is always present in myself *(my-self)*.

## The Observer or the Immortal Soul

Begin by looking within, the answer lies in you. Remember, to make progress, we must endure the challenges of life with self control. On this part of the cosmic journey, we are traveling inwards to the destination of infinity within, because the microcosm and the macrocosm are connected through our *chakras*, which are our bodies' energy centers. With the metaphor of the two birds sitting on a tree in our heart, we come to the realization that our true *Self* will follow us wherever we go, and even if we try to outrun it, it will always be with us. Our soul basks in the light of our hearts. We should let our heart skip a few beats if it must, but we have to keep running with it. We must not wait until it stops beating to realize our true *Self*. If we can stand still for a moment, we can view our life from a higher perspective.

## Timing Is Essential for Achieving Inner Peace

The part of us that seems like a stranger has been following us all along. We should get to know who that person is. Only you can know your true *Self*, because no one else can ever know yourself *(your-self)* better than you. Our true *Self* can feel like a stranger even though it has been residing inside of us all along. The true *Self* is here, and emphasis is placed in the present moment now; it is not the person who we once were or will be. How often do we allow our minds to be in the moment? In the first chapter, on our first destination, we learned the importance of being in the present moment. The illusions of the past, or future, rob us of experiencing happiness in the present moment. A life in balance is difficult to achieve in the past or future. Patience is a virtue because we can discover many aspects of our true *Self*, with time.

When I entered the world of energy, I saw that cosmic consciousness is everywhere. It pervades every molecule, whether animate or inanimate, and is ever present in all things. This river of molecules of light, of which all things are made, is known as *prana* in Sanskrit. These *prana* were called *lifetrons* in Yogananda's *Autobiography of a Yogi*. The power of the mystical universe is right here in front of our eyes, but it is normally invisible. Our thoughts have a profound effect on this life force.

We can use the power of thought to detach from drama and pain in many situations in life. We can use the knowledge of *lifetrons*, and that divine power to find solutions, and detach from suffering in any situation. When we understand that life *(lifetrons)* is in a constant state of flux, and it is always changing, we can therefore realize that it is not necessary to hold on to thoughts from the past that no longer serve us. The positive and negative emotions that we encounter on a daily basis, no matter how difficult, painful, or joyous, are to be experienced and let go. When we let go of both the positive and the negative experiences, without trying to hold on to either, we can be in the moment. Why not release them and go with the flow?

When we understand our true *Self*, we realize that life is like a continuous spiral of never-ending energy. Many times, we try to be in control of our life in order for us to have safety and security, and by doing that we block the flow of our lives. It is just as important to let go of the good times, as much as the bad times, yet many of us want to hold on to only the good memories. In the cosmic consciousness, we learn to live our lives like an empty vessel. Therefore, we become *lighter*, and we remain open to receiving new experiences.

**Life Is Just an Experience**

The journey through life was designed for our enjoyment, yet sometimes we get caught up in the business *(busy-ness)* of life which is routine, and that blocks us from experiencing synchronicities, or the divine flow. We suffer only when we take ourselves too seriously, and we forget that life is just an experience to learn about our true *Self*. Remember, as time goes by, our thoughts, memories, the seasons, the world, and our minds change.

Forever exists now! There is no future, and no past, because everything exists here, in this moment now. Past actions led up to the present moment. The future is only possibilities which are based on our current habits. In essence, the future is not a certainty. It is a probability of potential outcomes based on the actions we take now. We do not have to feel stuck in any situation. We can change anything. The common denominator to change is the decisions that we make. Our decisions shape our destiny.

**Even the Energy of Money Is Changing**

Traditionally, money was the primary or only reason considered in making a decision. However, in today's conscious society, many of us are seeking socially responsible, or enlightened, business networks and relationships. Accounting is the basis of business decisions. Take a look around, and see how many businesses that were thriving just a few years ago are still around today. What changed? Many accounting textbooks focus only on the measurable or objective aspects of the Law of Accountability, because there is no way to quantify the subjective nature of energy.

We should have faith in the power of change. By its very definition, faith is a belief in something that is beyond logic, and cannot be quantified. Banks, institutions, and businesses will change. However, the unquantifiable spirit of mankind can never be replaced by any quantity of money. True value is in the exchange of our time, energy, and services, which governs the rate of monetary exchange, and not the other way around. Many people still live in fear of the power that money holds over them. If we value ourselves, money loses its power over us.

Today, more and more, scientists are developing technologies that prove the subjective facts revealed by the Yogic Sciences thousands of years ago. I feel that no matter how many scientific devices we develop, we may never uncover all the secrets of the great mystery of life. A physical apparatus can never measure spiritual mechanisms, and can never be a replacement for our true *Self*. Only that which is vibrating at a spiritual frequency can measure infinite cosmic consciousness. The invisible forces of gravity, electricity, and magnetism operate regardless of what we as humanity believe. Universal forces are not dependent on the whims of mankind, and money is one of those forces.

We should cultivate both spiritual and material pursuits to be happy. Even though the pursuit of materialism and pleasures externally are temporary, they are necessary. Fleeting and ever changing like clouds, the happiness they bring never lasts, and we would not be too happy if we were starving, not having a place to live, and didn't have adequate transportation, therefore, the balance between the two explains earthly life in a nutshell. We must also pursue the permanence of the supreme soul, the higher *Self*, because lasting peace comes only from within.

As we grow, our consciousness changes. We may feel like we're missing out on something or feel unsatisfied. Sometimes we want things to be the way they once were. We feel a shift in our hearts, and wonder what is in store for our future. Let go of those pestering thoughts because they come from the logical mind, which is always seeking to be in control of everything. When we criticize ourselves (*our-self*) it gives the logical mind, or ego, power over us. With a personal inventory, we can release the grip of the logical mind and begin to see reality through cosmic goggles. The Law of Accountability is a bird's eye view of the collective cosmic consciousness.

## An Inventory of Our Life

As we begin to remember a part of our true *Self*, it seems like forever since we've taken an inventory of our life. There are many factors in taking a personal inventory. We can begin with an inventory analysis now. By precisely knowing our limits and boundaries, we can conquer the limitations of our bodies and minds. To be able to do this inventory of our life, we must first listen to our hearts. We learned the importance of following our hearts on our first destination, that truth resides in the chambers of our heart, and it is the home of our true *Self*. By knowing our true *Self*, we can relate to the world with clarity.

## Understanding Accounting for Inventory

There are a few terms that you'll need to know. We must first understand the definition of inventory which will help us to make a spiritual comparison. Two components in inventory are valuation and costing. Valuation is simple, and it refers to the value of an item. For goods or products, it is the number of items, multiplied by their cost. For services, valuation is the number of hours, multiplied by the price. Costing is how much an item costs. There are various methods to compute valuation of inventory such as LIFO, FIFO, etc. However, for simplicity purposes they will not be considered in our discussion.

One of the most important decisions that a business has to make is how to value its inventory. Inventory determines how much income tax a business has to pay, and how much profit it makes. Inventory is part of the balance sheet, and it is a current asset. Current assets are things that would benefit the business within one year. Now let's translate these two terms: valuation and costing, and see how they relate to a spiritual accounting.

## How We Value Ourselves Determines Our Self Worth

Our self worth is connected to our net worth. What this means is, if we have high self esteem and value ourselves, chances are we have high monetary valuation. When we have low self esteem, and do not value ourselves, we have low monetary valuation. We have been conditioned that our self worth comes from external sources, but that is not true value. *Self* worth is based on how much we have to give to others, and not on the things we want. Many of us have been conditioned to want money, and so we usually feel a lack or scarcity when it doesn't flow to us easily.

In a spiritual accounting, if we focus our minds on being of service to others with all the gifts, skills, and talents that we possess, our self worth grows because people are willing to pay for our services; but, they are not willing to pay for us wanting money. It would seem logical that by focusing on the spiritual basis and the services we have to offer, there will always be abundance in our lives.

Suze Orman explains these concepts, and how they affect our financial lives. In her book, *The Courage to Be Rich* (Riverhead: Penguin Group, 2002) she states that as our self worth increases, our net worth increases. She covers the importance of our emotions, and how they relate to our self worth. Hence, our monetary values, and financial lives are dependent on our self worth. What I would like to add is that when we identify with our higher *Self*, and see ourselves as children of the Divine, we become heirs to true abundance.

We can inherit the divine son or daughter's share of fortune. I found that as my *Self* worth increased, not only did my net worth increase, but my overall happiness increased. Remember, everything that exists in the material world first came from the spiritual world of ideas and thoughts. Therefore, with affirmations, a solid plan, consistent efforts, and positive thinking, anyone can change their financial destiny for the better.

## There Are Two Systems to Record Inventory: the Perpetual System and the Periodic System

The word perpetual means eternal or constantly updated. The perpetual system is used in grocery stores. Every time we buy an item, like cheese, the scanner reads the barcode of the item, and updates the accounting record in a computer. This perpetual system works well because it lets the manager know when to reorder more cheese. This way, when we go to the grocery store the shelves are not empty.

The periodic system of inventory is used in art galleries, antique cars, or companies with fewer, special or expensive items. It counts the number of pieces of art, or a car, each time one is sold. Periodic inventory is tracked by intervals of time which can be weekly, monthly, quarterly, semi-annually, or annually. It is not instantly updated with a barcode and scanner, like that of a perpetual system. Companies do a physical inventory count which simply means they count all the goods and products in stock. Usually, a physical inventory count is required at year end, regardless of which inventory system a company uses; it accounts for lost, damaged, or stolen items. With a physical inventory count, the value of the company's assets is updated to reflect the true value on hand.

## Inventory Systems and How They Relate to the Spiritual Aspect of Our Lives

Similar to the periodic and perpetual inventory systems, life has two parts. The perpetual part of our being is known as the soul, it is constantly updated in eternity, and it is everlasting; it is our true *Self*. The periodic part is like a period of time in our life, or it can also be seen as one lifetime. Birthdays celebrate the years of our lives. Every human being has a few major periods of their life: childhood, youth, adulthood, and old age. Most of us usually do not stop to take an inventory of our life when we are children. It is when we are in our adult years that this process begins. We can count the physical parts of our lives in days, months, and years. The bones, hair, body, and flesh can be weighed in pounds because they are tangible and easily measured, whereas, the perpetual part of us is intangible, and it cannot easily be measured.

The physical parts of our being are dying and regenerating each and every day, yet, we think that they are who we truly are. There really is no way to maintain the physical aspects of our bodies permanently. Even plastic surgeries must be maintained with special cold creams or injections to keep the skin from wrinkling. We have been able to make advances in technology, yet as of the date of this writing, modern technology has not been able to defeat death, eradicate all diseases, and stop the aging process altogether. In the first principle to understanding the accounting for life, we learned that death is its counterpart. We are in the process of dying since the day we are born, and nothing can or will ever change that fact. Therefore, the Yogis explain that the purpose of our life is to know our true *Self* because it is immortal in nature.

We can compare the perpetual and periodic inventory systems to our soul, which needs a physical body. When both aspects coexist in harmony, we experience inner peace and balance. The everlasting soul maintains the physical body, but not the other way around. A body without a soul is lifeless. One way to understand our higher *Self* and our little self is with an analogy that Yogananda gave on his CD, *Be a Smile Millionaire*. A wave is part of the ocean. The ocean can exist without the wave, but the wave cannot exist without the ocean. The same way the little self cannot exist without the higher *Self*.

In our personal inventory, we can add many aspects of our true *Self* to the list of items. The periodic inventory part of our lives can be measured, and it can be understood as the number of years in one lifetime. We are given a certain period of time to accomplish our goals, and live our divine purpose. Normally, most human beings have a life span of about seventy-six to one hundred years, although it varies demographically. For example, in some villages in Japan, the average villager lives over one hundred years. In a spiritual inventory, the reason we are here on earth for this short period of time, besides the mundane activities, is to get to know our perpetual side or eternal soul, our true *Self*.

**Know More About Yourself with a Personal Inventory**

Each moment of our lives, if valued, helps us reap the rewards of a bountiful harvest of inner peace and fulfillment. Even though it appears to be permanent and solid, our life is not set in stone. In evaluating the inventory of your life, consider the process emotionally, physically, financially, and spiritually. It is not necessary to change your job or career. You just need to be able to shine your divine light wherever you are.

The rewards of being of service to others, is one of life's greatest experiences. I would like to help you reconnect with your divine *Self* within. Once you've reconnected with your real identity, the Universal Law of Accountability aids you in manifesting your dreams. More valuable than emeralds, gold, and diamonds are the precious jewels that you cultivate on the inside. Like a master jeweler, you can carve the luster of a magnificent life from difficult and painful experiences.

In this place of purity, inner strength, and bliss you will find that we are indeed souls having experiences in human bodies. Even though there are no shortcuts to discovering your true *Self*, in terms of the lessons that we must learn, the time it takes to learn these lessons can be drastically reduced by practicing spiritual techniques.

We can take the express ride, and the gems of experiences that make up the totality of our being do not have to be missed along the way. One such technique for *Self* discovery is using questions. *Self* analysis opens the doorways to new thinking and inner knowing. You will be able to get closer to your true *Self* in the process.

**Begin by Taking a Personal Inventory with the Following Questions:**

1. Are you in alignment with your divine purpose?

2. How often do you challenge yourself to grow?

3. Do you resist change?

4. Do you attend continuing education programs, seminars, retreats, workshops, or classes for inner growth and self improvement?

5. Would you have to go back to school or take a training course to get in alignment with your purpose?

6. Can you seek the help of a group or groups to network with?

7. How much time do you spend trying to overcome challenges that hold you back from achieving your highest potential?

8. Can you consult with an expert? This will save you valuable time and energy from having to do it all by yourself.

9. What is your focus?

10. What do you think about all the time?

11. Who do you spend most of your time with?

12. How do you spend that time?

13. Is it focused just on you, or on helping others as well?

14. Do you fear the things that you have no control over?

15. Are you able to surrender and place your trust in a higher power, or do you worry about life?

16. Are you in a positive state of gratitude when you are asking for things, or do you make decisions in times of frustration?

17. Do you wish you had a better home, body, or car?

18. Do you focus on what you want, or do you focus on the things you do not have?

19. Is your mind in the now, or is it fearing for the future, or worrying about the past?

20. Are you content with what you already have, and seek more with an attitude that you are already successful?

21. Are you willing to do what it takes to get what you want in life, or can you create a new avenue for your success?

22. Do you set aside time for your well-being with exercise, proper nutrition, and meditation?

## Cooperation vs. Competition – The Divine Feminine and Masculine
## Variety Is the Spice of Life

How boring would it be if all the flowers in the world looked and smelled the same? Can you imagine only Blue Bells? Being innovators of our soul and inner growth sprinkles the joy of sunshine in the gardens of all hearts on the planet. Fragrant like the red, white, pink, peach, and crimson roses, we all have enough room to bloom. The divine scent of each flower pales in comparison to the magnitude, and beauty of the inventory of each human soul. Collectively we can light the way to divinity on earth. Together we can accomplish much more than we can individually. Yin and yang, black and white, up and down, good and evil, day and night, are ever following each other.

The divine feminine concepts balance and empower the masculine ways, and vice versa; the masculine enhances the feminine, and the dance of the two is the essence of all life. With cooperation, much more can be accomplished, and that would be in the highest and best good for all. Competition is the counterpart to cooperation, and it is a principle that serves the purpose of developing strength and character. However, fierce competition creates an imbalance. Eliminating a competitor is not always in the best interest of humanity in the long run. When power resides in the hands of a few, with royal families or military dictatorships, we end up with an oligarchy.

Masculine energies can be thought of as active, direct, and linear, whereas feminine can be thought of as flowing in a circular way, receptive, and softer. At times, it is important to employ the energies of a logical, direct, and linear left brain approach. Yet at other times, it is best to employ the feminine energies of the right creative brain. There is a middle point where the two are married in divine cooperation: left brain and right brain, mom and dad, masculine and feminine. Neither is better than the other, yet both combined surpasses either one individually.

It is this union of male and female, the linear and circular, which created us. This is where both components serve to make the other complete. Together they form a third component, which consists of something entirely different. It is the union of the circle and line that creates a spiral. We can ascend on a spiral or descend, but we can never remain in the same place, and it frees us from feeling stuck. The same way, our perpetual and periodic lives dance within each other, lifetime after lifetime, until we break free, and become enlightened beings.

## Spiral Thinking Is Cosmic In Nature

Our consciousness is moving from a linear to more dynamic spiral thinking. What this means is that we no longer see it as you and me, right and wrong, or us vs. them. Rather, we begin to think, how can we make this work? It is the evolution of our consciousness with a new understanding of our true *Self* filled with love. Newer technologies which use telekinesis, such as autopilots and robotics measure human thought frequencies. Scientists are using dolphins to create new sonar technologies. The ancient *Vedic* texts described the power of voice and thought command in ancient aircraft, which are resurfacing and are now coming to the forefront of cutting edge technologies once again.

In a spiritual inventory, we may find an entirely new part of ourselves residing inside the body composed of flesh and bones. The ancient Yogis called it the *atman* or soul. Ancient Shamans would try to integrate what scientists call the right and left hemispheres of the brain, to bring about transformational healing in a person. As we grow and become more compassionate, it is important to make time to create the balance of both sides of our being. Cooperation in these challenging times may prove to be our best protection against hardships globally.

In an infinite universe there is more than enough for everyone. If we are to evolve our monetary consciousness, then we must learn to appreciate another person's accomplishments and success. Even though cooperation may not fit society's current mold for success, it is based on the concept of unity. We as human beings need a quantum shift in thinking to regain control of our spiritual, physical, emotional, and financial lives. We can ask the following questions: Are we employing a consciousness of unity or division? Do we support other people's growth and dedication to a higher standard of living, or are we envious? Jealousy and anger eventually destroy the person who creates them. We were taught to feel as if we lack something. Ever seeking, humanity looks to fill the void with external measures, only to find disappointment in the long run.

The ancient Yogis gave us the knowledge of *dharma* which means our divine purpose, to surpass the elementary understanding of karma. The Yogis say Karmic Law is responsible for much of our success or suffering. If we were able to see millions of years in the past or future like the ancient Yogis, it would be easy to understand the current suffering on planet Earth. They explained that talented children who are considered geniuses have earned those skills at one point in their existence. What if this were true? It means that we all have a chance to fulfill every wish, even if it does not happen immediately. Therefore, success is not a matter of luck or chance, it comes by our efforts. This great message was assuring for me because I realized that not even death could take away our joy, and all of our efforts are successful eventually, because we learn and grow from them.

Something that we earned cannot be taken away from us. The Great Masters say, in a future incarnation we would be able to fulfill our heart's desires, even if we were not able to accomplish it in this lifetime. Why not live life to the fullest? Failure is not an option because there is no such thing as failure in the universe, only trial and error. Failure came from our societal conditioning, and from the education system. In a spiritual accounting, we can only fail when our physical bodies are in the grave, and for as long as we are alive, there is still time. Remember, it is better to have failed living our divine purpose than to have succeeded in living someone else's.

**To Find the Treasure Within, We Must Dig for It**

A personal inventory helps us to reconnect with our dreams, but it is strange how in a world of instant gratification, these philosophies may sound foreign. Many people would like to manifest their dreams, but expect the results instantly. Wishful thinking is good, because positive thoughts create opportunities; however, physical action must be taken in order for us to manifest something in the physical world. We were taught to borrow and demand the things that we want, but this way of manifesting our dreams and goals is not easily sustained. Pursuing our divine purpose is a much better way. If you are willing to sacrifice to obtain your dreams, then you will surely succeed. There is a price to be paid in time, money, or energy for anything to be accomplished successfully.

It is important that we focus on being grateful for all that we have. The feeling of gratitude allows for more abundance to flow into our lives. As the familiar saying goes, "The sun will come up in the morning, and set in the afternoon." This, we can count on. When we are in the moment, it helps to harmonize the three aspects of our being, the body, mind, and spirit. When we put forth the efforts, we always reap the harvest of success. By focusing our positive energies, we can create a better financial, emotional, physical, and spiritual life.

**The Real Secret to Eternal Happiness**

In the DVD *The Secret*, it showed that whatever we desire is available through the Law of Attraction. One very important factor that *The Secret* did not cover is the importance of our emotional state while manifesting our desires. In my experience, the state of mind that I was in when I visualized what I wanted was equally as important as my desire. The energy that I put into my creation was the energy that I experienced when my thoughts manifested. Hence, the Law of Karma, and cause and effect, were very real for me. If we focus intently on what we want, and work towards achieving it, there is no question whether or not we will get it. We are creating our lives all the time. The state of mind we create from is the emotion, or energy in motion, that we will experience when our desires are manifested.

It is important to be in a positive state when you are thinking about your future. Otherwise, if you create from a negative emotional state, when you receive that which you were seeking, it will be experienced with negativity. A negative thought leads to a negative outcome, and a positive intention leads to a positive outcome. That is one good reason for meditation because it allows us to create from a peaceful state of mind, and therefore, we experience more peace in our lives.

## Yogis, Meditation, and Time Revisited
## Surrender in the Spirit of Service

Meditation does not necessarily mean sitting in one place for hours. Work can be a moving meditation, if it is done in the spirit of service. We can reclaim our divinity if we choose to do so, anytime, anywhere, if we align our thoughts to love. It does not matter where we are or what we are doing. The only requirement is for us to have control of our thoughts. We are the masters of our destiny because of our free will. We can have a reality of our choosing if we truly wish it to be so, but we must be willing to do what it takes to earn it. Meditation opens the doorways to manifesting our desires with inner peace, and the manual for its use can be obtained directly from the higher *Self.*

We can begin to change our lives with affirmations, which are saying words of power repeatedly; they literally program our subconscious mind. Our thoughts are real and they transmit energies like a wireless device. Silently saying the cosmic sounds of Aum, Amen, Hum, Amin, or any spiritual word, can bring one in contact with divine power, so long as it is done with respect. These words will bring us into a state of balance. If we work with our thoughts concentrating on the Divine, in the attitude of service, while surrendering the outcome, it will free us from karma, doubts, and worries in our lives; thereby activating the principle of *dharma* which is our divine purpose.

We have been given a powerful mind which can follow our orders when we subdue the pleasure-seeking senses. The problem is that the mind runs out of our control with too many thoughts, like wild horses. The *Vedic* texts compare the senses to horses. The charioteer is the person in control of the senses. If we cannot control our senses, we can't steer the chariot which represents the mind, and the horses run wild. A mere word has no power on its own. When we believe in ourselves and have conviction, it gives us the power to control our destiny. We can harness the power of the mind like a divine charioteer. When we realize that we can only control our intentions, we can make contact with the cosmic mind.

These simple, yet profound, teachings of the Great Yogis reiterate that we are not the doers of anything, but it is only the Divine that does everything. Being of service to others can transform our lives. We gain peace of mind when we take action in alignment with our hearts. If we can follow the truths in our hearts, we can free ourselves from limiting beliefs, and connect with our true *Self*.

## Courage Amidst the Jungles of Daily Life
## Modern Ways vs. Ancient Ways – The True *Self*

Forested lands are missing from city life, and many of us are not able to spend time by ourselves. Venturing out to find a secluded spot in the woods to discover our higher *Self* is not always an option at lunch hour. Retreats are amazing havens for peace, but the serenity they provide is temporary. It is important to have at least one experience of complete deep serenity, and inner peace, so that you may be able to recall that experience in your daily life. However, it is not possible to live our entire life in a retreat setting, because we have to go back to the routine activities in our mundane life at some point. Our true *Self* does not have to be found, it resides within, even in the jungles of daily life.

## Walk the Talk

Now, as our journey comes to an end in this chapter of life, you can challenge yourself to bring this wisdom into mundane activities. The Universal Law of Accountability was revealed for me to share this wisdom with you. I assure you that enlightenment has been in your heart all along. It is said that the ancient masters and poets walked for days. They literally walked their talk. They worked without a computer or electricity, and studied by candle light. I once heard someone say that the poets of old, and their words, are still relevant to us today, because they earned the merits of their teachings. Even today, many writers make a living from quoting their words.

Modern conveniences have many advantages over the old ways. Yet sometimes, like cheap thrills, they don't leave a lasting mark on the soul, and they pass by like a bird in flight, once above the horizon, never to be seen again. I realized that neither the old ways, nor the modern ways, are better than the other. Many circumstances in the world led up to the present moment, and by honoring the now, we find that it contains the seeds for happiness. Modern technology can be great, however, it gets us to focus our attention outside of our self, which leads us farther away from our true *Self* that resides within. We can learn a lot from the ancients without having to reinvent the wheel. Ancient masters, such as Sri Yukteswar, were said to be as strong as thunder when it came to their principles. Throughout the ages, adversity and challenges came in different forms. Regardless of the obstacles, the objective to triumph over them will always remain the same, eon after eon.

The founding fathers, who established the Constitution of the United States of America, based it on the ancient principles of brotherhood and peace which came from the Iroquois Native Americans. They fought for freedom, and their efforts withstood the test of time. Similarly, ancient messages of the Yogis have relevance for our modern plights because their teachings were based on the immortal essence of the soul. While the western world developed awe-inspiring technology in the external world, the ancient Eastern mystics explored the *inner world* of cosmic consciousness. They gifted us with the ability to maintain our inner sanctum.

The soul resides in the higher *Self*, and ever-present it is never destroyed, and ever permanent. Our true *Self* alone is the pole star that can steer us through the murky waters in the impermanence of our life. Even though it can be difficult to experience the bliss of the soul amidst the crashing waves of turmoil, it is not impossible to do so. We can turn our attention inwards and seek solace even in the midst of chaos. We are all on this journey through life together. It is hard to believe how simple it can be, yet difficult, to walk the path of truth, and stay the course of our true *Self*. Even an experience of enlightenment is insufficient, because it requires consistent effort to remain in the enlightened state. The good news is that the ancients left a roadmap for us a long time ago.

## Know Our True *Self*

*Self* boundaries - We should know our limits by setting boundaries for ourselves.
*Self* acceptance - We should know how to be accepting of ourselves.
*Self* approval - We should know how to satisfy our needs by understanding that there are many elements that compose our true nature, body, mind, and spirit and seek self love.

*Self* reliance – We should know our interconnectedness to all life as part of co-creation. We should know how to live the simple life, and follow the ways of the earth, and know when to give and when to receive.

*Self* forgiveness - We should know our truth and divinity by letting go of negative energy, and by forgiving ourselves and others.

*Self* guidance - We should know how to look inside with introspection to activate our intuition to find clarity.

*Self* respect - We should know how to value, honor, and care for ourselves by spending time with our inner child and creativity.

*Self* responsibility - We should know how to be responsible by keeping our promises and living in integrity with our word.

*Self* preservation and rejuvenation - Silence is golden. We should know when to speak and when to keep still inside.

*Self* regulation - We should know how to cultivate humility, and how to be receptive, this will help us nurture our relationships.

*Self* sufficiency – We should know how to be content and live in balance.

*Self* realization - We should know how to recognize our higher *Self* by setting the time aside for meditation and contemplation to realize enlightenment.

# CHAPTER 3
## *Ancient Native Voices –*
## *A World Out of Balance*
## *Wisdom for a Life in Balance*

"Ceremonial Fire – Letting Go"

*Avatar* was one of the top grossing movies of all time. It packed the theaters when it came out in December of 2009. The movie, by James Cameron, took fifteen years to perfect. Amazing 3D effects, from out of this world, told a story about a military regime that wanted to destroy an entire village for its natural resources. The people were connected to a sacred tree where they heard the voices of their ancestors. The word *avatar* comes from Sanskrit; it translates as divinity in form, or a God who is reborn as a human being. Similar to principles in *Avatar*, our journey continues to explore our true nature as oneness.

To weave the web of one's fate or destiny is to remember one's connection to the myriad of living beings in existence. On our last destination, we learned about cosmic consciousness, the Law of Accountability, our true *Self*, and our interconnectedness with all that exists.

> "All things are connected.
> Whatever befalls the earth
> Befalls the sons of the earth.
> Man did not weave the web of life;

He is merely a strand in it.
Whatever he does to the web,
He does to himself."
– Chief Seattle

## We Begin with the Law of Accountability and the Environment

Many indigenous cultures and Native Americans understood environmental accountability to the planet Earth. They referred to the earth as Mother because she provides all that we need for survival, and they refer to oil as the earth's blood. She gives us the vitamins, minerals, and nutrients from the plants and animals to build our bodies. As I sat and meditated on the Divine Mother, I felt inspired by her to reclaim my divine birthrights of happiness, abundance, and inner peace which were endowed by the creator; may she inspire you to do the same. The norm of all life is peace. Wouldn't it be nice to see humanity reclaim it once more? Reality however, can prove otherwise as the struggle continues. The oil spills that destroy sea life, world wars, famine, economic crises, tsunamis, and droughts, lead to people's suffering.

1. Would we seek the inner wisdom of our soul if we didn't have a divine prompting or suffering?

2. Can desperate times lead people to cooperate with each other and seek strength from within?

3. Could these very planetary struggles lead us to the place we need to be in the future?

Native Americans understood The Law of Accountability as the concept of karma that carries from one life to another. They say we are responsible for the results of our actions for seven generations to come. Interconnectedness is to move our thinking from a finite to an infinite cosmic consciousness. In a finite consciousness, we think of things as having an ending, or, it's over. The Law of Accountability leaves ample room for infinite consciousness, and in an infinite world, all possibilities exist. Our thinking moves to building relationships, rather than burning our bridges. We do not see things as an end. We learn to leave room for mistakes, and account for growth with forgiveness.

In an infinite cosmic consciousness, we see things as a process, and they flow within cycles. Everything has a common thread and is connected to a larger system. Businesses move their attention to what is in the best interest of the customer and future generations. Instead of short term only profit motives, longer term profitable and sustainable measures are pursued.

## The Golden Spiral

The dynamics of this kind of thinking is not masculine or linear, nor is it circular, which is repetitive and feminine, it is spiral. A spiral is more than two dimensions and it is a 3D concept. The spiral is the interconnection of a circle and a line merged. The synthesis of the two forms a third component that is neither circle nor line, yet is composed of both. Everything in life is forever moving up or down the spiraling rings. It is known as the golden ratio. The Fibonacci spiral approximates the golden spiral, and it is the nature of everything. The Milky Way Galaxy that we live in has spiraling arms that extend into infinity. All life on Earth is finite. Everything with a beginning must end. Only that which lives for something greater than itself can outlast its own life expectancy, and live on infinitely.

## Cosmic Journey in the American Southwest

We now take our cosmic journey to the American Southwest, where we will learn about spirit and matter being one. Jonathan and I drove along the highway, and we felt a sense of eager anticipation as we were driving. After some time passed, we saw a pink haze far into the distance. Since we never saw such a thing, we didn't think much of it, until we were caught in the middle. All of the sudden, out of nowhere, we found ourselves in the midst of a dust storm. We felt vulnerable with the unpredictable situation. The sandstorm was like nothing we'd experienced before. Like a tornado it appeared in a matter of minutes and ferociously engulfed the highway ahead.

If you've ever driven through foggy white-out conditions, sleet, and heavy winds, this experience is similar with one exception; the sand is like something from an Indiana Jones movie. It hits the windshield and scratches the paint right off the car. Now if you were in a small car like mine, it would feel like moths headed for the candle flame. Pure terror ran through our veins. We were driving blindly with our hazard lights on. As we got closer we saw police lights, and sirens next to a trailer truck that toppled over onto the side of the road. In the spinning sand, powerful winds felt like 80 mph. Drivers were slowing down with their hazard lights on to salvage what was left of visibility.

We did what any red-blooded person does in a moment when they're faced with their mortality. We made a plea bargain with the Cosmic Creator. Something to the extent of, "If you get me out of this raging sandstorm alive, I promise I'll do anything you want." Most of us frantically make a promise to change some aspect of our life if we can make it through such a challenging experience. The way to the Hopis was blocked, and we had to turn around. The sun was going down and sand-out conditions prevented us from seeing the road. I could not help but remember the atrocious events of September 11, 2001.

On 9/11, I made the decision that I was going to change, and be true to myself. I remember the frantic phone call from my brother in Orlando. I was still in bed as I awoke to his voice and cried. Checking to see if I was in Manhattan that day, he said, "Bombs hit the Twin Towers." The World Financial Headquarters came crashing down. I remember, in a matter of moments my beloved life in New York City felt unsafe. The soldier's with M16s, Military tanks, and the bag searches felt eerie in the middle of Grand Central Station. I pray that those who died rest in peace, and the rescue helpers recover with the necessary medical attention they deserve. As I caught my breath, getting back to the moment, I noticed the wind gusts died down.

There was a calm feeling in the air. Eventually, I saw a sign for the Cameron Trading Post. We arrived in Cameron, and it was as if nothing had happened. The weather was beautiful. The sun was shining with no storm in sight. We ate some delicious Southwestern cactus candy that I'd never tasted before. It was like jelly beans, but soft and sticky with a lemony-sweet flavor. The Plaza at Cameron Trading Post had displays of Native craftsmanship, fine pottery, carved dolls, and many other items for sale. Even though our trip to visit the Hopis was unsuccessful this time, it was an enjoyable conclusion to a frightful experience.

**We Meet the Kachinas**

We saw the Hopis another time, when a tour guide took us to visit her friends in Hopi land. We now continue on our cosmic journey to see the Hopis, and learn more about their culture. They have been living continuously in Northern Arizona for more than ten thousand years. They live a very rural, simple, and humble life. Their name means people of peace. The Hopis carve dolls called *Kachinas*, which regard everything as having a spirit. The following is a definition from Wikipedia.org:

> "A kachina can represent anything that exists in the natural world or cosmos, from a revered ancestor to an element, a location, a quality,

a natural phenomenon, or a concept. There are more than 400 different kachinas in Hopi and Pueblo culture. The local pantheon of kachinas varies in each pueblo community; there may be kachinas for the sun, stars, thunderstorms, wind, corn, insects, and many other concepts. Kachinas are understood as having humanlike relationships; they may have uncles, sisters, and grandmothers, and may marry and have children. Although not worshipped, each is viewed as a powerful being who, if given veneration and respect, can use their particular power for human good, bringing rainfall, healing, fertility, or protection."

**The Legend of the Four Brothers**

The Hopis say they were given guardianship of the earth. They say, in the beginning, at the time of their creation story, humanity were four brothers: the red, the black, the white, and yellow. This legend is still alive in the medicine wheels placed on the land all over the Southwest. Medicine Wheel Ceremonies are common in Sedona.

Each brother was given guardianship over a direction; the red brother was the guardian of the earth. Today you will find that our foods such as wheat, corn, etc., came from the Native brothers. To the West, the black brother was given guardianship of the water, being the most humble and powerful. To the North, the white brother was given guardianship of fire. Modern electronics, cars, and airplanes have the spark of fire. To the South, the yellow brother was given guardianship of the wind. They teach us about using our breath and *chi*, which is the invisible energy that flows through all things. *Chi* is similar to *prana*, which are lifetrons and divine intelligent light.

The Hopis say that the four brothers were sent in four different directions, and they were supposed to come back together in unity to heal the Earth Mother; if we are able to come together, we will be able to prevent more destruction on the planet. We are responsible for protecting the delicate balance of life. It is our responsibility to care for Mother Earth, who provides everything for us.

Our tour guide introduced us to her longtime Hopi friend who had several children and grandchildren. She asked us to keep her name private. She sang some songs and took us to Prophecy Rock, and explained the lines in the rock to us. Our Hopi friend said the creator gave the Hopis a sacred covenant that they must live a spiritual life, and that would save them from destruction in the future. She then explained that their creator asked them not to follow the path of destruction, and provided warnings for the future generations who did not live in balance.

Our Hopi guide told a familiar tale about her people being saved from a great flood in the beginning of their creation, like that of Noah's Ark in the *Bible*. Naturally, her people made a sacred covenant with the Great Spirit at that time. It's funny how when we get caught in some cataclysmic event, whether a world financial crisis, sandstorm, tornado, or a great flood, we make a promise to change for the better. I learned some new words: *koyaanisqatsi*, which means life out of balance, and *esquali*, which means thank you. *Koyaanisqatsi* is a movie by Godfrey Reggio. The movie depicts the beauty of the natural world, and the industrialized world in stark contrast.

**Earth's Balance Sheet: Assets, Liabilities, and Equity**

We continued on our journey to see the bigger picture from a bird's eye view. If we were to do a balance sheet of the Earth today, we would realize that our planet is in a position of loss. The balance sheet for the entire planet would show alarming results in its current state. If we take an inventory of the number of endangered species and populations, it would produce terrible results. The concept of the balance sheet is one that is permanent in nature, as compared to the income statement.

*Balance* in accounting refers to the outstanding balance, for example, on a bank account or credit card. In a balance sheet, it can refer to the positive balance which is an asset, or negative balances which are loans and credit cards also known as liabilities. A *liability* can be short term, which means less than a year, or it can be long term, which means more than a year. Most of us are familiar with the concept of bills, which are liabilities. The term accrued liabilities includes things we are all familiar with such as rent, sales taxes, and payroll. *Accrue* means that they build up steadily over time.

*Equity* is another component of the balance sheet, commonly referred to as net worth. The equity that goes forward on a balance sheet year after year, factors in the *retained earnings*. Retained earnings are simply all the money that a business has accumulated from the profits each year cumulatively since it began. To help you understand the balance sheet, I would have to take a step back and provide an explanation of the income statement. The income statement, as we learned earlier, measures the profit or loss for a period of time, such as monthly, quarterly, or annually. The net income of a business is known as profit, and it is added to the retained earnings on the balance sheet; a net loss is subtracted from retained earnings.

## A Cosmic Accounting

*Depreciation* is a concept that is used for assets, such as buildings, equipment, or cars. Anything that cannot be written off in one year, as an expense, has to be depreciated into several years. For example, the IRS would not normally allow a person to write off the entire purchase price of a new car as an expense for a business in one year. However, they will allow for the depreciation of the purchase price over a few years. Normally the cost, minus any salvage value, is divided into three, five, or seven year periods. Without improvements, buildings would look run down, and vanish into thin air over time. From a cosmic perspective, liabilities in terms of lives lost from manmade catastrophes, would far outweigh any investment.

- What would happen if we apply this concept of the balance sheet to planet Earth?
- How many years would it take for us to rebuild the forests and natural resources depleted?
- How many future communities and human lives are endangered?
- What kind of net loss will the BP oil spill report on their financial statements?
- Is anyone taking an inventory of the sea life and fish that are lost?
- How about the human lives that are threatened by the toxins from poisoned air, water, and deforested land?

## Meeting a Great Chief and the Great Creator

As I stared at prophecy rock, I recalled the words of a Great Native Chief from a dream that I had many years earlier in 1999. He explained that we were accountable for the earth, and he asked me to deliver a sacred message to humanity. The Great Chief went on to say that their Creator appeared to his ancestors as a man who spoke with them. This Great Spirit taught them how to live in balance, what foods to eat, and how to plant seeds and harvest them. The Great Being gave his people instructions on how to live, and inscribed them on sacred stone tablets.

Their people were to live a spiritual existence, and keep the earth in balance, and that was their *dharma*, or divine purpose. The Great Chief said his people are the keepers of the earth. His ancestors were told to perform ceremonies to hold the earth in balance; a practice which is continued to this day. The true, or traditional Hopis, do not spread scare tactics, but at the same time they are not afraid to share facts about the destruction of our planet. As I think about these ancient cultures, so simple and humble,

I wonder how many of us would hold their ways in high esteem if we saw their humble abodes.

The Great Spirit showed the Chief a vision of a time to come of droughts, earthquakes, storms, tsunamis, tornadoes, and wars happening all over our planet. I thought to myself, maybe the Chief was just watching the news on TV. The Great Chief said to me, "Go now my child, you have seen through my eyes a fearful possibility for the earth." He again instructed me to bring the following message to humanity. He said, "You must remind your fellow brothers and sisters that we are all connected, and we must return the balance to spirit and nature. The four brothers must come back together to heal Mother Earth."

I pray that my words will reach all ancient cultures in peace and prosperity. The important thing to remember is that we must live in balance. I do not think it is feasible for us in the Modern Age of Information and Technology to turn back the hands of time, and live as simply as the Hopis. Our modern lives are complex, and we are dependent on telecommunications. However, I feel that it is our duty to live and respect the ancient ways of the indigenous cultures around the world. Even though we may not choose to live their simple ways, we should respect and honor the important place that they hold for our planet.

Our modern society by its nature is more focused on the materialistic side of life. Even today in Manaus, Brazil, people face what the Native Americans faced centuries ago. On March 27, 2010, James Cameron attended a conference to raise awareness, and protect the Amazon from deforestation. It seems his movie *Avatar* was not just science-fiction. I feel that it is time to allow indigenous cultures the freedom to continue living in a natural way. Their ways, though foreign to us, are not savage, civilization and industrialization have taken their rights away. Barbaric acts of war, terror, rape, and destruction are not the best means to "civilize" people. If we do not allow them to freely perform their sacred duties, we hinder the progress of all life which leads to an imbalance on earth.

In the dream state, the Great Chief saw me off on my journey. I left with a bit of enthusiasm and hope. If you have seen the movie *Dumb and Dumber* with Jim Carrey, I felt like Lloyd when he asked Mary if they might be together. Her response was, there is a one in a million chance. Lloyd's reply was, "So you're telling me there's a chance? Yeah!" That's how I feel about our human condition. Though the chances are slim, hope still remains.

## The Great Sickness Called Greed Is Devouring Our World

The vision of the Great Chief started to disappear, and he said, "With just a thought, you have the power to change, and stop raging storms." He explained to me that the destruction on the planet was happening because of the great sickness he called greed. He said our planet is like an airplane. If it's going down, then we're all going down with it. If it crashes, all of us fall, not just the pilot. The Chief's departing words were, "Be well my child and think good thoughts of peace." As I look back on the dream, the Great Chief did not have an MBA, but he was a Master of life. He pointed out one single cause of many financial problems in the world, greedy people. Greed has its roots in fear and scarcity, because when we feel that there's not enough, we compete with each other ruthlessly to get our share. Greedy people want the lion's share for themselves.

Gandhi said, "Earth provides enough to satisfy every man's need, but not every man's greed." Fear is an emotion with a devouring nature, and it is ever increasing like a raging storm. We must not allow fear to take away our happiness. We should try to make a firm decision to remain calm in the midst of the storms of life. The green movement is bringing our attention to the Law of Environmental Accountability with global warming, and other issues that our planet faces. Indigenous people are protectors of the earth. They regard her as Mother Earth, and honor every aspect of life with ceremony. The Hopis say that we are moving out of balance with the earth, and it is the cause for many natural disasters.

Christopher Columbus rediscovered America where Native Americans were living for thousands of years before his arrival. Columbus thought he was in India, and called them Indians, or did he? America was already populated, and home to the Indigenous peoples of this land which they referred to as "Turtle Island." The Natives were able to see their reflection in the Hudson River. The water was pure and clear, and one could drink from it. Trees such as grapes, peaches, and apples were hanging down to the ground, overloaded with fruits.

**We Meet a Great Chief in Real Life**

My trip to visit family took an unexpected turn, and I was about to meet a Great Chief in real life. It was a bitter cold day in December of 2009. We flew into Boston and arrived at Jonathan's parents' residence to spend Christmas. As I sat with Mr. Eastman at his kitchen table, I did an intuitive reading for him and heard the voice of a native elder close to him. I asked him a few questions and before we knew it, in a few days we were driving through a cold winter night in upstate New York.

We were on our way to meet the Chief Faith Keeper of the Onondaga Nation of the Haudenosaunee, North America, otherwise known as the Iroquois Confederacy or Six Nations. The members of the Confederacy are: the Onondaga, the Mohawk, the Seneca, the Cayuga, the Oneida, and the Tuscarora. The Chief, whose name was Oren Lyons, generously gave us his time, and invited us to a gathering that would be in Canyon de Chelly, Arizona, in February 2010. The following are his words as written in the book, *Voice of Indigenous Peoples* (Clear Light Publishers, 1994, Page 31):

> "Greetings, it is a part of our tradition to start with a prayer. I would like you all to pray for world peace and harmony. So, if you would stand up so that we may join our minds together as one...I call for world peace and harmony. May peace be with you, thank you... Indeed, the quest is a renewal of what we enjoyed before the coming of our white brothers from across the sea. We lived contentedly under the *Gayaneshakgowa, the Great Law of Peace*. We were instructed to create societies based upon the principles of peace, equity, justice, and the power of the 'good mind.'
>
> Our societies are based upon great democratic principles of authority in the people and of equal responsibilities for the men and women... Our leaders were instructed to be men of vision and to make every decision on behalf of the seventh generation to come, to have compassion and love for those generations yet unborn. We were instructed to give thanks for all that sustains us. Thus we created great ceremonies of thanksgiving for the life-giving forces of the natural world-with the understanding that as long as we carried out our ceremonies, life would continue.
>
> We were told that the seed is the Law. Indeed, it is the Law of Life. It is the Law of Regeneration. Within the seed is the mysterious and spiritual force of life and creation. Our mothers nurture and guard that seed, and we respect and love them for that, just as we love *Etenoha*, Mother Earth, for the same spiritual work and mystery."

Chief Lyons has been in an appeal process with the United Nations to repeal the *Doctrine of Discovery* and to regard the indigenous peoples of the world as human beings. According to Mr. Lyons, they are still considered a non-existent race as decreed by the Doctrine. The Chief, along with nineteen other leaders, brought their message to the United Nations to no avail. After meeting him, I realized he shares a powerful message about the Law of Accountability.

Chief Oren Lyons said, "It seems that we are living in a time of prophesies, a time of definition and decisions. We are the generations with the responsibility and option to choose the path of life with a future for our children or the life and path that defies the laws of regeneration. Even though you and I are in different boats-you in your boat and we in our canoe-we share the same river of life. What befalls me befalls you. And downstream, downstream is this river of life our children will pay for our selfishness, for our greed and for our lack of vision."

**Cosmic Accountability**

I feel that The Law of Accountability will take its course because this Universal Cosmic Law is not about any one of us, but all of us collectively. We are all interconnected. From a cosmic accounting perspective, it does not matter what something costs any one individual alone, rather, it factors in the price we all pay for the misdeeds, or good deeds, of the few. The cosmic energy and molecules are not stamped with dollar signs. Rather, the Universal Laws record an accounting of each and every thought that we have. We must remember that the energy of the balance sheet carries forward, and it affects future periods. It is one financial statement that is permanent in nature. We should ask ourselves the following questions:

- What will deforestation mean for the generations to come?
- What value can be placed on the lives of endangered species and wildlife lost?
- Is it possible for us to stop destroying the planet?
- What alternative, renewable resources and energy can we develop?
- How can an industrialized nation move to a spiritually conscious nation?
- Can we consider the ramifications of our decisions, and their impact on all life?
- How will the business world keep up with the changes of the modern spiritual era?

The following ancient American Indian proverb sums up cosmic accountability on the balance sheet, "Treat the earth well, it was not given to you by your parents, it was loaned to you by your children. We do not inherit the earth from our ancestors; we borrow it from our children." The way to clean up the environmental mess is to create a system of accountability for companies.

The corporations scoff at clean up, but it is the very support that our planet desperately needs in order to be in balance. When we go to work, our hours are recorded by human resources personnel as earnings with payroll. The concept of savings, earnings, and investments play an important role in staying in balance. Companies who build it into their price structure to give back to the earth will find that the Divine Mother shows her appreciation in unforeseen, profitable ways. In cosmic accountability the Divine Laws are very precise.

Companies that we once thought would fail are thriving. Yet, some corporate conglomerates with blue chip stocks that we thought would be a secure retirement, and a good rate of return on investment, have failed; a few such companies were Enron, AIG, and Lehman Brothers.

As the earth transitions, there is tremendous fear about people losing their jobs. As of July 2011, unemployment is still at an all time high since the economic crisis of November 2008. I can only imagine what the lumberjack felt with the discovery of coal and oil. The same excitement that an oil man had in the early 1900s is the same excitement we should have to pursue renewable sources of power, such as wind, hydro, and solar. Instead of being afraid of change, we should embrace it, and realize that change can be for the betterment of all. Solar and wind technologies can create newer jobs.

- What if our economy ran on natural fuel sources such as solar power?
- Would there be any clean up cost for natural and biodegradable fuel sources?

## STRATEGY FOR ENLIGHTENMENT

**Since the dawn of time and the very beginning of cosmic consciousness, time has been cyclical with spiral thinking. Everything moves in an ebb and flow, day and night, expansion and recession, times of prosperity, and times of scarcity. The point of our human existence is not to fear the ebb and flow, because we live on a revolving planet with cycles of time, day and night, and even the seasons. Rather, we should learn how to cultivate balance, that is, the middle point. By understanding balance, we realize that we can dance in both the good times and the bad times by comfortably accepting and acknowledging both, but never allowing either one to affect our peace and stability. When we live by the universal divine principles of balance, we awaken our inner wisdom.**

## Transitions Are Not New – The Age of Industrialization and Technology

With the legends of Atlantis and ancient history, maybe the indigenous cultures are reminding us of a certain demise. In the ancient *Vedic* texts, aircrafts were described thousands of years before their discovery by the Wright brothers in 1890. I went to a lecture in Sedona which showed us evidence of the antigravity and solar spacecrafts with the Tesla experiments. In ancient cities such as Mohenjo-daro, blueprints existed to build helicopters and airplanes. It is even spoken of in the *Vedic* texts about atomic warfare, because at Mohenjo-daro bodies were found that had extremely high radioactive components.

We should not fool ourselves into believing that we are meant to live on primitive fossil fuels, such as oil. Were it not for the greedy and power hungry, the masses would not experience such pain because solar powered and wind technologies would create more jobs than we can handle. The same way humanity moved from the Age of Hunters and Gatherers, to the Age of Agriculture, to the Age of Industrialization, to the Age of Technology, and into the Age of Information, we are about to make another shift. Our world is crying out for the Age of Enlightened Cosmic Consciousness. I propose we move into an Age of Enlightened Technology in harmony with Mother Earth, and thereby creating an economic boom and prosperity once again.

We can become stronger, and use the pain during transitional times to serve us collectively, and co-create a better world. What we cannot do individually we can accomplish together. We can reach for the ever-new experience of total freedom. The solution for a world out of balance is a simple one; we must share its resources, care for each other, and be accountable to our planet. The antidote to fear and greed depends on the choices that we make. The Great Chief explained the power of choice, and the importance of positive thoughts in maintaining inner peace and balance, individually and globally. From my personal experience of being in the *prana*, which is the divine intelligent light, I saw that the decisions we make have a tremendous impact on each other, Mother Earth, and our entire Universe.

## Our Decisions Affect Galactic Consciousness – You Can Get Back in Balance

We now continue on our journey. You will get a chance to learn about the power of decisions in relation to light, as we enter the enlightened consciousness. We enter the realm of infinite possibilities with these new ideas to conquer our fears, and co-create the life of our dreams. If you can understand yourself, and know what your responsibility is, then you can learn how to use information to live in balance in a world that is out of balance. Rather than being disempowered by destruction, change, and chaos, you can feel empowered knowing how to cope, and effect positive change. By being of service to each other, we create interconnectedness and bring our minds together.

Our connection to each other brings the balance necessary to achieve success. What we achieve individually is felt by all. Even though achieving balance on a personal level is quite a challenge, it can be done. If we can get in balance individually, it will naturally lead us to being in balance collectively. Being in balance is a personal process which is different for everyone. Focusing on one thing at a time is good because we can accomplish more in a shorter time frame. However, when we focus on one area for too long, our life can fall out of balance. One example is during tax season, there were times when I was so caught up in work that I did nothing else but prepare tax returns for fifteen to twenty hours per day.

At other times, during the holidays, all that mattered was family, fun, and friends. To strike the right balance does not mean perfection with every aspect of life at all times. For me, balance does not mean that I get to be with my family for the whole year, nor does it mean I get to have my cake and eat it too. There are even times when I do not get a moment to meditate, or feel peace. Yet that never stopped me from trying to create a life in balance. What is important is having the right tools, and knowing how to get back in balance if I become imbalanced. The key to staying in balance is, knowing how to get back in balance if we are off course.

Sacrifice is a necessary part of being in balance. Getting back in balance can mean sacrificing a slice of cheese cake or ice cream when that is all I desire. Yet, at other times it may mean eating a whole cheese cake or cup of ice cream. There are no outer measures for balance; rather, it is the feeling of inner peace which crowns the successful knowing that I am in balance.

I came to understand that balance is not trying to measure up to the images on the television screen either. On our second destination, we learned the importance of our true *Self*. Balance is the knowing that our being is rooted in the higher *Self*. It does not mean that we will never experience negative emotions either. The ways in which we cope, and react to experiences shape our destiny. The Great Yogis express the importance of our reaction to everyday life. Emotional reactions carry experiences to the karmic level to be experienced from one life to the next.

## Innovators – Integrating the Body, Mind, and Spirit

If we ignore any one component of the physical, emotional, or spiritual aspects of our being, it leads to imbalance. Understanding the Law of Accountability helps us achieve the cosmic state of equilibrium. We learn to go with the flow knowing that our decisions and choices have consequences, and thereby we let go of petty little things, and we open our hearts by giving and receiving. Balance is an understanding of how to use the power within to benefit others. It is in giving that we activate the power of the Law of Receiving. When we share our gifts, they bring us happiness, and joy naturally overflows from a space of creativity. We become innovators. The natural state of the universe, cosmos, nature, plants, and all life is peace. However, the modern man's nature is stress, overwork, fear, and scarcity.

Balance doesn't always mean fifty-fifty, where two very different things strike a middle point somewhere smack dead in the middle. Balance can be something that is more fluid, and in constant motion; it is like the spiraling arms of our Milky Way Galaxy more familiarly recognized by the Yin Yang symbol. We become mesmerized when we see the Olympics, and a gymnast does a balancing act by moving a little to the left, to the right, up and down, spinning their bodies, and then makes an astounding move. When we understand that balance takes some effort to achieve, and remain open to change, we are well on our way to achieving it.

## Fifty – Fifty Isn't Always the Answer

When we think only in the fifty-fifty logical way, it leads to all kinds of difficulties. A true representation of balance is not, you scratch my back and I'll scratch yours, or you give me a dollar and then I give you back a dollar. That is not truly giving and receiving. Instead, give what you have more than enough of, but do not give away something that you do not have, with the thought of it returning to you. This is the concept of debt, it becomes an "I owe you."

Knowing when to give and when to receive is understanding balance. We should give, knowing that we will receive what we need when we need it through synchronicities. We should not fear that there isn't enough money. Many of us like the flow of money coming to us, but we fear when we let it go. True abundance is knowing that cash has to circulate, and in accounting this is known as the Cash Flow Cycle. If we keep an open heart and mind, divine abundance flows constantly and effortlessly into and out of our lives, like the blood flowing in our veins.

## Life Is Not As Simple As Riding a Bicycle

One of my favorite memories growing up was learning how to ride a bicycle, and the example gives a good comparison to balance. If you or anyone you know has learned to ride a bicycle, then you know the effort that it takes to do so. Achieving balance requires the same skills: attention to the now, energy, dedication, focus, and looking ahead to steer clear of obstacles in the way, such as cars, trees, and bumps.

I learned to ride later than most people, when I was a teenager. I needed a little push to be sure I would be able to ride, so I had to ask for some help. One of my favorite cousins, Shashie, gave me the push off I needed by grabbing hold of the seat, and he sent me peddling. It was quite fun. I couldn't use training wheels, so I was swept off, and away I went. The same way, everyone can achieve balance with a little push. The challenge is in the learning stages, like riding a bike. Once you learn how to pedal the bike and move with it, it is easy to remember, and virtually impossible to forget. There are days when it will be easy to remain in balance, and days when it will be challenging.

Things that once felt good no longer feel the same. To better understand this point, you can watch one of your favorite movies from your childhood. Do you feel the same about the movie as you did when you were a child? The movie has not changed. Our perceptions changed. Likewise, as you become more and more aware of your true *Self*, you will be happy doing the things that are in harmony with it, and it becomes much more difficult for you to deny your truth. In this way, if you are feeling stuck or unsatisfied with life, you will be able to change it with just your thoughts. Depending on your connection to your true *Self*, repetitive thoughts, affirmations, and the connection to your subconscious, conscious, and super-conscious mind can easily be reprogrammed, because the intensity of your belief systems will magnetize your dreams to you.

The following is a list of components for the spiritual balance sheet. You can add these to the balance sheet of life to help you bring yourself back in balance.

## Contemplate the Following Concepts that Would Make You Feel More Balanced:

- Service – Understanding the Law of Giving and Receiving
- Exercise – Taking care of your physical body
- Being Healthy – Eating a balanced diet
- Silence

- Spending time in nature
- Listening to healing music
- *Mantras* – Repeating sacred sounds that evoke healing on a cellular level. It reprograms our DNA with light
- Imagination – Visualizing what you want
- Surrendering – Letting go of things that no longer serve you
- Communication – Requesting help when needed and lovingly speaking our truth
- *Dharma* – Living your divine purpose: taking action in alignment with your heart
- Integrity – Being honest with yourself
- Charitable – Giving without attachments
- Receiving – Remaining open to new experiences
- Synchronicities – Going with the flow
- Courageousness – Standing in your principles
- Inner Peace – Meditation, self inquiry, introspection, and contemplation
- Stability – Building foundations by saving for your future and your family or children
- Gratitude – Filling yourself with contentment

**Humanity Is Progressing Towards Enlightened Cosmic Consciousness**

Our Scientists are doing a great job of finding evidence to support ancient teachings. It is evident if we look at the wisdom of each new generation. We as humanity are evolving into higher beings. As the Earth moves into alignment with the Galactic Center, actions that were once considered dark and evil, whether on an individual basis or global scale will surface more and more to be healed. Systems that are based on the dark nature of humanity and greed will no longer be supported by the underlying collective cosmic consciousness, which is yearning to experience a higher vibration of enlightenment and love.

# CHAPTER 4
## *Reclaiming Your Divine Self –*
## *Realizing Enlightenment*
## *Spiritual Accountability*
## *Our Nature As Beings of Light*

"Immortality – Light of Consciousness"

**Our Nature As Beings of Light**

On our last destination, we got a general understanding of environmental accountability. We continue on our cosmic journey together, and we now build upon that foundation to understand spiritual accountability. Unlike the balancing act while riding a bicycle, you won't get taken for a ride on this destination. In the cosmic plan we are not banking on a miracle; the cosmic bank does not need a bailout because it is ever flowing with infinite abundance. Spiritual Accountability shows us a better and synchronized way where we can use our will, thoughts, and power to heal the world financially.

We expand our thinking on a cosmic level to see that our financial security is not in stocks, bonds, and real estate values, which change over time. Many people would not be impoverished if wealth came from personal abilities alone because they work tirelessly. Rather, our financial security comes from the cosmic mind, and our goodwill in relationships with others.

These relationships can be with customers, vendors, friends, coworkers, employers, neighbors, a personal banker, and family. The networks in our lives are some of our most valuable resources.

We must consider each other in our decisions and their impact on the planet. Many successful companies invest in their people knowing that they are some of its most valuable assets. Emphasis should be placed on the benefits of efficiency and effectiveness. The bottom line and profits are truly all that matter for any business to be successful from an accounting perspective. A crucial area for a successful business should encompass continuing education, and training their employees.

## *Spirit-Wealth-Empowerment* Are One Energy

It was in the winter of 2009. At that time, the world financial climate was still rocky, and it was at a point of frustration globally. I woke up blurry eyed one morning with the words *"Spirit Wealth Empowerment"* resounding in my ears. I walked over to the computer to see if the domain name was available, and to my amazement it was. I clearly felt the connection of those three words, and I felt that those powerful words express the divine guidance and synchronicities. The Great Masters were showing me a spiritual connection to wealth.

In reality, it seemed as if not much had changed since Yogananda's time. Instead of the Great Depression, we had a world financial crisis in November 2008, and the recession dragged on into 2012. It was worse than the stock market crash of the 1930s. Many people lost confidence in the economy because of the crisis. History repeats itself often enough for us to realize that there has to be a better way. Yogananda said, in his book *How to Be a Success*, the Great Depression proved that when the wealthiest nation on earth can be suddenly thrown into poverty, divine laws govern our financial lives. There is a divine hand which moves all things.

## Meeting a New Ascended Master: Master Kuthumi

The Law of Accountability and synchronicity were at play. It was still the winter of 2009 in December, and I met a man who I connected with instantly. He was a former software engineer for Microsoft, and he had just recently moved to Arizona. He was teaching Nada Kriya Yoga in Seattle, Washington. He invited us to his house one afternoon, and I felt like I had known him for a long time. He wanted to establish a music school in Sedona, and sang a few classical Indian chants for us. His house was simple, clean, and just magical. We could not part. We sat together and talked for hours. It felt like we had known each other for lifetimes. As we looked around his house, a picture of Mahavatar Babaji caught my eye. We could not stop sharing the amazing stories and synchronicities about the Great Masters.

As we parted, the dark night sky seemed lit up in the entire mountainous area. We drove on Highway 89A between Sedona and Cottonwood, and it felt like celestial beings were all around us. I remember feeling that something great was happening. I looked up in the sky, and I had a vision of billions of tiny star-like Angels, enveloping the earth with their arms connecting with each other as if they were cuddling a delicate baby. I heard the message intuitively, "Humanity has chosen to ascend their level of consciousness to peace. We are here to help you in this transitional time of chaos." In that moment, I felt that we all have guardian angels. Every time I asked for guidance, protection, or help, it was as if they were ever-present, and willing to provide assistance. As the *Bible* saying goes, "Ask and ye shall receive."

1. Have you ever been in a time of crisis when you asked an angel for help?

2. Did your angel respond with a clue that left you speechless?

We continued driving on Highway 89A on the way home, and I heard the name "Master Kuthumi, Master Kuthumi, Master Kuthumi." I did not know much about Master Kuthumi, and it was more of an annoyance. My connection to Yogananda and love for him was very strong. I enjoyed meditating on Yogananda's energy of strict discipline, and the spiritual feeling of floating in the sky when I connected with him. I did not want to connect with any other masters. I was loyal to the point of attachment with Yogananda.

Sometimes we think that the difficulties we face in any given moment will be permanent. The veil of suffering and ignorance clouds our judgment, and that is when we are most susceptible and vulnerable. In those difficult times, we must seek inner peace, and know that the good times may be only a few moments away. Our reactions to the struggles we face shape our destiny. Even in the worst of times, we should maintain a positive outlook, and they will eventually change for the better. Trust me, this is much easier said than done.

For three days I was in a state of sadness, and I never felt such sorrow. It was the kind of sadness that left me feeling empty, hopeless, and without any courage. So I took a picture of Mahavatar Babaji and stared into his eyes. I humbly prayed to him, and asked why I was so sad. Intuitively, I heard, "I sent Master Kuthumi to work with you and in resistance, you told him to wait." I had ignored the name Master Kuthumi since driving on the highway, thinking it was unimportant.

I put down Mahavatar Babaji's photo, and tears flowed down my cheeks. Was I ready for Master Kuthumi? The answer was no. I had so much to do. Even I struggle during transitions. After meditating on Babaji, the good news is that my intuition revealed that it took me only three days instead of two and a half years to realize that I was off course from my *dharma*.

1. How many times do you feel stuck or like something is not quite right?

2. Are you moving with your divine intuition?

3. Do you resist the flow of synchronicities?

If you ever feel out of sync, take a moment to reflect on what the source may be. You might find quite a surprise, and it may be the thing you least expected. I quickly learned that it is important to go with the flow and be accepting of change. At times it can be difficult, but with time, change brings us closer to happiness. After all, the only constant in an ever-changing world is change. Caroline Myss in *Sacred Contracts* explained that sometimes suffering is due to spiritual depression. I feel that we all know deep in our hearts when we are off course. Sometimes we stay a course that is against our intuition out of fear of the unknown.

Even though it took a few weeks, eventually I felt ready to meditate on Master Kuthumi's image. What I know from meditating on Master Kuthumi is that he is an earth-plane Ascended Master, whereas Yogananda is a spirit-plane Ascended Master. For me, that meant when I work with Master Kuthumi I would get to eat more, and heavier foods such as meat and dairy, to feel grounded. Whereas, with my meditations on Yogananda I was fasting for days at a time. I ate only a vegetarian diet in order for my mind to reach the high spiritual planes of super-consciousness. I felt like I was floating on clouds. The experiences while meditating on the Great Masters are out of this world.

If you would like to connect with one of the ascended masters, remember you can look at their picture, and by looking into their eyes with reverence, and humbly making a request, you can connect with them. I would like to share a discussion with you about your experiences after meditating with the Great Masters. We can share in the joy of their divine presence via Social Media on our website: *www.indeara.com*, Blog, YouTube Channels, and Facebook. If you would like to share your ideas with me, please refer to the "Resources" page at the back of the book for more information to connect with us.

I decided to do a Google search for the name Master Kuthumi. He is thought to be Koot Hoomi Lal Singh of the late 1800's. I did not know too much about the Great Master in terms of his history. The following quote was taken from wikipedia.org to reference him:

> "The *Masters of the Ancient Wisdom* are the beings in the Spiritual Hierarchy of the planet Earth as a whole as identified by the Theosophists Madame Blavatsky, C.W. Leadbeater, Alice A. Bailey, and Benjamin Creme…Master Kuthumi is also called Koot Hoomi. It is said, one of his earlier incarnations was as Pythagoras, the Greek philosopher and mathematician. Also, it is said that Master Kuthumi was Saint Francis of Assisi."

The following quote describing Master Kuthumi is taken from spiritlibrary. org:

> "Master Kuthumi led an extremely secluded life, affording to a public record of him that is at best somewhat fragmented. Born in the early nineteenth century, Mahatma Kuthumi was a Punjabi whose family had settled in Kashmir. He attended Oxford University in 1850. His remaining years were spent at his lamasery in Shigatse, Tibet.

**Balance – Family Reunion**

On our last destination, we learned the importance of balance in our lives. Our cosmic journey continues now, and at this point in time it was December 17, 2009, a few days before Christmas. We were packing presents, and we were busy with preparations to meet our families. I feel that the holidays bring balance to the missing link of family in our lives during the rest of the busy work year. We were going back home to visit and spend the holidays on the East Coast, in New York and Massachusetts. Both Jonathan and I have pretty big families. I hope you will enjoy our trip.

Jonathan took the digital camera, and he snapped a few pictures while we were packing to go. A photo is a precise moment in time. In this case of celebration, it represented a connection and happiness with our families. The thought of hugs, kisses, love, eggnog, presents, and the kids made me glow. As I was sitting in the airplane, I remembered something that came up when I packed my bags preparing to go to the airport.

*Indeara Hanoomansingh*

## Reminiscing About a Century's Old Tradition with My Grandmother

As I looked up at the fireplace, the picture of my siblings and parents from decades ago brought back memories, and I reminisced about when Mom died. I remembered in 1982, Grandma sold her little home at age sixty-six to raise all of us. When I looked back at what she did for us, I realized how much Grandma meant to me. My beloved grandmother lives in Guyana and she is now ninety years old. It has been many years since I last saw her, and I miss her very much. She still grows her food in her little garden, and prepares her meals according to *Ayurveda*, which is a Sanskrit word that means the knowledge of life. Special spices and foods are composed of the elements of life in a holistic way; each person is considered *vata* (air), *pita* (fire), or *khapa* (earth and water).

Grandma was raised in the ancient *Vedic* customs almost a century ago. She imparted much wisdom, and fueled my passion for the Sanskrit teachings. With her gentle but firm nature, each and every day, she instilled values in me which seem non-existent in the modern era. My Grandmother would say having guests is like a visit from God, and she recommended that we treat them with the utmost respect. In her tradition, serving guests was like a patronizing ceremony. She offered the best food and drink to any guest staying at our home.

On the other hand, my grandfather was a devout Catholic, and he believed that "sparing the rod spoils the child." Grandpa was a staunch disciplinarian. Mostly he was abusive domestically, and I thought he was plain old mean and I avoided him at all costs. Everyone in my family was afraid of Grandpa. He passed away in 1996. Grandma told us tales of his extremely violent outbursts, and a time when he beat her within an inch of her life and wrapped her body up in a sheet to be disposed of. She bravely went against tradition and divorced him after he left her for dead. She raised my father and his siblings on her own as a single mother. I love my grandmother because she never made me choose between my mother's and my father's spiritual beliefs; my father was a baptized Christian, and my mother was Hindu. I thought it was normal and quite natural to grow up open-minded spiritually with Hinduism and Christianity.

## In Flight to New York and Massachusetts

My daydreaming ended as the pilot announced the plane's arrival at JFK International Airport. I wondered if it would be a drama filled holiday season, or a joyous occasion. I guess with family, a little of both can be expected. We were exhilarated because we hadn't seen the family for almost a year. The little ones had now grown up and were taller than me, and I surely wanted to spend time with them. It was a short vacation, and there were many people to visit in New York. I couldn't believe how quickly my nephew Brian had grown up when he said, "You can't buy me presents that teach me how to count or do my ABCs anymore."

## Did Master Kuthumi Say Eating More Food?

In our family, food was a custom to be offered to guests as a great sign of respect. Some home cooking from my eldest sister Donna is worth the two and a half hour drive to Phoenix Sky Harbor Airport, and the seven hour layover flight to New York City. During the holidays, food, family, and fun are a theme for us. We had a great time! We rang in the New Year for 2010 with the ball dropping in New York City, and we danced up a storm as we watched the Black Eyed Peas concert in Las Vegas on TV. We clanked our red wine glasses and cheered "Happy New Year!!! Yeahhhh!!!" The next day, my sisters and I visited our step mother who is a great cook, and I loved her food. I ate as much of the traditional Guyanese style chow mein as I could. When we departed her apartment the temperatures were so cold, I felt like my nose would be shattered to pieces like crushing ice to make a frozen drink, and my hair felt like peanut brittle in a two year old Eskimo's mouth.

We ran to the car, got in, slammed the door, and turned on the heat. We then drove to Long Island to my Aunt's house. The winter white snowstorms on the highways felt like we were at the North Pole. The arctic weather was bitter cold with snow and icy roads which made the trip longer, but it was nice to be able to spend time chatting with my sisters on the way. When we got to my auntie's home, it was late. We slid and slipped up to her front door. She made some great lamb curry with hot roti-pita bread, and after sipping hot tea my sisters left. Auntie Christina and I chatted into the wee hours of the morning until we got tired, and we went to sleep.

The next day, my aunt brought me to my uncle Chait's house in Queens. I only had a few hours before checking in at the airport. Gosh I love Master Kuthumi, and all the home cooking. My Uncle laid out a buffet of foods, and there were many different Indian dishes. We ate to our heart's content. Everything was warm, sweet, salty, spicy, and oh so delicious. I loved my trip to New York.

On January 4, 2010, Jonathan and I arrived back in Sedona in the twilight hours of the morning. As much as I loved the vacation, when I got back, I promised myself not to ever take such a long one again. I know for sure I will, but when I am so busy, I swear it is so tough to leave for more than a week.

There was so much to do, that I thought I would go nuts trying to catch up for about three weeks after the trip. But I sure wish we could get together with our families more often. Maybe I will get to do it again next year. I enjoyed the profound sense of balance and peace with them.

## Spiritual Principles Merge with Accrual Accounting

On February 12, 2010, I sat in a building located on Dry Creek Road in Sedona, and thoughts of the great Mahavatar Babaji were immersed in my mind and heart. Once again, I began writing for our dreams to take flight, individually and collectively. Whenever I meditate on Babaji it is almost as if I can hear the Great Master's words. He has proven to me time and time again, through people I meet, that he is alive and present in our consciousness today.

The Great Master explained that one's success or failure can be attributed to tendencies in the past. The Yogis explained the concept of reincarnation in which the actions of one lifetime affect the next life. It is like the accrual concept in accounting in which transactions affect more than one period. We learned, on our second destination, that our efforts are never wasted. Let's apply the accrual concept of accounting to the spiritual concept of karma. We will expand on the example from the chapter on inventory, where we viewed one lifetime as one period and take these principles to a spiritual financial statement. In the same way, the accrual concept affects more than one period in accounting. The sales or expenses from one period, affect the next period. An accounting period can be yearly, monthly, or quarterly. A spiritual period can be perpetual, everlasting, or eternal which never dies.

A few of these concepts are reiterated from earlier for clarity purposes, and your understanding, because accounting principles build step by step to make up financial statements. The income statement affects one period such as one year. The balance sheet, however, is perpetual. Each year, the net income, or loss, gets carried forward to the next year on the balance sheet. A net income increases, or gets added to the beginning balance of retained earnings on the balance sheet. Net losses are subtracted from the retained earnings. Net income is added to retained earnings. Remember, retained earnings are simply all the income that a business carries on the balance sheet from year to year.

## Bypassing Karma with the Law of Accountability

We can understand the spiritual concept of Accountability with the concept of karma. Good karma increases our balance in life; bad karma, on the other hand, takes away from our balance and inner peace. It sows the seeds of disharmonious financial, emotional, physical, and spiritual relationships with money, friends, family, coworkers, or the IRS. When we willingly help others, we increase our store of good karma. When we harm others, we increase bad karma. The saying, "What goes around comes around" is a representation of karma and the spiritual Law of Accountability.

## STRATEGY FOR ENLIGHTENMENT

**Continuous actions that benefit others accrue into good deeds. In the universal mind, if one gives money, their time, or love, it does not matter. Rendering service with an open and loving heart, without the expectation of receiving anything in return, allows us to bypass the Law of Karma. If one gives with the expectation of getting it back, then it is not giving a gift, rather, it is considered a loan to the other person. Giving with a free heart is the greatest thing one can do to benefit the world and accrue good karma.**

The Yogis say attachment to the outcome of our actions binds us to the karmic wheel, lifetime after lifetime. If you have more than enough oranges, give oranges. If you have more than enough apples, then give apples. If you have more than enough love, then give love unconditionally. If you have kindness, then give kindness. In this act of giving, you will activate the powerful Cosmic Law of Receiving. The universe does not care what kind of service you are giving. It is the intention behind our thoughts which counts.

The invisible Law of Accountability records the act of giving, hence, the sister complementary Universal Law of Receiving is activated. Thereby, the Law of Reciprocity activates the Law of Synchronicity, which allows you to get what you need when you need it. Synchronicity is basically divine timing; it is what we term meaningful coincidences. To reciprocate something means to give back in return, reply, or respond. These principles are the basis of the spiritual understanding of accrual accounting. The accrual concept in accounting has basically two underlying principles: the Revenue Recognition Principle and the Matching Principle. In any given system, there are principles or rules which keep the body or organization together; in our example these are known as universal, divine, or cosmic laws.

### The Revenue Recognition Principle and the Realized Soul – Our True *Self*

The Revenue Recognition Principle states that a business recognizes revenue only when the goods are sold or when the services are rendered, not when cash is collected. The seller must perform the services or deliver the goods. In accounting language, money collected up front is treated as a liability. The seller must hold the money as if they owe the customer until they deliver the goods or services. This one accounting principle sums up one of the greatest spiritual messages of the *Vedic* texts. *Seva* is the Sanskrit word for service. Service is the interconnecting fiber of all life. Practicing selfless service leads us to the realization of the concept of interdependence.

The matching principle states that expenses incurred in one period may apply to revenue from another period. Hence, the accrual concept in accounting can be differentiated from the cash basis of accounting. Cash basis treats an expense when the cash is paid. For example, if you buy a stereo, it is considered an expense when cash is paid for it, but when you pay for it in installment payments, it is considered as an accrual basis of accounting. A cash basis accounting system recognizes revenues when cash is received.

The Realization Principle in Accounting is related to revenues. It must be within a period of time such as a month, quarter, or year because it gets recorded on the Income Statement. The corresponding Matching Principle relates to expenses. Expenses are thought of as incurred for the purpose of producing revenue. In my first introductory class to accounting, the text book, *Accounting: The Basis for Business Decisions, Tenth Edition*, explains the concept of offsetting expenses against revenue on a basis of "cause and effect," and it is called The Matching Principle.

In the Revenue Realization principle, cash and its consequences in the material world would have no bearing on the realized soul. Similarly, if we wanted to become *Self* realized beings, according to the *Vedic* texts, *Self* realization must be earned, and we don't become enlightened beings by wishing, begging, borrowing, paying for or buying it, and chance or luck has nothing to do with it. The service we render to each other is one path to help us reach *Self* realization. How can we realize enlightenment with service?

This opens up the discussion about the Law of Intention, and its manifestation in our lives. Let's take, for example, we go to the grocery store to buy milk. We give cash to the cashier, but instead of putting the milk in the bag, she hands us a coupon for milk. Would you walk away from the store with a coupon for the cash you just paid? No, of course not, we should get a bottle of milk for the cash we paid, only then the transaction is realized and completed. In another example, let's say you go to the doctor. Would you walk away from their office and pay them if they did not treat you? This is another example of the Revenue Realization Principle.

# STRATEGY FOR ENLIGHTENMENT

Service strips money of the power that it holds over us. We must think of others and try to understand their thinking. We should ask ourselves how we can be of service to our family, job and employer, community, or business. What are their needs? What can I do to help them? This is how simple it is to shift our thinking with the energy of money. It should not have any power over us. To receive money, we need to produce a product that people need and value, or provide a service.

## Money and Enlightenment

Our current thinking in society is dominated by the thought that there is not enough money in the world, and what's in it for me? From an enlightened cosmic perspective, I beg to differ. Money comes from paper, and paper comes from trees. There is plenty of ink and paper to print money. The energy of money is how much we are willing to give of ourselves to get it. Think about it for a moment, if we are not willing to give, what will we receive? According to Yogananda, if we can accept that we are children of the divine, to whom all the riches of the earth and universe belong, then we can reclaim our divine birthright of abundance. We must learn to be on a loving, grateful vibration to attract and keep wealth. If we learn to love money and appreciate it, it will grow. If we don't value money, it depreciates in value.

## Faith in the Divine vs. Selling Our Souls

In *Sacred Contracts* (Crown Publishing: Harmony Books, 2001, Page 118), Caroline Myss explores the archetype of the prostitute in terms of energy:

> "The act of prostitution is generally associated with selling one's body for money, but to my mind that is perhaps the least significant example of the Prostitute archetype. The Prostitute thrives most bountifully in subtle ways and in ordinary, everyday circumstances. It comes into play most clearly when our survival is threatened. Its core issue is how much you are willing to sell of yourself-your morals, your integrity, your intellect, your word, your body, or your soul-for the sake of physical security.
>
> The Prostitute archetype also dramatically embodies and tests the power of faith. If you have faith no one can buy you. You know that you can take care of yourself and also that the Divine is looking out

for you. Without faith, however, you will eventually meet the price you cannot turn down."

The entire *Vedic* teachings constitute a wealth of knowledge over thousands of years. In our discussion I cover only a few topics from my own experiences. *Dharma* is simply our divine purpose or duty. When we live our *dharma*, our life will be based on the principles of faith. By rendering service in alignment with the higher divine intelligence, we can experience more synchronicities. The act of faith is not easy to accomplish. It is almost as if when all the odds are stacked against us and there seems to be no way out, we must find a way to go deeper in, and face the challenges. To become *Self* realized, we must have faith and belief in a higher power, and be of service to others. We do not have to sell our souls for money. We just have to be willing to provide a service that is beneficial to our communities and society without compromising our values.

The ancient Yogis were able to see thousands of years in the future. In India, a tradition called reading Nadi leaves is passed down from the saints of the past. They wrote the destinies of future generations on palm leaves. Palm leaves, which match a person's fingerprint, can reveal their destiny. They also reveal the actions one can take to change the course of their destiny. We do not have to search our soul's entire history from conception to present day to try and nullify the negative karmic consequences of our past actions. Our efforts to be of service, while surrendering the outcome, can change the course of our destiny. Our *dharma* changes everything! It is like a domino effect. The action of one person changes the entire cosmos. What changes can you effect?

In the Indigenous and Eastern Societies, the accrual concept is not foreign. Emphasis is placed on the wisdom of previous generations. It is not uncommon to honor one's ancestors in many of those cultures. In Japan, there is a village where almost all of the villagers live past one hundred years old, and their age is respected as a sign of accomplishment. Even though the Eastern Societies are advanced with modern technological ways of life, they still maintain a balance with their ancient culture. Technology can be good in many ways and like anything on earth, balance is the key to its success.

**Accrual Accounting and Enlightenment**

Our journey continues inward to discover enlightenment with the accrual concept. We begin our *realization of enlightenment* by looking for physical evidence and clues left by the ancient ones. Almost all ancient traditions have examples of this *light*. The Mayans talk about the cosmic Galactic Center, and they say humanity is awakening to their *light* or luminous bodies. The ancient Yogis call it The Golden Age or Sat Yuga-The Age of Truth. Our sun's *light* was revered by ancient cultures.

Even though there have been many amazing discoveries, our modern scientists have yet to discover the secrets of the Galactic Center. NASA made public a report on solar flares, which are explosions on the sun's atmosphere that release a tremendous amount of energy. NASA's findings coincide with ancient teachings. Our Sun is a star and it contains 99.86% of the mass in the Solar System.

## There Is More to Sunlight than Meets the Imagination

Through *photo*-synthesis, carbon dioxide is changed into oxygen which supports almost all life on our planet. It is undeniable that the sun exerts a tremendous thermal, gravitational, and electromagnetic influence in our Milky Way Galaxy. Remember earlier in the book, we did an accounting with a *photograph* or picture of our life. A photon is simply *light energy*.

I am happy to have endured some of the Physiology lectures in my pre-med classes in college. As many of you may already know, our emotions and moods can be affected by sun*light*. Scientists are now beginning to understand a complex relationship with sun*light*, melatonin, and serotonin. Serotonin is a neurotransmitter which regulates sleep, sensory perception, mood, depression, body temperature, noise sensitivity, and photophobia, which is sensitivity to light. Melatonin is a hormone that controls sleep. The web of life is connected by a biological clock. The circadian rhythm is roughly a twenty-four hour cycle in the biochemical, physiological, or behavioral processes of living entities, including plants, animals, fungi, and bacteria.

More developments in the scientific arena that shed *light* on the ancient teachings came from the Japanese scientist, Masaru Emoto. It was a beautiful night when we met Dr. Emoto at his Seminar in Sedona. In his book *The Hidden Messages in Water*, he exposed small samples of purified water to music. Dr. Emoto video taped images, words, sounds, and pictures as it was freezing. He then *photo*-graphed the images of the water as it crystallized.

Positive words, such as "love" and "thank you" created the most beautiful snowflake like crystals. Negative words, such as "demon" formed grimy dark images in the crystals. He explained that music made with love can be experienced on a cellular level. It feels good, whereas music that is done in hate feels destructive. Dr. Emoto's studies scientifically proved the power of positive thoughts on the mind.

This explains the reason why music is universal. Imagine the missing ingredient in grandma's secret recipe is no secret at all. It was her energy and thoughts as she prepared the food. Something cooked with love can be healing versus something cooked in anger. Imagine how profoundly our thoughts and intentions affect the environment around us. As we begin to understand spiritual accountability, consider the following questions:

- How would you change your life if you knew that your thoughts can make you feel happy, sad, sick, or peaceful?
- What kinds of food would you eat if you knew that your chef's intentions would affect you on a cellular level?
- What kinds of music would you listen to?
- Who would be your friends if you knew how their thoughts affected you?
- How would you treat other people if you knew that they were another you?
- What words would you choose to speak if you knew the impact it had on your emotions and our planet?
- What kind of wishes would you make for the world's financial, environmental, and spiritual situation?
- How could our thoughts change the economic outlook if we all believed in our divine birthright of abundance, rather than lack and scarcity?
- What companies would you support?
- What would this do for education standards for our children and the school systems?
- How would our value system change?

## Reprogramming Our DNA with Sound – *Mantras*

A long time ago, the ancient Yogis of India came up with a system to unlock the power of the energy centers along the spinal column, which control our DNA, known as *mantras*. The Sanskrit language is based on fifty-one letters in the alphabet, and each sound corresponds to a place along our spinal column which affects different glands. The Yogis devised a plan to eliminate suffering using sounds with *mantras*. *Man*, means to think. *Manas*, means mind. The suffix *tra*, means tools or instruments, hence, a literal translation of *mantra* is, instrument of thought.

They said wealth, good health, and all other means of happiness have been granted by the Heavenly Father and Divine Mother through these sounds, because the human being is governed by their thoughts. Repeating *mantras* is an entire science within the *Vedic* texts, and even one *mantra* repeated consistently throughout one's life can lead to enlightenment. *Mantras* were used to protect the mind from negative thoughts. The ancient yogis said it was very important, and recommended that we do *mantras*, because they bring peace and relaxation to sooth our minds.

One particular *Mantra* is called the *Gayatri Mantra*, which activates all twenty-four glands in the body. The following is the *Gayatri Mantra*:

> *Aum Bhur Bhuva Swaha,*
> *Tat Savitur Varianyam,*
> *Bhargo Devasyah Dheemahi,*
> *Diyo Yo Nah Prachodayat,*
>
> *Om Shanti Shanti Shantihi*

### Gayatri Mantra English Translation (Original source – unknown):

*"Oh God, the basis of all life, Who is self-existent, Who is free from all pains and Whose contact frees the soul from all troubles, Who pervades the Universe and sustains all, the Creator and Energizer of the whole Universe, the Giver of happiness, Who is worthy of acceptance, the most excellent, Who is Pure and the Purifier of all, let us embrace that very God, so that He may direct our mental faculties in the right direction."*

### Gayatri Mantra Alternate Translation (Article by ShantiMayi):

*"Throughout all realms of experience 'That' essential nature illuminating existence is the adorable One. May all beings perceive through subtle and meditative intellect the magnificent brilliance of enlightened awareness."*

In the book *Let There Be Light* (Dinshah Health Society, 1996, Page 95), Darius Dinshah shows the equivalency of sound frequencies and *light*. Each musical note is shown to correspond to a color. The human body is composed of more than seventy percent water. Perhaps it would be reasonable to assume that sounds and our thoughts affect our bodies. From my telepathic experiences, thoughts are real energies, and they can be transmitted over long distances. How many times did you pick up the phone to call someone and they've just called you? Or how many times have you thought of someone and they called you? This is the energy known as telepathy or thought transference. Thoughts emit a certain sound vibration. When I meditate and close my eyes, I can hear the dim sound of *Om* like a *light* bulb.

In ancient times, there were apprentices and master craftsman. Knowledge was passed down orally from the teacher to the student. If the student possessed the right qualities, they were accepted by the master.

The Guru simply showed the way to one's true *Self*. The Gurus of old sacrificed everything for the disciple, and their satisfaction came only from the en*light*enment of the student. The ancient Yogis taught the student how to access the guru within. The following definition of a guru is taken from wikipedia.org:

> Guru is composed of the syllables *gu* and *ru*, the former signifying 'darkness', and the latter signifying 'the destroyer of that [darkness]', hence a guru is one characterized as someone who dispels spiritual ignorance (darkness), with spiritual illumination (light) -as per Advaya-Tāraka Upanishad (verse 16)[citation needed],
>
> The syllable gu means shadows
> The syllable ru, he who disperses them,
> Because of the power to disperse darkness
> the guru is thus named.
>
> – Advayataraka Upanishad 14-18, verse 5
>
> The word *guru*, a noun, means "teacher" or spiritual master in Sanskrit and in other languages derived from Sanskrit, such as Hindi, Marathi, Bengali, Gujarati and Nepali, or influenced by Sanskrit, such as Indonesian and also Malays. Guru is also used in other Indo-European languages, such as Persian from time to time to refer to a wise and knowledgeable figure who can guide and shed light in the time of need.

**Knowledge That Has Been Hidden for Centuries**

The time has come for us to realize our thoughts and their far-reaching consequences. Perhaps that is why Mahavatar Babaji sent Master Kuthumi to work with me. He is a world teacher who wants to reveal the hidden knowledge to us; we are all alchemists who can create worlds, galaxies, and destinies through sounds and *mantras*. Our highest potential is indeed there, but like a precious stone, it needs to be carved and shaped to reveal its brilliant magnificence. These words are based on my personal experiences after meditation on the Great Masters.

With today's busy lifestyles, mankind does not have an entire lifetime to dedicate to *Self* awareness. Children are taught in a school system that is inadequate for the development of their full potential. Spiritual principles are needed to reconnect us to our higher *Self* and true nature. The solutions are not found on the outside, they come from within, and as we learned earlier, meditation unlocks those secrets.

## Meditation and Spiritual Accountability

On our first destination, we know that the ancients left a clear road map for our success, and now we will explore it. The most important thing that a human being can do to eliminate stresses of the mind is meditation. It allows us to connect to the divine wisdom within, and our inner guru and teacher. If we can make contact with the innermost *Self*, then we can expect to find some sense of peace and stability. The ancients knew how to use meditation to achieve balance, healing, miracles, and travel to other galaxies. Certainly miracles can be real possibilities. Climbing a mountain seems like an insurmountable task, but we can climb to the summit if we take it one step at a time. If we make one choice at time, we will be able to climb above chaos in the world.

## What Is the State of Enlightenment Worth to You?

Congratulations on your cosmic journey of life thus far. Due to societal conditioning, many people in the world neither contemplate their life nor attempt to understand it. In effect, when you take the time to contemplate and meditate, it will change your life because it leads to *Self* realization and spiritual accountability. You can change how you relate to everything and everyone with this new insight, and it helps prevent problems that might surface.

Knowledge of your true nature can guide you towards riches, successful business, good health, great career, a happy relationship, wonderful friendships, and a fulfilling life. It took me several years to go through the *Life Balance Process for Inner Transformation*™. Traditionally a student dedicated twelve years to accomplish such a feat. However, I have been able to teach this process to many people, with lasting and permanent changes in their life in a much shorter period of time.

## *STRATEGY FOR ENLIGHTENMENT*

**The Law of Accountability helps us to become responsible. It brings us one step closer to knowing our infinite true *Self*. While others are too busy finding faults, and trying to fix other people, the enlightened person basks in the sunshine of inner peace from within. He or she takes the time to look in the mirror at their self with the**

awareness that they have choices. They have not allowed themselves to become mechanical in their thinking, and jaded by society. They know they cannot manipulate the image in the mirror, but must work on themselves first then the mirror reflects back truth.

Like a good soldier who mounts the stallion and directs it into battle, the realized being wages war on their inner pity, petty emotions of negativity, and doubt. They are replaced with the divine nectar of meditation, the ambrosia of the mind. The logical mind which was used to working twenty-four hour days, seven days a week, ceases. Uneasy and uncomfortable feelings of guilt, shame, and pain are transformed. The soul is realized! Life's struggles become a challenge to be overcome. Victory is seen as a chance to render devoted service with joy. Everything that was a constant battle ends. Duality becomes a unified field of oneness, and everyone becomes a mirror for us.

- What would happen if we watched less TV with the heartbreaking news of the world, and instead turned on our mental antennas to receive and transmit divine messages? Our imagination can create a healthier and more beautiful life.
- What would happen if we listened to our children and realized they hold the reigns to the future, not us?

**Spiritual Accountability Isn't A One Size Fits All**

We should keep up with current events on television programs, but we should program our minds and create the vision for a better world. Remember, we are accountable to our true *Self* for our words, thoughts, deeds, and actions. In the end, no one else is responsible for us. There are as many ways to realize enlightenment as there are human beings on the planet. Each of us experiences life through our own lens.

If five different people experience the same event, we will get five different reports depending on the person, because each person has a unique perspective. Even if they were to conduct themselves in the exact same manner, no two people can ever see things exactly the same way. If I were to ask you what a peach tastes like, you would give me the best description possible. However, until I eat a peach I will not know. If I just brushed my teeth, the peach will have a toothpaste taste. Our sensory organs are different. Depending on what you ate before, the peach taste will be affected by the flavors in your mouth.

What feels great to some may seem like utter torture to another person. A good example of this is one of my cousins and his experience moving. He listened to one of my uncles and moved to Florida. My uncle who moved to Florida loved it there because he loved the nature and peace. He retired, and thought it was heaven to be away from the city. So my cousin took his advice, packed up, and moved his family to Florida, expecting to be happy there. After a few months, he packed his stuff again, but this time, he moved back to New York. I asked him, "What happened? I thought you'd be happy there." He told me that Florida was hot, boring, and the quiet made him so miserable. He said he missed the city lights, the people, and the nightlife in the city that never sleeps.

In the same way, becoming enlightened is a personal experience. The road to enlightenment is a personal journey, and no one can walk it for you. You cannot buy it, trade it, barter it, will it, sell it, or give it away. It must be *realized* or earned like the *Revenue Realization Principle* in accounting; services must be exchanged for money to be realized. Another way to describe the personal journey to enlightenment is that it must be experienced, not theorized. Anyone can connect to their innermost feelings while meditating. Each person connects to their higher *Self* in a different way. We can only reference external descriptions. Being of service to others is a moving meditation and a personal process for everyone.

Dr. Deepak Chopra says we are spiritual beings having a human experience. Each one of us has the key to the chest of golden light. It lies hidden within the vault of our hearts. Yet, sometimes we grip the keys so tightly. The fear of what would happen hinders us from unlocking the chest. Many of us fear the unknown, and we hang on to security as time slips away. The Yogis would urge us not to miss this chance of a lifetime by fearing change in our lives. This fear keeps us inside the darkness of ignorance; like the murky shadows, fear of poverty and death grips our hearts. So many people live in fear until their life ends.

They live their later years wondering why they didn't take a chance with their *dharma*; their life was stolen with time, in regret about what could have been. Don't miss the chance to experience your immortal essence because of fear. In the end, the magnificence of our true *Self* in the mystery of life is worth all the pain and suffering. Spiritual accountability cleans the soul of man, and it lets us become, as Gandhi said, the change we wish to see in the world.

## Death Is a Certainty – Move Beyond Its Consciousness

There is only one thing for sure with absolute one hundred percent certainty, our bodies will die one day. When someone dies and we go to the funeral home, we say the body has arrived, and we do not say, the name of the person, has arrived. The name of the person was given by their parents at the time of their birth. The nameless, formless soul is eternal in the world of spirit. Not even our parents can lay claim to our souls. Another way to say this is, in about one hundred years, almost all of us alive today will not be living. Why fear death? It is our common destiny. What should be feared more than death is how we choose to live our lives now. Our days are numbered, so make them count! Thus begins the accounting of our life.

In the words of Dr. Wayne Dyer, "Remember that progress would be impossible if we always did things the way we always have. The ability to participate in miracles true miracles in your life happens when you open your mind to your limitless potential." We cannot escape negativity while we live on the earth. Yet, we can change the ways in which we live to experience bliss, inner peace, happiness, and joy. We do not have to quit our jobs, or give up our careers or professions, all we have to do is bring our spirit into our work, like the ancients who lived with passion. This will transform the world into an Enlightened Age of passionate works.

To assimilate the wisdom of the ancient ones and leave a legacy of financial freedom, humanity must remember that money is simply a medium of exchange. The true valued possessions are in the invaluable services we give to each other. Remember, currency is always changing; we no longer have the greenback dollar, or currency backed by gold, nor do we have ancient cultures' money which was once shells, beads, feathers, and grains. Remember, the commodities markets today continue that system of money. True value is in the food, love, service, and time that we give to one another. We must believe we deserve our divine share in order to receive it.

## We Are All Beings of *Light*

The word *"Jyoti"* means *light* in Sanskrit. The ancient yogis of India taught an art called *Jyotish* which is known as the science of *light*. Today, a version of it exists as astrology, which means the study of the *light* from the stars. The sages of the past, like Sri Yukteswar, were able to perform miracles with the knowledge of its science. We as humanity have been separated in darkness for a long time. We have been conditioned to value our self worth based on external factors, and we have not been free to be what we truly are, beings of *light*. We are all immortal *light* beings.

Each individual has free will and the right to choose in any given situation. From my own experience of en*light*enment, I like to call it *Making Empowered Decisions*™. To realize one's *Self* as *light* is to be wise, and have the ability to foresee consequences. This is where all future realities of a person's life are based on the outcome of a decision. It is known as concurrent parallel realities, where the future is only probable or a possibility, and it is not permanent.

## My Experience of Enlightenment

When I was absorbed in the intelligent stream of enlightenment, the energy that I was immersed in was liquid like water, yet felt light as air. It was neither wet nor dry, and sparkled like the most brilliant light that I had ever seen. It was neither moonlight nor sunshine. All of existence was just there! My perception of physical reality vanished into thin air. I became an inner *light* which reached up to the moon and passed through trees, rocks, and carpet simultaneously. I was as tall as the moon, and as small as a tiny speck of dust, and everything was alive and had a consciousness.

My consciousness was present, and pervading every molecule and atom of existence. Everything knew everything and everyone knew everyone. Bliss beyond bliss and love beyond words, it was like everything unconditionally loved each other. I wanted more than anything else to stay in that place of peace, and never wanted to come back into my physical body which felt like a cage for my soul. As I was coming back to my body, I was asked to teach people how to *Make Empowered Decisions*™.

What we believe becomes our reality. What would happen if we chose to believe in a world filled with prosperity, abundance, and unconditional love? Wouldn't we open ourselves to a potential for abundance, prosperity, and unconditional love? The example that I was given by this experience is that we have choices. The intelligent divine light communicated with me, and said if there was a rumor that their will be a nuclear attack in Sedona, the *inner world* of enlightened consciousness works like a voting process, where our votes actually count. If I say, no, I do not want to have a nuclear attack in Sedona then the molecules rearrange themselves because they respond to my thoughts and move to protect Sedona. Our thoughts affect our physical environment. Therefore, if we all believe in a recession, it prolongs it. If we all believe that it should end, then the solution to a prosperous and thriving economy reenters our consciousness. Anything can change!

I looked through enlightened eyes and saw that the world was like looking through trillions of specks of light; each particle was intelligent. In another example, if the television news broadcasts that there will be a tornado. We can speak to the *inner world* molecules, and ask the spirit of light within the tornado to protect us and not touch ground. We can end droughts, famine, wars, and poverty with this consciousness. All we have to do is use the power of our intention or thought.

## Affirmations – The Power of Thought to Change Our Reality

Yogananda said if someone is experiencing scarcity and a poor financial situation, they can change it. If they believe with all their heart with repeated affirmations that they are wealthy, even without a penny, they will eventually emerge from poverty. In his little pocket book *Scientific Healing Affirmations*, Yogananda said to repeat the affirmation "I am getting richer and richer." In the case one is experiencing poor health affirm that "I am healthy."

Over time, positive thoughts will draw to you the people and circumstances that you need to get out of the despair or negative situations. Depending on the individual's conviction, the power of thought can instantly transform our lives by a mere wish. For others who are not as convicted and whose mind and energy are scattered, it would take more than a mere wish, and much longer to accomplish their dreams, but surely if they do not give up, they too will eventually triumph.

As I continued on this amazing journey through life, the synchronicities grew. If only we believe, indeed our lives can be happy. We as human beings complicate our lives unnecessarily. It's not easy for me to express the ideas about enlightenment on a planet filled with dualistic concepts, because we exist in a world filled with opposites. Contrary to our chemistry and physics books from high school, likes do not repel each other in the world of energy; rather, likes attract and opposites repel, and complementary objects go hand in hand.

We should now realize that this spiritual journey of accountability is an individual trip for each and every one of us. In realizing enlightenment, we all have unique identities, personalities, and physical characteristics. We are part of a whole, but we are not the sum of the parts. Many people get a glimpse of the wondrous existence beyond the body and call themselves God. I do not believe that my experience of enlightenment should create an ego personality that somehow I became God the Supreme. I am still human and learn from my mistakes every day. In Yogananda's words, if someone were to hit us on the head with a brick, "our God will escape from us."

## *STRATEGY FOR ENLIGHTENMENT*

Enlightenment is about the humility to know that we are part of divinity. In a previous example, on his *Become A Smile Millionaire* CD, The Great Master said that "a wave is not the ocean. The ocean can live without the wave, but the wave cannot live without the ocean." We are one with consciousness. The physical world manifests from our minds and thoughts. The unmanifest creates the manifested world, and not the other way around. The universe is calling out for us to remember that we are part of the ocean. This life is filled with the motion picture of drama. **We should not forget our *light* bodies are one with the entire universe.**

For suffering to cease we must transcend the physical. Our reality is nothing more than a hologram of thoughts and images, and what we fill our minds with becomes our reality. If we inherently believe in good, and that others mean us well, then that will be the forthcoming reality of our existence. We must give our gratitude for the gifts we receive, and the things we have so that they may increase. If we believe that we are wealthy, then it would be easier to acquire the consciousness of wealth. However, if we fill our thoughts with poverty and lack, how can we possibly acquire wealth?

## Affirmations Lead the Way
## Actions Make Our Desires Become Reality

In a modern world filled with bills and material pursuits, we cannot pretend to sit in a meditation posture all day, and become happy either. Affirmative thoughts will only lead us to the ways of fulfilling our desires, but we must take physical action in order for them to manifest. We have human bodies that need to be clothed and cared for. The pains of hunger hurt no matter how enlightened someone is. Remember, it is not necessary to drive a luxury car and have a multimillion dollar mansion to acquire happiness. However, it is necessary to have adequate transportation and a home. So enlightenment is not this nirvana on a cloud somewhere, at least not for as long as we are in a human body.

## A Spiritual Solution - Change Fears to Success

Enlightenment is knowledge put into practice, and *Self* realization is when we take action with awareness; it is our inner knowing. What would be the use of knowing how to do something, but not doing it? The energy of money is in the doing, not the knowing. Only the wise practice what they know, while the ignorant make wishes. Fears are like treacherous demons that lurk amongst thoughts of success. They are just waiting for a chance to steal our peace of mind. We must not allow them the chance to take hold of the mind.

After careful planning, we can take action one step at a time. It may take some time, but anyone can achieve their dreams. A realized soul knows that a few little pleasures are not the entirety of existence. The pursuit of a balanced life should be our goal, and we should avoid the extremes of life. Living in harmony is to be good to those closest to us, and it is the easiest thing to practice to become an enlightened soul, but this is much easier said than done. Forgiveness and unconditionally loving our friends, family, and coworkers is the first doorway to inner peace. What other possibility is there for the enlightened soul?

## The Modern Yogi and Yogini Triumph – Metaphorically They Exist In the Cities of Life

We cannot escape the responsibilities of our modern lives, yet at the same time, the possibility for enlightenment exists in our daily routines. Meditating alone in the jungles will not give the qualities that the modern day yogi needs. It is not easy to be a modern day yogi or yogini. Angelic and Demonic influences are everywhere, metaphorically and symbolically. The myths of creation may yet prove to be real. In the jungles of modern life roam the untamed wild animals. They lurk amongst the leopard prints and alligator boots in the cities of life. Angels and Demons alike, roam amongst the cafes, and in the highways of life too. Nomads can be found on sidewalks, in deserts, and in the lands of metropolitan lights.

The cave-like hologram has changed to cityscapes. Mankind still has much to face, and many challenges to overcome even more so today than to live in a secluded cave, and think that enlightenment is to be found there. The media portrays the bloodsucking vampires wearing new shades; these creatures are worshipped in the movies and on television. Yet still, they drink the blood of man in broad daylight like the cash sucked out from circulation.

Children's minds are vied for by violent games and movies, and yet it is all a drama. When we make the choice, we can begin to break free from the reigns of terror, darkness, and ignorance, and that is true enlightenment. Denying the existence of evil for an idealistic view that this earth is perfect is a farce. We live in light and shadows, and therefore negativity cannot be avoided all together. So we must become stronger in our hearts and minds to overcome these inner evil tendencies. Victory over adversity plants the seeds for enlightenment. What better place than the discipline of work and family life to begin lifting ourselves out of the physical illusions to become enlightened?

## Humanity Wakes Up with Spiritual Accountability

Trickery came from the alluring power of deception used by the greedy and power hungry to manipulate our minds when we were young. The suffering of humanity will not cease if mankind does not wake up to the stark reality that we are our own saviors. External factors can only do so much. We must help ourselves. We are the ones who must be spiritually accountable for our lives.

We must not focus on controlling others, but rather on controlling our own thoughts. We must not focus on the faults of others for they will become our faults; rather, we must improve on our shortcomings. We must focus not on the evils of the world. Rather, we must think about how much good we can do for others. In this way, we will be able to overcome every obstacle that stands in our way. We should shower praises of gratitude to our guardian angels, guides, heavenly and earthly protectors, and those holy ones that are invisible, and yet always close by and waiting to assist us.

## *CHANNELED MESSAGE – FROM AN ANGELIC RACE*

The following words flowed onto the paper as I was writing this chapter, "Guardians of Earth and Humanity, we are an Angelic Race of Humans given the job by the Divine to wash away the sins of mankind who were inherently good by nature. Peace is natural, and it is nature's way. There will be things put into place in times to come, that for those who follow the spiritual and blissful ways, will meet with divine justice, and all will be well. The Law of Karma is precise and accurate. Work hard now and save time for later." I interpreted the message to mean we are the generation that indeed must pave the way to change the course of destiny.

## *END OF CHANNELED MESSAGE*

## *STRATEGY FOR ENLIGHTENMENT*

**We inherited a world filled with karmic debt. Enlightenment is the wisdom knowing that we cannot possibly know all that there is to the great mystery. It is the knowing that there is more to life and humanity than just a few thousand years of our written history. There is more to know about the distant past and the future of the cosmos. Newer technologies such as DROID Smart Phones and Star Maps, are bringing the cosmic consciousness to our reality. What we call the great mystery of life is the acceptance of the unknown, for in it contains the seeds for all forms of existence.**

Enlightenment is doing our *dharma* or divine purpose in the spirit of service, without attachment to the outcome. Our duty is all that we can do. It is the job well done, and the role we were given. It is the unconditional service that we provide for each other. Despite our differences, we are indeed part of one earth, and interconnected. We share a common destiny with the stars.

We are the enlightened souls that we seek. If only this wall of flesh is removed, then we can see clearly that we are all beings of light. If we can accept that we were created in the image of greatness, we can begin to remind ourselves of that truth. The struggles and suffering that we face are the temporary characters in the plays of our lives. Enlightenment is to know that our human bodies are like vehicles which can be used as instruments for profound experiences. Our true identity cannot be housed in the physical body for long.

The *Vedas* says the body is like a garment that the soul embodies from one life to the next, and it is like changing clothes from day to day. Our logical mind would find it inconceivable to understand the age of enlightened beings to be millions of years old. Most of us cringe at the fact that we will one day be close to a hundred years old, but the immortal essence will one day escape the flesh. Death is not the end, rather it is a beginning! Like the wave that must return to the ocean, so the soul will one day return home to the Cosmic Creator; this realization is the highest goal of human life.

# CHAPTER 5
## *Ancient Vedic Wisdom –*
## *Moving Beyond Enlightenment*
## *The Cosmic Plan – Key to Wealth*

"Lord Nataraja – Cosmic Dancer – A Metaphysical Reality"

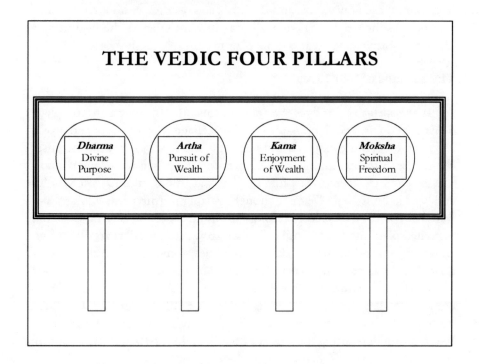

## Divinity in Form

After realizing the amazing experience of enlightenment, I wanted more than anything else to maintain that sense of inner peace. I wondered how I could bring that spiritual experience into the mundane. After all, I am living in a human body, and it is the home of the spirit. I thought to myself, surely there must be a way. I meditated and remembered that there were energy centers in the human body called *chakras*; these energy centers operate invisibly, but they can be detected with night vision and infrared technologies. Many modern technologies are proving our existence as beings of light. I found it amazing that the answers I was seeking were not out of my reach. We simply have to apply our daily activities to the divine principles, and we can experience synchronicities in our lives. Realizing enlightenment is only part of our journey in the cosmic plan. We can bring our spirit into our work and routine activities to move beyond enlightenment, and live like divinity in form.

We continue on our journey now, it was the spring of 2010 and I picked up where I left off in the winter of 2009. The winter chill purified the air and it turned out to be a beautiful spring day with the peach, apricot, and pear trees in full bloom. The little fruits were taking form on the branches. I had hoped that the peach tree wouldn't freeze its buds off, because if the frost comes, the flowers die, and the birds and deer go without fruits for the summer. As the seasons change, all of nature experiences the beginning of life in the spring. The great cosmic plan for our lives is the same.

## The Seasons of Our Lives

In the spring of our lives, we are born tiny infants, and we are completely dependent on others for our survival. The teenage years of youth and growth are when everything expands and hurts; growth is always painful because it challenges us to stretch. It is a time when the heat of sensuality and passions, like the summer, seem to last forever. The warmth of summer sure was fun, and warmed our soul. We once thought getting to thirty was a long ways a way. The leaves change color during fall, and the cool breeze allows us time to contemplate and relax. Similarly, as we grow into the fall years of our lives, we transition, and the heat of our personalities from the youthful years cools down. In our later years, we can finally feel independent.

During the winter of our lives, on the surface, we may look like the branches of the trees which are rigid. Yet, beneath the surface, new life is waiting to be born. A tremendous difference exists between the Eastern and Western thinking during the winter of our lives. In the Eastern traditions, the elderly are welcomed into society with great respect. In the spring, summer, and fall years of their lives they sacrificed and contributed to their societies, families, and the upbringing of children. In the Western Societies, we do not value old age as we do in the East because we're chasing a forever young image.

In our youth, we once believed we could change the world and fix its problems, but as we get into the fall years of our lives we begin to accept reality as it is; we've put the rebellious teenager within, to rest. In the winter years of our lives we retire, relax, and rest into the rigidity of the physical body. It is then, that we finally have the time to contemplate our eternal spirits, and ever new, it grows younger as we age. We must accept our bodies as vehicles encased in flesh and bones, and realize that we don't live forever. As our society grows older with the baby boomers, we have precious time to change our consciousness to respect the aging process, and growing older.

## The Little Things Can Seem Overwhelming

At times, mundane and simple tasks can overwhelm us. Once I completed the chores around the house, I felt a sense of ease. I tried to take a deep breath in, and realized how difficult it was to just breathe through tension. Something as simple as taking the time to notice our breath feels so good. A funny thought crossed my mind, what if I tried to breathe just once? One big gulp, and not take a breath again. What would happen? I guess I surely wouldn't be alive, and laughed out loud at the thought. I wondered why we do something a few times then stop.

We've been conditioned to get it done now, pronto, and fast. We live in a finite reality. Sometimes the faster we move, the more we get out of balance. We can step into an infinite reality knowing that everything has continuity, and we can relieve tremendous stress, because the little things we do consistently change the course of our lives. We chart our own destiny.

There is much to say about taking the time to write one page or paragraph at a time, year after year. Then kaboom! Just like that, a tremendous task of writing a book is accomplished. The key was not giving up, I persevered in my efforts. The same principle applies to almost everything in life. For example, if we take one step to promote our business each and every day to three people, it would be over one thousand promotions in a year. Remember, nothing great was accomplished overnight.

## Mahavatar Babaji's Presence Was Revealed Once More

Sometimes I wondered if the world of enlightenment could really be right in front of my eyes. While I wrote, I always felt the presence of Mahavatar

Babaji. At times, I questioned whether he was real or if he even exists in our reality. Was he just a figment of my imagination? I knew the importance of breath, breathing, and exercise, yet somehow it eluded me. I would begin a routine, and then I would falter. I couldn't seem to be able to have a fixed schedule to exercise, because the opportunity escaped me often. In my heart I wished that there was a way that I could do *Kriya Yoga*, which is breathing and yoga techniques that Babaji taught Lahiri Mahasaya, and they were passed on to Yogananda from Sri Yukteswar.

In my heart there are a few passions, and one of them is children and their well-being. So I became a Big Sister for a young girl here in Sedona. She filled my heart's desire to care for a child. One day I took her for a little shopping. We were at a local metaphysical store in Sedona. She played with fairy dust and magic bracelets. We were browsing, and she and I decided to look at some videos that were for sale. She said in words that made me laugh "What is Ba---b---a-u-jeeee's... Ba---b---a-u-jeeee's... Ba---b---a-u-jeeee's Kriya yoga?" I laughed out loud, and with tears of gratitude in my heart, I knew the Master guided us to the video. It is called *Babaji's Kriya Hatha Yoga*, with Durga Ahlund and Marshall Govindan. They give a good demonstration of yoga postures dedicated to Mahavatar Babaji.

The intensity in my heart to bring the teachings of the Great Masters in my daily routine grew stronger with each new day. Another synchronicity to confirm Babaji's presence came in the form of an email. I received a message which said that a man was coming from India who met Mahavatar Babaji in the Himalayas almost thirty years ago. Many years ago, he had a severe heart condition and doctors gave him only three months to live. This man said that he went to meditate in the Himalayas and Mahavatar Babaji healed him completely.

Sometimes it is humbling to know that the great masters can be so close by and miraculous. This Swami is now teaching *Kriya Yoga* to students in the West, and he visited Sedona. I was very happy to meet this teacher. I learned some baby steps in breathing. It is like deep breathing in, and then breathing out, with double breaths in and out. It felt so good. He was an engineer who now teaches free *Kriya Yoga* techniques. He said it was better that he earned a living than to be a burden to society. He had never charged a fee, or asked for donations, and he refused to accept money for teaching *Kriya Yoga*.

While I was trying to synchronize spirituality in my accounting work, I was wondering, "If this man met Babaji, was my work in conflict with the Great Master?" It made no sense to me. I wondered how his teachings related to the practical business world which functions only with money. After all, in ancient times bartering proved to be inadequate, and so did carrying around heavy coins of gold, silver, and bronze. I meditated on Mahavatar Babaji, and

I inquired in stillness for him to please resolve the conflicting ideas about spirituality and money.

My inner turmoil subsided when I recalled a story from *Autobiography of a Yogi* that Yogananda shared about when Sri Yukteswar sent him a telepathic message. Sri Yukteswar was delayed and could not be on the nine o'clock train to meet Yogananda and his friend. The same telepathic message from Sri Yukteswar that he would be late was sent to both Yogananda and his friend. Yogananda was able to receive Sri Yukteswar's message telepathically, but his friend could not. Sri Yukteswar said that Yogananda was able to receive the message because he was receptive. Meanwhile, his friend could not hear him because his mental microphone was not connected. When we are connected to our higher *Self*, our intuition is clear and we can receive messages from the Great Masters.

## Divine Guidance Is All Around – Are We Open to Receiving It?

We can indeed move beyond enlightenment if we are open to receiving messages from the cosmic plan. We are all given divine guidance from the Great Masters. Some of us listen to them in our meditations. Meanwhile others just ignore their heartfelt hunches. I must admit that I was one of those stubborn people who ignored my intuition all the time. I would knowingly ignore my heart because I was more concerned about what other people thought of me. In my mind the Joneses were real. Later on, I found that I should not have dishonored the divine guidance. At times I felt like I had to stumble and fall to learn my own lessons. I endured much suffering due to lack of trust in my intuition. The most pain I ever suffered was due to my lack of faith in my true *Self*, and not following my heart. I learned the hard way not to ignore my hunches. Now I listen!

## Spirit and Money Revisited

I continually tried to bring the truth about spirit into my daily life, but the perplexing issue about the separation of the monetary and spiritual world persisted. Were money and spirit indeed one? I was really curious about saints who do not touch money, and people who do not collect money for their spiritual work. I was baffled. How did they survive? The situation persisted for a few weeks with inner turmoil. After all, I was an accountant. How could the world function without money? Over the previous fifteen years I was trained as a business person knowing that money was needed for our survival. The need for money in our lives was of primary importance. Money gave us food, clothing, cars, homes, and basically everything.

We arrived at the Sedona Library where the Swami was giving a talk about his experiences. I meditated deeply in silence with the question and surrendered to the wisdom that came through my intuition. I was in the presence of the Swami. I trusted that he was sharing his honest feelings. As we did the *Kriya Yoga* breathing techniques, I asked the question again. How could he be doing this for free with no attachment to receiving money? He did have to pay for the space and amenities. The answer came to me while doing *Kriya Yoga* for a few seconds. It was almost as if someone hit send on one hundred emails. My mind's inbox was flooded full in an instant. The telepathic message was delivered. The answer was simple: money is the end result! It is a tangible, physical component of spiritual energies. Everything first emerges from our thoughts, including the services we exchange with each other for money.

Even Yogananda taught that we use money; however, he said that the divine alone gives us our sustenance. We were taught that we need money first, and that our survival depends on it. In my intuitive revelation I saw the opposite was true. If we provide a service with a free and unconditional spirit, then money flows effortlessly. We were taught to think backwards. Almost opposite in perspective, the Swami made sense; what he was saying was that we should give our services and talents to benefit each other, and by valuing ourselves we receive monetary compensation.

The cosmic plan does not record that we must give dollars to receive dollars. The universal currency and the currency of spirit are the opposite of our financial system. We provide a service, and money is the medium of exchange for that service. Service is known as *dharma*. *Dharma* is our divine duty, or the service we give to others, and without the exchange of goods or services, there is no monetary exchange.

## The *Vedic* Four Pillars of Life
### *Dharma*, *Artha*, *Kama*, and *Moksha*

We should balance the four tenets of the *Vedic* principles: *dharma*, *artha*, *kama*, and *moksha*. Remember, *dharma* is our divine purpose or sacred duty, therefore, it is our responsibilities, and no one else can fulfill our *dharma* for us. *Artha* is the acquisition, and the pursuit of wealth and materialistic possessions. *Kama* is the enjoyment of wealth. *Moksha* is spiritual liberation and the release of attachments to materialistic possessions. Each step, when progressed one at a time, can lead us to an enjoyable existence.

*Dharma* is the first step. Our purpose is to render service in connection with the cosmic plan for the highest and best good of everyone. The second step, *artha*, is to create wealth to be enjoyed by our children, families, and society. When we support systems, institutions, and businesses that are in service of the highest and best good for mankind, everyone benefits. The third step, *kama*, is the enjoyment of wealth with a lifestyle that brings us pleasures and happiness. The fourth and final step is to reach *moksha*, or spiritual liberation.

How can one reach *moksha* if they have never lived their *dharma*? Wouldn't their entire life be filled with suffering? I believe that enlightenment for the modern yogi is to live the same principles of discipline, self control, endurance, inner peace, unconditional love, and controlling their desires. These requirements are still the same since ancient times. The level of psychological traits that we must acquire has not changed for thousands of years.

## The Modern Day Yogi or Yogini – Self Control in Spending

The primary difference is that a modern day yogi does not sit on a tiger skin, rather he or she sits on a couch. The modern yogi may not always be current with trends because the few pieces of clothing that they have are sufficient. This does not mean that they do not go shopping. It simply means that they have self control, and do not live beyond their means on credit and installment plans.

Credit card companies are merciless with the interest rates they charge. The lines of credit ceased, but the desires of man continue to be insatiable. The banking system is just a mere representation for our collective consciousness. When our collective thoughts change, the banking system will mirror that change for us, and so will the financial, economic, and monetary systems. On the level of spiritual accountability, we are all responsible for the chaos of the current economic system. Now that we know better, we can see it crumbling before our eyes. We must not fear the changes. We should intend for the highest and best good for all of humanity with a banking system that is accountable to us.

## My Credit Card Balances – I Once Contracted into Debt and Slavery

Remember, in the language of accounting, if service is not rendered then it is considered a liability or an "I owe you," and it leads to debt. Do we normally provide a service to receive a debt? The answer is no! In my teenage years, I once thought that credit was like free money and could easily be spent, and I had every intention of repaying my credit card balances in full. However, when the greedy credit card companies decided to raise interest rates to forty-two percent, it was an impossible feat to repay outstanding balances. I now realize that no one can take our freedom away unless we agree to it. The credit card companies came up with extensive ads on television programming to entice me, so I was naïve and easily fooled, and I gladly contracted away my peace of mind for a piece of plastic. If I had taken the advice of my father, I would have saved about a decade of suffering.

I guess I needed to be humbled by the experience of debt to learn from my own mistakes. My father though, was quite brilliant. He said, "I work so hard for my money and they are asking me for one hundred dollars for annual fees, what for?" In a mad furry, he taught me a lesson about how much he valued credit cards. I was only sixteen at the time. He got a pair of scissors and cut the credit card offer up into pieces. I saw my dreams of all the shoes that were lost, the dresses I could have been wearing, and all the nights I could have had out, shredded in front of my eyes, and I was devastated. That day my father became a human shredding machine. My dad said, "I will never allow them to take my money." He was furious and angry, and he was having a fit. He threw the shriveled up pieces of plastic credit card in the trash. Being a rebellious teenager, that act of his made me want the credit card even more.

That was almost two decades ago. Credit limits have gone up to platinum status, and on top of that, installment payments, student loans, and car payments have changed the dynamics of our financial world. It took many years, but I regretted not listening to my dad. I quickly realized that if I continued to pay the interest only, I would not be able to pay off the principal balance in a lifetime. This issue was not a personal one; our nation has the highest national deficit in its history. Our generation has to face this situation of debt with much more severe consequences than generations in the past. We have a huge burden to bear because of inflation, and we can no longer get on the city bus for fifteen cents, and we certainly can no longer buy a house for ten thousand dollars in cash.

Social Security retirement income can barely keep up with the cost of living with inflation on the rise. In the sad state of personal finances, something dawned on me. How many people were going through this same dilemma? I set my mind on conquering this problem. I was determined to find a permanent solution knowing that things first manifest from our thoughts. I knew that the answer would be based on spiritual principles. I wanted to learn more and teach others how to overcome this same obstacle.

## *STRATEGY FOR ENLIGHTENMENT*

### Freedom from Debt

**Sometimes, to know how much it hurts, we have to walk a mile in another person's shoes. As I walked that path for a few years, I had**

**had enough. I wanted to be debt free, and I wanted to free the world from financial misery and debt consciousness forever. As I began this process, the energy of money was revealed to me. Now I understand clearly what the source of debt is. Usually, a contented person who is filled with ever-flowing gratitude for what they have is not indebted. Ever willing, they give their service to others. Their self worth and value comes not from what they want from others, but rather from what they have to offer.**

On the other hand, when I amassed debt, my self worth was low, and I always needed to buy something to make me feel good. So I realized that to become debt free, I had to take my self worth to *Self* worth, and once I valued myself, I no longer needed external factors. I stopped buying on credit cards and replaced it with spending on my debit card. The good old fashioned way helped to relieve financial stress because if I had cash, I could buy what I wanted on a budget, but when I had no cash I could not spend.

Once upon a time, during prosperous financial years, a lot of money was circulating in society. The economy was doing well, but lack of savings and planning led to overspending on lines of credit backed by mortgages. For those who improved their homes, it was not so bad, but for those who spent it lavishly, they lived in regret. I started to uncover a pattern in millions of people's lives. Though I had liked the advantages of a credit card, I realized if I could not earn enough to repay the full balance within thirty days, then it became a slavery card. If I did not repay the full balance, I was enslaved to repay the interest on the balances, and if I didn't, then my credit score would go down. A monthly review of my credit report was as painful as getting an "F" on a report card.

Extensive credit card debt is like a karmic debt. Like a hamster, we run round and round the wheel of existence, and we acquire debts to be repaid life after life. The amusements of advertising tell us that we are somehow imperfect. I believe we are divinity in flesh, and as co-creators with our Divine Mother and Father, we can change our destiny, because our heavenly parents did not make us as defective models in spirit. Each of us is a soul, and we are the inheritors of our own karma, yet we were conditioned to be like someone else, and like the models whose pictures are Photoshopped, we're expected to look unrealistic.

Maybe if we cut off the legs of the deer, oh so thin and long, we can attach them to the rabbit and see how high the rabbit can jump. Maybe we can Photoshop a mouse's head onto a donkey and see what an ass it is. The Law of Acceptance seems foreign and it was replaced with a fascist, one size fits all. We are taught to deny growing older, but of course we cannot resist the facts of life. According to the *Vedas*, the planet Earth is a planet of death, disease, and old age. No man has escaped it! This does not mean that we should not beautify our bodies, minds, and spirits. In fact, we should be motivated to accept who we are. It simply means that the true love which we seek in the mirrors of life is just a façade to our true *Self* and spirit. Insatiable desires can never fill an empty heart, and they can only lead us into debt. The true vessel we seek is unity with our higher *Self.* What we long for more than anything is a connection to our true *Self* and our nature as enlightened beings.

## Enlightened Community

Enlightenment is to be content with one's lot, yet tirelessly striving to benefit the lives of others by building communities for prosperity and peace. The word unity is in community. It represents a unified cosmic consciousness striving towards a common goal. When we earn for more than ourselves, we begin to take an enlightened approach towards money. One of the most powerful subtle laws for wealth and success has to do with helping others because it activates a powerful source to provide for more than our needs. According to the *Vedas*, one of the highest *dharma* is to earn money for charitable causes. If we can allow for the divine flow of money to be acquired and used for spiritual purposes, we may find ourselves tremendously happy.

## *STRATEGY FOR ENLIGHTENMENT*

**Charitable giving alone is not the epitome of enlightenment. We must learn to receive as well, and receiving is not the same as taking. The Yogis say the habit of taking, and our attachments, keep us bound to the endless pit of desires, and that binds us to the karmic wheel, lifetime after lifetime. This is not a new concept. At some point in our lives if we come across a fortune, it is not advantageous to give away all of our money to others, neither is it beneficial to spread one million dollars in one million hands. Rather, it is better to use that one million dollars to invest in a project that would generate sufficient income for the long term, then distribute that wealth in a way that benefits society.**

## The Enlightened Consciousness of Money Is Changing

Enlightened money is officially changing to another currency. Even though physical cash will always be around, the energy required to receive abundant cash flow is now changing to service because the manufacturing jobs have been outsourced internationally. It becomes increasingly important to value ourselves and have self worth. There is a new principle of networking and sharing. Dollar bills do not have legs, and money cannot walk to us. Money comes to us from people. At the core of wealth is the energy of respect. We should respect others in order to receive cash, and maintain its flow. Those who network well and share with others will reap the rewards of profitable returns. Those who thought that they could hoard their wealth find themselves in deep regret, and they live in fear of losing their lot. Remember, nothing ever stays the same, and money is no exception.

Especially now that humanity is at the juncture of a wonderful and great cosmic event which occurs once in 25,600 years; we are at the gateway of a new thinking and revived consciousness. A renaissance of new thoughts that lay dormant is reawakening now. Mankind has been on the planet far longer than some idiosyncratic texts claim. Our society has been evolving for a very long time. Galactic consciousness is not new to this Earth because the ancients knew about this change thousands of years ago.

## *Dharma* or Divine Purpose Is the First of the Four *Vedic* Pillars for Balance

Our *dharma* becomes so simple with this new understanding, and indeed it is the interconnecting fiber of all life. Nature understands this well. Our food reaches us with this Cosmic Law of *Dharma*. In the world of nature, a deer gives deer meat. The squirrels help us plant trees by forgetting where they buried their pine nuts. The rabbits dig holes which regulate the irrigation and temperature for the roots. The ants carry little pieces of food and build ant hills to communicate a strategy in nature. The buffalo sits and eats all day so they can give meat to feed many. The cows give their milk so that our bones can grow healthy. Animals sacrifice and give of themselves for our well-being. What can we as humanity do to return the balance to the natural world?

In the cosmic plan of life, it seems we as humans are the only ones that are totally confused about our *dharma*. I bet nature looks at us like lost children, bewildered by our environment. They must look at the maze of our daily lives and question how long before we collapse. We think the jungles are filled with wild animals. Maybe the animals think we are the ones living in cages. They might say, "At least they are able to roam free." They have not lost their connection to Mother Earth, and they survive. Mankind lost the connection to the principles of Mother Nature and therefore we suffer, and live in fear for our basic survival needs. An interesting statistic is that not one animal died in the Indian Ocean Tsunami in the 2004. How did the animals know to escape such a deluge? What intelligence governs the natural world? Have we become dependent on artificiality and lost connection to our true nature?

## Poverty Is a Disease – We Can Cure It with Spiritual Accountability

Society has a major dis-ease, known as poverty. We should look at it as a disease, and like any disease, it is treatable. Financial healing is necessary to cure the illness that leads to lack of abundance, and like any other disease, it has symptoms. These symptoms are usually prevalent in personalities that have endless unfulfilled desires of wanting bigger, better, or more of something. We sometimes think more money is the solution. Cash is an immediate fix, or is it? Cash seems to be a cure-all remedy to overcome the disease of poverty. The need for cash to immediately repay loans and credit can prove to be very effective. However, if one does not change their thinking, they will forever be caught in the web of impoverished thinking. For example, some people win millions in the lottery, and lose it all. Their money consciousness never changed, and so they lost it all.

Another thing that is required to cure the disease of poverty is to put preventative measures in place. One preventative measure for poverty is consistent and constant effort. This is the reason why consistent work pays off in the long run. We have to believe we are worthy to receive the divine son and daughter's share. It may be better to live within one's means, than to acquire more stuff on plastic or high interest loans. Painful as it may seem, we can take responsibility and begin the process of healing financially. We can get a glimpse of the eternal spirit, and live beyond enlightenment with abundance in spiritual accountability.

The *Vedic* texts were not only designed to lead us to the experience of enlightenment. They were written for us to live our lives as immortal souls. We can escape the clutches of *Maya*, which means illusion, karmic debt, and death. We can grow angelic wings while living on earth by being of service, and living our *dharma*. The Great Masters would say we should not die twice, but we should die only once in body, and reach for the state of all existence beyond death when all suffering ends. Each soul has a specific karma for wealth built up over lifetimes. Why get caught up in the karmic wheel of debt life after life?

It is amazing, once we surrender our desires, how open we become to realizing our true *Self*. With these simple thoughts, and maintaining a positive outlook for the future, miraculously, the fears about debt and money begin to diminish. It is almost as if they vanish into thin air. Our monetary consciousness can change! Thoughts about money having power over our happiness go away. If we focus our life force on giving what we have to give in service to others, we become abundant so long as we place a value on our service, and have a high self worth. For example, when I had time, I provided my services to anyone that needed my help without concerns for my needs. I wasted no time worrying about paying my bills, and provided the best service I could.

One day, in my meditations on the Law of Accountability, the spiritual answer to my questions about our survival, and our dependence on money poured into my thoughts. I was relieved! I realized that money doesn't give us the chance to live our *dharma*; it was the other way around. Many of us think that once we have a large sum of money, we will be able to live the life we want to live, and do the things we want to do, I beg to differ. When we take action towards our dreams, little by little, it opens the doorway to financial resources and the money needed to live our *dharma*. After meditating on Mahavatar Babaji, I realized that the *dharma* of a person is known. Everyone knows in their heart what they want to do. The question is will we do it?

## Do We Unnecessarily Complicate Our Lives?

The problem with humanity is that we complicate things. The grass always seems greener on the other side. Due to lack of clarity between the heart and head, we sometimes get confused as to which path to take. We humans seem to have an innate ability to sabotage ourselves by complicating our lives, and we tend to go against our hearts. It is no wonder why heart attacks rank amongst the highest killers of our society. When we deny our greatest gift to each other, we cheat ourselves and everyone else of that joy.

Caroline Myss states in *Sacred Contacts* (Harmony Books: Crown Publishing, 2001, Page 122):

> "We all have the archetype of the Saboteur. The saboteur is the guardian of choice. Like the Prostitute archetype, it is a neutral energy. It reflects our fears to take responsibility for ourselves and what we create. It is most connected to our issues for survival. Acts of courage and listening to our heart takes the saboteur's power away. Fears cannot control our lives. The only way to experience the power of choice is to listen to our intuition and gut instincts."

The great force which governs all life in the cosmos, even down to the intricate details of photosynthesis, digestion, and the innumerable miracles of life, is not dumb. The Laws of the Universe are exact and precise. The *dharma* of an individual should not be stifled by what others think. We should not allow that madness to govern our lives. We should follow our hearts and live our purpose. We should not throw caution to the wind either. Remember, we can build it one step at a time. Trust me, if I can do it, a stubborn person who took years to follow my intuition, anyone can do it.

## *Dharma* and the Law of Accountability

If I think about it logically, how could the great universe be unintelligent? We were taught to beg, pray, or blame others and external factors when things go wrong. In the cosmic plan of life, after eons of existence, the Law of Accountability is at the forefront once again. We are the ones responsible for our lives. In the famous words of Lao Tzu, "We must unlearn our learning," then we can connect to the infinite intelligence. If the great cosmos are sending email messages to deliver us from suffering, maybe we should open and read them once in a while. If we allow ourselves to receive the messages of the Divine, we can begin to see our lives transform.

Our duties and *dharma* are like parenting which never ends, because once we're a parent, our responsibilities to our children are endless. Even if the children grow up, get married, or have children of their own, we are still parents. Even though we change, *dharma* is a continuous process that changes with us. Understanding our *dharma* allows us to connect to the infinite cosmic consciousness. There is no rush to infinity, and the past, present, and future exist in this moment now. The understanding of *dharma* or divine purpose, gives humanity power and divine protection because it is a Universal Cosmic Principle. The entire universe is governed by *dharma*, and planet Earth is no exception.

*Dharma* can be further explained with the following: The *dharma* of a student is to study. The *dharma* of a worker is to be of service. The *dharma* of a tree is photosynthesis and reaching towards the light. The *dharma* of the IRS is to wisely use our taxes, and redistribute the money to serve the needs of the people. The *dharma* of a government is to serve its constituents. The *dharma* of the earth is to provide for humanity and the natural world. The *dharma* of a writer is to write. The *dharma* of a singer is to sing. As the saying goes, the birds sing not because they have to, but because they have a song. The writer who writes for money is a marketing person. The writer who writes because they have a book of ideas with a message to share is an author. Money is earned from selling both books just the same. One writer has a *dharma* to write, while the other writer writes because the information they submit must be approved for a retail market. Like the Journalists who risk their lives on the battlefields of life to share a story with the public, I write to inspire truth, and that is my *dharma*.

We should be free to bring our spirit into our work to benefit others. The bodies of courageous ones as well as cowards have a place amongst dust in the end. Remember, throughout our cosmic journey and on our second destination, we learned the importance of being true to our *Self.* The path to *dharma* that we take determines whether we are living or dying. Our heart lets us know clearly when we are on the right or wrong path. The question is: Will we listen to our hearts? The answer does not come from outside of our *Self.* Our *dharma* supports us, and it is in alignment with our hearts. However, karma does not support us, and is not in alignment with our hearts. Mostly, when we go against our *dharma*, it causes tremendous suffering in our lives.

In Dr. Wayne Dyer's *10 Secrets for Success and Inner Peace,* one of those secrets is, "Don't die with your music still inside of you." It is not failure that we should worry about, but at the end of our days, will we look back with joy and gratitude, or will we look back with regret and say, "I wish I had?" *Dharma* is understanding that life is a never-ending process, in our everlasting connections with the cosmos. In the cosmic plan, everyone's music needs an expression to make the symphony of souls.

## *Chakras* – Wheels of Light: Balancing the Energy Centers in the Body

Scientists say that everything in the universe is energy, and we are no exception. *Chakras* are energy centers in our bodies. I will give a brief and simple understanding of the human *chakra* system. The word *chakra* means wheel in Sanskrit. We have energy fields that are spinning around our bodies, which are composed of various colors of radiant *light.* There are many *chakras* in the physical body which can be seen as the human aura. *Chakras* are normally invisible to the human eye. However, with practice and training, anyone can see these circles of light whirling around our bodies. For a more in depth understanding of *chakras*, I recommend the works of Dr. Deepak Chopra, Caroline Myss, and Ted Andrews.

Some of you may already be familiar with the work of Dr. Chopra on balancing the energy fields of light. We will begin our understanding of how they apply to our nature as beings of light. In his book *Animal-Wise,* Ted Andrews gives an elaborate way for us to connect with our inner *totem* pole and *chakra* system. A *totem* is a Native word which means spirit guide or symbolic power animal. Ted Andrews elaborates with diagrams and exercises for anyone wishing to learn more about *chakras.* Also, Caroline Myss gives a great example of *chakras* using the archetypal wheels of light in *Sacred*

*Contracts*. It is based on astrological houses, and symbolic representations of the invisible energies which govern our lives.

For our discussion purposes, we will cover only the basic *chakras* as I have experienced them. We only need to know that in the Law of Accountability, our words, deeds, thoughts, and actions are being invisibly recorded in our body's energy centers. We cannot lie to ourselves! Our actions are being recorded and accounted for within our own being. This invisible energy body is called the *astral* or light body. The information stored in our *chakras* affects us for more than one lifetime.

Modern science calls it the human aura, and for an understanding of *chakras*, it's better that we experience them. I created a video that is available on our website to help you connect with them. The following is a basic description of the *chakras*:

1) The first *chakra* is located at the base of the spine, and its light is red. It is responsible for our stability on the planet. Also, it is connected to our ability to manifest our desires.
2) The second *chakra* is located just below the navel, and its light is orange. It is our connection to each other, the place where we share power, and our interactions with sensuality; it is also the center for money and finances.
3) The third *chakra's* light is yellow, and it is the center for our self worth. The yogis say when a person becomes enlightened, the yellow color turns green, and the golden light is transformed into the heart *chakra*. We find the saying that such a person has a "heart of gold."
4) The heart *chakra* is the fourth energy center in the human body, and its light is normally green. This center in the body is responsible for our emotional well-being.
5) The fifth *chakra* is located at the throat center, and its light is sky blue. Funny, when we are down we say we are feeling blue. According to the yogis, this *chakra* is where we carry our past karma. So when we say, "A weight has been lifted from my shoulders" or "You've got a chip on your shoulder," this all makes sense. The ancient mystics used the science of sounds (*mantras*) to unblock these energy centers. The throat is the communication center in the body.
6) The sixth *chakra* is located in between the eyebrows, and it is commonly known as the third eye. It houses our intuitive and psychic abilities. Its light is indigo blue.
7) The seventh *chakra's* light is purple, and it is our connection to the cosmic consciousness at the crown of our head. It is in the shape of

a multicolored lotus petal turned up, and we look like magnificent beings dazzling with rainbow lights.
8) The eighth *chakra* is responsible for our connection to our higher *Self*, and frequencies of enlightenment. It connects us to the universe and when this *chakra* opens, we expand our awareness to experience the grandeur of oneness with all of existence. If we can open this *chakra*, we know that all is one, and we are all interconnected.

## A Higher Perspective

My eighth *chakra* was open from an early age, and I have had many spiritual and other-worldly experiences since I was a child. I always knew we could reach for the stars. Many children still have the ability to connect with the cosmic intelligence. Yogis describe our *chakras* as galaxies and universes in the human body. Hence, they created *jyotish* and astrology, which is the study of our astral bodies, light bodies, and our auras. These energy centers are doorways and portals to infinite universes within our Universe. This can make a lot of sense only if we view ourselves from an eighth *chakra* perspective, which is the enlightened perspective. Since the eighth *chakra* is located at the crown of the head, it is literally a higher perspective.

We are filled with a thousand rays of light, but I can't imagine sharing my story about reaching for the stars, with a mole; it would think I am crazy, since all it sees is dirt and roots. If, however, I told an eagle that we can connect to the stars, the eagle would probably spread its wings, and ask me which star system I am referring to.

Similarly, we are all viewing our life experiences through different energy centers in the body. Not only do we have individual personalities, but we view experiences from different perspectives based on our past life experiences, and past situations which are stored in our spiritual DNA. The spiritual DNA is encoded in the astral body of light in our *chakras*. We can access the guiding *light* of intuition depending on which perspective we take. Some of us can see the light of wisdom, meanwhile others can't. Everybody is part of the grand cosmic plan regardless if they can experience enlightenment or not! An enlightened perspective gives us a sense of peace and freedom within.

If the upper chakras are not open, it's virtually impossible to feel inner peace because we are disconnected from our higher *Self*. The circumstances in our life are not always our fault, but rather they are cosmic illusions of life just happening. We feel like this life is real, however, it is temporary. The roller coaster of emotions in our lives can feel so real. Like a movie reel, we cry, yell, feel up and down, then it's over, such is the frailty of our human existence.

The message of spiritual accountability is clear. We can come to the realization that no one controls our destiny because the higher Cosmic Laws are impersonal in nature. We as humanity can begin empowering ourselves by practicing the Divine Law of Accountability. We can achieve a dynamic existence and live in balance. Each aspect of the *Vedic* four pillars has to be experienced: living one's purpose, acquiring wealth, enjoying life, and feeling spiritual freedom, which leads to a happy existence.

In theory, realizing enlightenment and a life in balance sounds great, however, in practice it is very difficult. An easy way to explain this is: What good is a college education if we do not practice what we've learned? Would my accounting degree be worth anything without practical work experience or a job? The cost of education is very high, but the piece of paper is worthless if we cannot apply the theoretical principles to practical life.

**Cooking the Books**

In theory, accounting entries have presented us with financial information. Theoretical application of accounting has been misused by some financial institutions. They presented inaccurate financial statements to the public that cost many people their livelihoods. Making fraudulent entries in accounting is known as "cooking the books." In theory, a financial statement or journal entry can fix the books, but a journal entry cannot undo the damages and losses to a person's life, nor can it fix a financial crisis. The Comic Laws work the same for all of us.

In the book of life, the Cosmic Law of Accountability is not dependent on the whims of financial institutions or mankind. Imagine what chaos we would have if the heavenly bodies' movements depended on what we think. Though we may not immediately recognize its power, the Law of Accountability cannot be bribed or tampered with because it coincides with the Divine Law of Justice. The Yogis explain that justice is eventually served, even if it takes thousands of years. *Dharma* is therefore supreme, and surpasses our understanding with the logical mind. It can only be experienced. When we cultivate *dharma*, we cultivate the spirit of inner wealth beyond measure, and we can manifest our desires more easily.

**The Second *Vedic* Pillar for Balance Is *Artha*–The Pursuit of Wealth**

I understood my *dharma* or divine purpose is giving the best service that I can give, and my best changes from day to day. All we can do is our very best in any given moment. I realized my *dharma* is to bring joy and plant the seeds of empowerment for humanity to reclaim divinity, and alleviate our suffering. I give to you freely my wealth of spiritual knowledge, inner peace, synchronicities, the *Life Balance Process for Inner Transformation*™, caring for others, and the unquantifiable treasures of my unconditional love. I feel wealthy in the spirit of life. However, I admit I am no expert on the acquisition of billions of dollars. It would be better to reference the works of millionaires and billionaires who have succeeded in amassing fortunes. If the stars smile on me and I amass a fortune of billions, I will be sure to share those strategies with you.

**The Rat Race**

When I look back at the foolishness of my conditioning, I pursued money like a mad slave working over twenty hours a day, seven days a week. When the logical mind ruled, I worked tirelessly and endlessly until my eyesight was so weak that I needed glasses. I raced to work with adrenaline rushing through my veins, and felt like a rat injected with too much steroids. Mostly, I allowed my heart to get into a panic about being a few minutes late. Sometimes I revel in my ignorance about the thought of how I could possibly be late in an infinite universe, and it makes me chuckle. That gave me an even better reason to laugh out loud about the idea of procrastination in eternity.

We should not be afraid if there are not many jobs or enough work for us. We can use our *dharma* to change the world around us. Living our purpose is the power that protects us from all suffering, whether spiritual, emotional, or physical, it automatically brings balance in our lives. Our mind is a powerful tool that can accomplish anything our heart desires. When we focus our mind and energy upon a goal consistently for long enough periods of time, it makes our success a certainty. By focusing our minds on a task at hand, we change our reality. When we understand spiritual accountability, it will help us align with our divine purpose.

**Hang On – Help Is Here**

I must admit, I searched everywhere for a solution to our current economic, political, societal, and financial issues. I thought that there had to be a better way for humanity to live. I remembered the words of the Great Masters as I meditated on them. They said wealth is our divine birthright. The Great Masters said that we must believe that we are divine children and we must seek wealth with the thought of doing good deeds for ourselves, and our planet. Focusing our attention on success and prosperity helps a lot. A few thoughts of success do not counteract thoughts of failure and doubt.

Rather, each and every day, we must cast away all fears about poverty and claim the divinity within.

I tried these teachings for about a month. Then one day, out of the blue, I received a text message to consolidate my credit card debt. The process took what seemed like minutes to wipe away years of financial burdens. This solution may not be the only solution out there, or even the right one for you. What I do know for sure is that if you live your *dharma*, the intelligent universe surely will send divine aid to help you find the right solutions, as it has done for me.

There are times on this journey when there is a dark tunnel of debt, mortgages, and bills to pay. We should try to remember that this is not the only reason we are here on earth, nor is it reflective of our true *Self*. Sometimes there is ignorance and darkness, and there may be times when we want to give up on this ride through life, or feel we may want it to be over with, but we must hang in there. We can get on this journey of our life's purpose or *dharma* which shows us the infinite possibilities of hope, courage, strength, and determination. I assure you there is a light at the end of the tunnel. Anyone can find a way out of the darkness. If we make the choice now to be led from the ignorance of darkness to the light of wisdom, the feelings of being stuck can change and be transformed, now. One thought changes the world!

**Real Savages – Rip Off for $24**

I stayed focused on my *dharma*, and could not help but to think of billions of people on the planet who this message could help. Wealth was relative to the time and place where we lived. Living in Arizona, I realized the frontiers of the "Wild Wild West" were won in the battlefields of the gold rush. Many lives were trampled over to attain the golden nuggets. The legend states that Native Americans sold Manhattan for twenty-four dollars. Imagine what a rip off that purchase was without royalties or rental income. Native Americans were called "savages" because their value system was different. They did not value the gold which they considered to be the veins of Mother Earth.

They were like the Eastern mystics who valued the knowledge in the golden fields of enlightenment. Imagine how it would feel when we reach the state of enlightenment, and realize what a rip off it was to have sold our souls, on planet Earth, for a little bit of comfort. Natives valued the riches of nature and its preservation for generations to come. The trains that ran through these lands brought immigrants from everywhere during the Industrial Revolution. The coal miners and lumberjacks built our great United States.

The parallels of life, time and again, repeat themselves. The Gold Rush was like the carrot dangling in front of the donkey's head, and we were taught the same beliefs. Somehow I thought money would be the solution to end the suffering of humanity and all of our problems. Like the game "Pin the Tail on the Donkey," I was the one blindfolded when I was pinned with the reality of our existence. Nothing could be farther from the truth!

## STRATEGY FOR ENLIGHTENMENT

**The real riches of gold came with the realization that our thoughts control our reality. Mankind suffers, because of ignorance, and not knowing about the true Law of Abundance. By now we should know that believing in lack and scarcity causes us to experience it. We can reclaim our divine birthright as children of the One Creator, and receive our divine share for the services we give to others. We should realize that without being of service to others, we have no share to claim.**

### *Lakshmi*, the *Vedic* Goddess of Wealth

In the *Vedic* texts the Goddess of wealth is *Lakshmi*. She embodies a beautiful woman who wears a red sari with golden coins flowing from her palms. Goddess *Lakshmi* is the abode of fortune, far above the poverty consciousness of earthly thinking. She presides over the following forms of wealth: fame, knowledge, courage and strength, victory, good children, valor, gold, gems and other valuables, grains in abundance, happiness, bliss, intelligence, beauty, higher aim, high thinking and higher meditation, morality and ethics, good health, and long life. The forms of her manifestation of prosperity are: grains, courage, elephants, progeny, victory, knowledge, and money.

Once, I wondered if such a goddess exists. Would I be able to connect to her? Would she grace me with wealth? I desired it. My meditations revealed that on a human level, we see them as different beings, but from a spiritual perspective they are all part of the same cosmic consciousness; it is something inconceivable to our human understanding. In a state of desperation I folded my palms and prayed to her. I said, "Oh Mother, I am afraid to approach you, but please reveal thy form. Divine Mother in the form of abundance, what would you give this humble child?" I said, "Please mother, more than anything else in the world I want to be a writer. Please provide financial resources to meet my obligations." It took a few weeks until I got a response.

## DIVINE TRANSMISSION – A CHANNELED MESSAGE

### Master Kuthumi Answers My Call for Help and He Can Do the Same for You

One day, I felt a thought run through my mind. I clearly connected with Master Kuthumi. As I looked into his eyes and meditated, I intuitively and telepathically heard, "Don't think about your needs. Surrender to the Divine your physical needs. Focus on providing a service, and helping others achieve their dreams while you are in the process of accomplishing your dreams. Do not give anything that you have to beg, borrow, or ask for. Just give what you can. Give Indeara to the world." That was it! Sometimes we think that we have to be perfect, but that is not the case at all.

## END OF CHANNELED MESSAGE

All we have to give is our best. We cannot give anything else. When we are not in integrity with our true *Self*, lies eventually surface to destroy our dreams. After all, this is why we are here on earth. It took some time for me to be able to understand this message and be myself. Each time I tried, my conditioning as an accountant came up and I wanted to check my bank balance. Did I make enough to pay for everything that I was responsible for? Mostly I was afraid of giving up the security of my accounting business. Whenever I ventured in a new direction I got overwhelmed. Crying was the only thing that helped. In humility, after the tears subsided, I decided to have faith no matter what.

### When I Could Cry No More

How could the Great Creator who holds the Earth and Moon in orbit forsake one little soul? I placed all my financial concerns in the hands of the Great Masters, and wrote to my heart's content. More than life itself, I wanted to spend eternity writing and helping people. My beloved world of enlightenment and peace could not crumble over the slices of bread that I need for sustenance. Far away from the mundane concerns, I could meditate forever in some far away cave, but reality proved otherwise. I thought to myself, I could not give up my car and all the bills, and escape to some far away land. When I could cry no more, I kept on going. It was then that I received the blessing from the Divine Mother *Lakshmi*. At this point, I prayed each and every day. Maybe my faith was being tested. Maybe I had to be deserving of sharing this message with you. The Great Masters are not without firm discipline.

The gurus of the *Vedic* tradition, like Sri Yukteswar, said that they absorb the karma of the disciple. For example, Sri Yukteswar helped Yogananda bypass much karma. Yogananda said that not everyone can be a millionaire. No matter how hard one tries, everyone can never be a Henry Ford. However, everyone can reach enlightenment.

The Goddess *Lakshmi's* dazzling beauty came to me in the form of courage to live my *dharma*. I felt so inspired after thinking about the Divine Mother in the form of the Goddess of Courage. It was then that I telepathically received the message that she is the energy of flow, synchronicity, physical activity, and service. It is not the money we want or need that is valued by the cosmic plan. It is the service, or things we are willing to do and give in order to receive money. Think about it realistically for a moment, can we eat money? No, of course not, we can eat the food that money buys us. Think about the answers to the following questions:

- What kind of service can you provide to others?
- How can that benefit their lives?
- How can you form a network or alliance to benefit your community?

How simple the understanding of wealth has become. It is just a physical manifestation of great ideas. As I edited these words, I felt such gratitude, and I also felt thoroughly like a fool. The Divine Mother has given so much to mankind. So much of her abundance has blessed us. How could we be ungrateful? How could we ever ask for more than we deserve? I developed a personal relationship with the Divine Mother.

**Spiritual Powers and Synchronicities – Prayers Work**

Each day, I pray the following words, let me be of service, use me for thy will, not mine. My life never goes the way I plan it anymore. All my plans have gone awry. I gave them up willingly for the peace of mind that comes with the synchronicities in connection with the cosmic plan. I prayed and said, "Lord I place all my business and personal financial needs at thy holy feet. I trust you, but I do not know how to trust." Within one week, more synchronicities began. I realized then, that there is indeed a divine intelligence, which is alive and can respond to us; it knows our needs and thoughts. We must be very clear about our decisions, then surely we can effect change in our lives. It is important to note that some decisions really do not make a big difference in our lives, meanwhile, there are some decisions which impact us tremendously.

One such decision that made a huge difference in my peace of mind was when I decided to make the Divine Mother my business partner. As with all things connected to the higher power and synchronicities, I happened to be at a bookstore, and came across *The One Minute Millionaire: The Enlightened Way to Wealth* written by Mark Victor Hansen and Robert G. Allen. I got familiar with this book and it was very helpful to me. I learned about the higher power, where they recommended that we make God our business partner. I surrendered my logical ego mind to the energy of flow, and I began to move in alignment with my dreams. My every wish has been fulfilled.

Why does the situation of debt exist in the first place? Who created debt and why? The permanent solution to the cycle of debt is cash. If we can detach from the situation and look at it from a fresh perspective, then surely we can find a solution. The first step to making empowered decisions is to understand that life is not a constant, and there are changes in life all the time. A king can become a pauper, and a pauper can become a king.

## With Great Power Comes Great Responsibility

We can achieve inner peace and balance by understanding our nature as beings of light. Power entices everyone, and money represents power. To hold on to either one, we must develop a backbone and have strength because with money comes great power. A theme in the blockbuster movie *Spider-Man* was, "With great power comes great responsibility." If someone can manage power then they can hold on to money. Some people misuse their power, and they take advantage of others with manipulation and the negative use of money. Usually those people meet with misfortune because the Law of Accountability is at play.

## *Alakshmi*, the Goddess of Misfortune

Some people associate money with being evil because greed left a trail of death and pain along the way. The pursuit of riches by some is covered in blood, tainted by human trafficking and slavery, and plagued by violence and wars. However, for the enlightened person, money is neutral and has no power over them. The value of money is not in a piece of paper. The true value and power of money lies in the energy of goods or services that are exchanged. We have to be engaged in the flow in order to receive currency, and share it with others to keep it circulating.

Now that we've met the Goddess of Fortune, *Lakshmi*, we will meet her sister, the Goddess of Misfortune. Since we live in a dualistic world, it is only natural to know her counterpart, *Alakshmi*. Everyone loves the beautiful form of *Lakshmi*. However, without the blessings of her elder sister, no one can be wealthy. Money has power, and power is not something that just materializes, it must be earned. Who might be the elder sister to the Goddess of Wealth? I am a big basketball fan, and I won't say who my favorite team is so that I won't offend anyone. One of my favorite coaches in the NBA refers to this elder sister all the time. I see him coaching his team and he says, "Come on guys… let's overcome adversity."

The elder sister to the Goddess of Fortune is adversity. *Alakshmi* represents the exact opposite of the Goddess of Wealth. Her characteristics are unhygienic conditions, lethargy, laziness, quarrels, fighting, poverty and scarcity, lack of courage and respect, and ignorance. The *Vedic* metaphors can help modern man understand the underlying spiritual principles of wealth. To better understand, we should consider the following questions:

- What happens if we do not clean the house for a month?
- What happens if we do not exercise for a year?
- What happens if we do not get a car wash for a few months?
- What happens if we do not take a shower every day?
- What happens if we don't brush our teeth every day?
- What happens if we don't take out the trash?
- What happens if we don't go to work every day?

I think by now you get the point. My point is that we do not have to do anything to attract misfortune. It is always present on earth in every aspect of our lives. The energies for suffering, sickness, and poverty arrive on their own. We must defeat those negative qualities of poverty, or *Alakshmi*, and overcome adversity to attract wealth or *Lakshmi*.

**How Can We Combat Adversity to Gain Wealth?**

No one can conquer this ugly foe to the beautiful Goddess by themselves. This is where we realize that the Cosmic Consciousness encompasses all actions. How can anyone possibly overcome these obstacles alone? When we remember that we are interconnected and part of one team called humanity, it becomes easier to defeat adversity. The days of the Lone Ranger are gone. The Lone Ranger prepared us and gave us the skills needed to contribute to each other. We should now bring our strengths and individual contributions to the table with a collaborative mentality. We should not take from others. Rather, we must focus on what we have to share.

As the level of our consciousness raises with a team mentality, network marketing companies are on the rise because many people work hard to try to get out of the box. We have to take calculated and carefully planned actions. What defeats *Alakshmi* more than anything else? The solution is simple, we have to be consistent with disciplined efforts, and persist through adversity. Consistency is one of the greatest characteristics because our habits shape our destiny. Also, consistency is one of the foundational principles of accounting.

## Equity in the Balance of Life
## Money, Past, Present, and Future: The Ultimate Game of Balance

Balancing the past, present, and future is no easy feat. Most of us balance the checkbook often. If we look back at our check register, we will see this balancing act very clearly. Everything in our life can be classified into three categories. Our entire life can be seen as time: past, present, or future. Accounting transactions record the past. Economics focuses on forecasts, and projections for the future. Our nation is in debt and we are always accounting for the past. Many people find it difficult to get ahead. Liabilities are past transactions while sales goals are the present moment. Many people find it difficult to save because they are so far behind in debt that they cannot get ahead with savings. Current earnings are constantly paying for the past. How can we stop the trend?

## Budgeting and Savings

There have been so many excellent books written on budgets that I do not want to reinvent the process in this chapter. Suze Orman has a great workbook for budgets. If you can understand budgeting principles, then you can easily find a way to do one, but first you must understand budgeting. We must not be foolish about financial principles, we must be wise. Yes, the Divine does provide for our needs, but we must have a plan for savings. Without a savings plan, inner peace is much more difficult. This does not mean that the budgeting plan that we create is etched in stone.

A budget is a plan for consistent efforts to be disciplined in our spending. Budgeting is simply a way that allows us to have self control when spending. It lets us know that we can't spend money that is set aside for important necessities, and it teaches us to plan ahead. A simple budget is to list all of our expenses and needs including fun money, and car repairs, and then we multiply the monthly budget by twelve, we should ideally aim for one year savings. Sometimes knowing the reasons why a budget is important, and how money really works, allows us to achieve balance.

Savings can be set aside for future spending or investments. If we can think about and plan for the future, then we never have to concern ourselves with the present moment. We would not have to balance the checkbook every day to see if there is enough money in the bank. When we learn self control from the budgeting process, we can appreciate the feeling of relief from constantly stressing to get more.

With salaries and minimum wage just barely covering the cost of a lunch sandwich, many people have to think outside the box. Sometimes they begin a small business, but without proper planning, they soon realize what they got themselves into. It is important that a small business owner consult with an accountant before, or very soon after, they start an enterprise. Entrepreneurs can tremendously benefit from the wealth of knowledge that accountants can provide for their businesses. Any good accountant should be able to help you create a budget.

## The Third *Vedic* Pillar for Balance Is *Kama*

We now bring our understanding to *kama*, the enjoyment of wealth. Many of us will not have any problem with experiencing pleasures, because most of us, deep down inside, daydream about winning the jackpot and how we would spend our fortunes. Our society is designed to fulfill every comfort of our existence with commercials that are designed to entice us to spend.

We can enjoy a luxurious beautiful multimillion dollar mansion made of marble, crystals, stemware, fine china made of silver, plates made of gold, and any delicious delicacies we can think of. Spas and retreats with ayurvedic remedies that can soothe the body, mind, and spirit with healing sounds, hot stones, honey, and milk baths. Cucumber stress relief for the eyes, chocolate covered facials, and hazelnut oil massages. There are all kinds of sensual pleasures that can be experienced as well. However, I will not elaborate on them, and I will leave that up to the writers of Romance Novels. I trust that we can surely find many ways to have fun.

## The Fourth *Vedic* Pillar for Balance Is *Moksha:* Spiritual Liberation

The most important part that the Eastern mystics play in our modern lives is teaching us the process of *moksha*, which means spiritual freedom, and it is a perspective that we in the West can benefit from. I would like to honor Yogananda's Master, Swami Sri Yukteswar, to give you a glimpse of *moksha*, which is the culmination and synthesis of the divine teachings of the Yogis of India. Yogananda shared his Master's firsthand experience of liberation at death in *Autobiography of a Yogi* (Crystal Clarity Publishers, 1946, 2005). You can read all about it in the chapter called *Resurrection of Sri Yukteswar*. *Moksha* is the ability to conquer death and be resurrected like Jesus Christ. After his death, Sri Yukteswar rearranged cosmic atoms and created a real body made up of flesh and blood to visit Yogananda.

## Conquering Death – Life After Dying

Sri Yukteswar explained to Yogananda that he was in another world called *Illumined Astral Planet*. Yogananda pleaded with Sri Yukteswar to know more about the astral cosmos, and Sri Yukteswar explained that there were many astral beings in the cosmos. There is no question whether there are other life forms in the universe. Our scientists and astrophysicists should be busy trying to communicate with the beings from other planets. Those inhabitants travel from one planet to another with masses of *light*, and through meditation and advanced spiritual techniques, I have been able to communicate with many beings from many different planetary systems. Sri Yukteswar explained that the astral worlds are infinitely beautiful with no bacteria, insects, or snakes. I have seen lapis lazuli castles, rainbow colored lakes, and golden sparkling rain in my meditations and lucid dreams. Even though planet Earth is exquisitely beautiful, the magnificence and grandeur of astral living is beyond compare.

It is no wonder the realized men and women of India happily surrender material desires. It seems that they can manifest much more in the astral worlds. As one Yogi put it bluntly, why would he need a few gold trinkets on Earth, when he has seen heavenly palaces made of solid gold? The yogis referred to the life energies as *prana*, which is a creative and divine intelligent light force, and unlike atoms and electrons, *prana* is a conscious intelligence. We live in an intelligent, and living, breathing Universe. All we have to do to connect with it is step away from the drama of life's activities. It is quite a reality!

## Our Immortal Existence
## Our Journey Culminates in the Fields of Gold

How can anyone access these amazing spiritual worlds? We will be able to access the energy fields of light with *Self* love. I like to call these dimensions "fields of gold." The emotion of love is the gate code that gives us access to the inner worlds of peace, and abundance. Love acts like a password to activate all the functions in the bigger picture of life. The emotion of love is the entry way into the unseen worlds of light.

Dr. Deepak Chopra's *The Way of the Wizard* gives a good example of the inner worlds of light. He said, "The basis of everything in the wizard's world rests upon the insight, 'All this is myself.' Therefore, in accepting the world as it is, the wizard views everything in the light of self-acceptance, which is the light of love." The Lakota Native Americans have a simple prayer called *Mitakuye Oyasin*, which means we are all related or all my relations; it acknowledges everyone and everything on Earth, and beyond.

## STRATEGY FOR ENLIGHTENMENT

**Namaste! Mitakuye Oyasin! Ubuntu! They mean greetings in Hindi, Lakota, and Bantu. I bow to the spirit in you. These simple words generate respect, compassion, and love for one another. We create a sacred bond, and connect with each other with a greeting. They are usually accompanied by a smile, clasping the hands in prayer, or a profound sense of reverence for the soul. The spirit as well as the physical body of a person is honored. These greetings create a gesture of sacredness, and acknowledgement of the other person as ourself, and thereby we strengthen the bond to each other on a deeper level. The one energy is the *light* within all of us. We stop to consciously recognize the *light* of divinity in another person. It is the realization that each person is connected to us, and for just a moment our individuality becomes a part of the collective cosmic consciousness.**

We conclude our journey on the *Vedic* Four Pillars and realize that we can live in balance, and be happy with the four-fold path regardless of race, color, or creed. *Dharma* is our divine purpose and the first step, without it there can be no happiness. *Artha*, or acquiring wealth, is the second step and without it we could not enjoy life on earth. *Kama*, the third step, is the enjoyment of life's pleasures without which we certainly could not be happy. Finally, *moksha* is spiritual liberation. We must bear in mind that we are here for a limited number of years, and we must treasure each moment. We should feel life in every breath.

*Moksha* exposes the temporary nature of life on planet Earth. Our lives, which seem so real, come to an end one day. What if it were true that there are indeed cosmic realities beyond our wildest dreams? We battle with each other on earth to be number one, the greatest, the first, the best, the world's greatest etc. Our logical little self with an ego-concentrated mind, tells us there is the chosen one. There seems to be enough room for only the chosen ones and the elite; however, underneath the canvas of the universe with the specks of dazzling lights across the Milky Way, humanity is seen like intricate diamonds gleaming across the pitch black skies. We are all given the exact same opportunity to become immortals.

Religion is not the goal, it is the way. We are born into a religion or choose a spiritual path which resonates with and suits our personality. Whichever path we take, whether it is Hinduism, Buddhism, Christianity, or Islam, it does not matter. In the end, we must all abandon and give up the path like we give up the body. The true consciousness of Christ, Krishna, or Buddha is that we are the enlightened ones that we seek.

Cosmic accountability is to know that we are one being, and one cosmic consciousness, and we make up the Universe. We are all children of the cosmos, and the Great Cosmic Law of Spiritual Accountability does not play favorites. The goal is spiritual liberation, or *moksha*, to become one with the universe. We are divinity in flesh, and we must release all possessions that we once held in our life, when we enter the cosmic stream of consciousness and into our immortal bodies of light.

On our journey we traveled beyond the illusions, to the Galactic Center of creation where there is more than enough for all. Our nature is beings of love and light, formless, endless, infinite light of divine intelligence. Even though there seems to be magic and mysticism around this very alluring phenomenon, there is really nothing sophisticated or amazing about this. All things in the Universe are sacred, and part of the cosmic plan. Everything is composed of the one light behind existence. *Mitakuye Oyasin! Namaste! Ubuntu!*

Together we can weave the fabric of our lives with color, intent, love, and inner peace, with the right decisions. Our thoughts are sewn into the intricate fabrics interconnected to all life in the Universe. We all have a magic carpet to weave. At times, each needle that passes through the hole, each color of emotion, seems like an insurmountable task.

The cosmic accounting of each soul records every word, deed, thought, and action we take in every moment of our lives. The aura of our magic carpet represents a dot in the masterpiece, on the canvas of life. Will we weave a tapestry of intrinsic value filled with love and inner peace? Or will we contribute to one of devastation on the planet? The choice is yours and always has been. We can custom make something of real value to heal and bring balance to the circle of life. We can move beyond enlightenment and into cosmic consciousness for the greatest benefit of all. Life is so much better than we have ever known. We are endowed with the greatest power. As children of the Divine, we were born with the gift and ability to change our reality based on our thoughts, actions, and choices, and with *moksha*, our souls are eternally free if we can surrender the outcome of our decisions.

# CHAPTER 6
*Make Empowered Decisions –*
*Uncover the Power of Personal Choice*
*Magical Miracles in Accountability*

"Thrilled – Expression of Gratitude"

"What goes around comes around truly means: what you give out you get back, at all times, and being fully conscious of this, is a step toward enlightenment."

--Jonathan Eastman--

On our last destination, we gained a new understanding of our energy centers known as *chakras*, with the ancient *Vedic* wisdom. We also learned about the aura which is the energy field of light that surrounds our bodies. We learned about subtle universal laws of the inner and invisible, unseen worlds that are part of our reality as much as the physical. Even though our eyes may not be able see them, they coexist in time and space simultaneously. The Law of Cosmic Accountability accounts for our words, thoughts, deeds, and actions. Many people who are successful have always considered these subtle universal laws in their decisions.

Napoleon Hill said, "Whatever the mind can conceive and believe, it can achieve." In his book *Think and Grow Rich*, he outlined the principles and power of The Universal Law of Thought. If we think about it logically, a desk cannot be made without a carpenter. He first had an idea to make a desk, then he got the wood, and carved the top and legs using tools like a saw and a hammer, and with nails he put it all together. Hence, the carpenter used his thoughts first then he crafted something for us to write on. In the same way, a house is built with blueprints from an architect. Cars, trains, and anything physical we can think of, are made possible with the subtle energies of the Law of Thought.

We can utilize the truly amazing invisible and intangible creative energies to manifest something that is physical and tangible. It requires merging of the heart and spirit to create something physical. For us to learn more about the Law of Accountability, we continue on our journey on this train of thought, with a new understanding of cosmic consciousness. You see, our ride through life does not have to be painful, because it is shaped by our thoughts. We can choose to make our world what we want it to be. Thoughts are like seeds. We must plant them in fertile soil and nurture them until they bear fruit. It is in the darkness of the dirt that seeds are planted, and the manure which fertilizes them. In the same way, we must transform negativity, pain, and adversity in order to make our dreams a reality.

## How Does the Law of Accountability Affect Our Thoughts? What Is Cosmic Accountability?

Simply put, it is responsibility which is "response" and "abilities." The Law of Accountability means that we must be responsible for our thoughts, and we are also accountable for our actions. If we make a promise to someone, we must fulfill that responsibility to the best of our abilities. When we keep our promises, it gives our word power; our word is the bond of our spirit. The Law of Accountability strips the "blame game" of its power, because we can no longer point the finger at someone else and blame them for our suffering. The Law of Accountability calls to the forefront the Law of Forgiveness in understanding that no one is to be blamed. Rather, the effects of our choices are far-reaching, much more than we could ever understand in one lifetime. Remember, on our second destination we learned that we must be true to our *Self* by listening to our hearts, and only then can our spirits soar.

At times, I feel that we made an agreement with spirit when we became humans, and deep within, that sacred covenant is beckoning us to live our life to its fullest. At this point in our evolution, there are so many issues at the forefront for humanity to deal with. Now is the time for us to change our thoughts, and make them in alignment with our true *Self*. As Don Miguel Ruiz states in *The Four Agreements*, to be happy we must "keep our word." We must try and live with integrity, and not go back on our word; it is accepting full responsibility for each word we speak. Do you remember your soul's promise, or have you forgotten your promises to yourself?

Accepting responsibility does not have to be overwhelming because the key to understanding the Law of Accountability is that we have choices. We have to remember that there are many alternative choices in any course of action, we have options. Our lives are not permanent and set in stone, remember, we can change anything with the power of thought. When we live in accordance with the Law of Accountability, it strengthens our will. As the saying goes, "Where there is a will there is a way."

We empower ourselves to make the right decisions by being responsible. Remember, accepting responsibility does not mean that we are at fault, because to point outside of ourselves is disempowering. We can have integrity acknowledging when something is out of alignment with our true *Self*, so that we may correct it. We can avoid the blame game, and some examples include the following: the dog ate my homework, my boss, my wife, my husband, my job, men, women, girls, boys, my kids, my parents, my grandparents, the school, the government, corporations, the banks, and the list goes on and on.

## STRATEGY FOR ENLIGHTENMENT

**Have you heard someone recently say, "I'm sorry, I was at fault, and I would like to learn what I can do to make this situation better. Would you please understand that I am a mirror for you, and vice versa? You are a mirror for me, and therefore you and I are one in the same being. Let us work together in divine harmony and realize that it is not your fault. If it is always someone or something out there, would it be possible for us to rectify the situation?"**

**We should not give our power away to external circumstances, or point the finger in blame. As the familiar saying goes, "What goes around comes around." We also know it as, "What you reap is what you sow." It does not matter what we call it, the message is the same. What we do to others eventually returns to us.**

Responsibilities sometimes lead us to feeling more burdens, and the burdens lead us to blame others because their beliefs and our beliefs are not in agreement, and we feel it is their fault. However, the enlightened person accepts responsibility, and does not blame others by realizing that each soul is entitled to their own belief system. Beliefs are simply our thoughts and the things that we believe to be true.

I would like to share an example about my experience with the "blame game." In the concept of reincarnation and the native belief about seven generations to come, "what goes around comes around" proves to be true. My father used to blame me for virtually everything that ever went wrong. Here is a hypothetical example, somehow, if the neighbor's cat got stuck in the tree, and got wet because it was raining, and there was lightning and thunder, my dad would blame me for everything. For most of my teenage years, I had tremendous annoyance and frustration towards him.

Today I look back and contemplate the relationship with my father, and I realized what my father used to say quite often. He often said his dad, my grandfather, blamed him for everything. It took me almost twenty years to realize that blame leads to a vicious cycle in the karmic wheel of existence. In order to get off the karmic wheel, and enter into an enlightened consciousness, we have to understand the Law of Accountability.

In essence, a true understanding in the meaning of the Law of Accountability and accepting responsibility for our thoughts, our deeds, and our actions can not only bring about inner peace in our lives; however, when we accept self responsibility we can end all arguments and disagreements on planet Earth, including saving our marriages, relationships, and communities. Thereby, we bring about a healing for the higher *Self*, and we enter into cosmic consciousness. If we cannot accept responsibility we can never become an enlightened being, because accepting responsibility is a condition to becoming enlightened. An enlightened being will always look at their thoughts for the cause of their suffering and transform those limiting beliefs, rather than blaming someone else.

If something is really bothering us, then we should be the person to take responsibility and change it, because many situations were ingrained in our consciousness from early childhood and societal conditioning. Collectively, we are tolerating those thoughts even though it might not be something that we know on a conscious level. I did not fully understand the power of my thoughts until I meditated on the Great Masters. How could any of us have known thoughts to be real things of that magnitude? Gandhi said, "Outward peace is useless without inner peace."

Once our individual inner consciousness reflects change, our outer world will become a mirror and change with us, and together we can change the world. We do not have to wear protective clothing, and fight with riot police to effect change. All we have to do is use our intention and thoughts, and the powerful *inner world* responds to us, and that kind of change is lasting.

## Success and The Law of Accountability

We can plant the seeds for success with thoughts of success, and we must not get discouraged even if we fail. We should remember that failures act as stimulants to our spiritual and material growth; it is the best time for sowing the seeds of success. Accountability is one of life's greatest lessons. In its lesson, we learn the importance of taking responsibility for all of our thoughts, deeds, and actions. As children we learned accountability when someone explained our actions to us. How did you learn accountability, was it with love, lectures, scolding, or anger? Accountability is about the wisdom that comes to us with experience, and age is not a factor because some children are very old souls.

We cannot be like ignorant children and sweep the important issues of our world under the rug. It is one thing to claim ignorance, and not knowing. Yet, it is an entirely different story to claim stupidity. We are not all ignorant. We know better. Therefore, from a higher perspective we are required to act upon our knowledge and be accountable.

Being accountable helps us to realize that things are interconnected like the Moon, Stars, Sun, and Earth. They are individual heavenly bodies on their own, but they are also part of our solar system and Universe. The same way a business does not operate in a vacuum, everything around us is interconnected. What affects one aspect of society affects all. How does accountability help a business to be successful long term regardless of economic conditions?

## How Can The Law of Accountability Help Businesses?

Once I had a discussion with a wise man. His name was A. Roy Horn. He wrote the book *Heroes, Sages, and Madmen*. He said that the same force that keeps the planets moving in orbit, and holds the sun in place surely has enough foresight and ability to care for any one person. I pondered that thought for some time. If the message was not clear enough, I saw a YouTube video on a Swami who said that God takes care of even our pets and all their needs are provided. How could he not provide for our needs? After a few weeks it began to sink in. The following three main aspects, when in balance, can make businesses thrive:

1. Products and Services: Who is responsible for adding value to your company's products and services?

2. Sales and Marketing: Who is responsible for selling the goods and services to customers?

3. Accounting: Who is responsible for paying taxes and other legal requirements for your business?

On this destination of our cosmic journey, we learn a powerful message that our efforts, not luck, are responsible for our success. Our personal and professional lives are interconnected, and both can be successful with the Law of Accountability. Even though achieving success is not dependent on thoughts alone, nothing can be successful without first laying the foundations with the intent for success. Our efforts accrue over time, and also from this life to the next; it is non-refundable and transferable. We inherit our divine share by accepting responsibility.

If we have integrity, we can be confident, and confidence is such an important factor for ultimate success. It leads us to clarity of mind, and a clear conscience to make the right choices. During my experience in the *prana*, which is the divine intelligent light of enlightenment, it was shown to me that depending on the choices we make, our entire life can change in an instant. The Law of Accountability brings peace and stability to rebuild our world which has crumbled economically.

**The Accounting Flow Chart: A Decision Making Tool**

On this destination, we will explore a new approach to problem solving with a concise version of the *Accounting Decision Making Flow Chart*. By now we should understand the importance of our thoughts, because it is crucial to *Make Empowered Decisions*™. The Flow Chart helps us to understand things in a simple step by step manner, and it uses symbols and geometrical shapes. To keep it simple, I will apply only the concepts of the first step in a Flow Chart listed below. Are you going to make a decision? What will you decide? "Yes" means we proceed further, and at each step we draw a line and attach another diamond shape below. "No" means the Chart stops with the line to the right, and we do not go further.

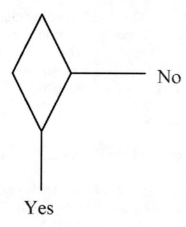

It is interesting that in the *inner world* of consciousness a "maybe" just means that we will have to wait and the *inner world* only responds to either a "yes" or a "no," to proceed or not proceed. The decisions we make are crucial to our well-being, happiness, peace of mind, and stability. Whatever the decision is, we should be willing to accept responsibility for the outcomes we've made, whether positive or negative. If a certain outcome does not suit us, we can change it by making another decision. Remember, to *Make Empowered Decisions*™, we can only control our thoughts and intention, and we have to surrender the outcome in complete faith in the Universal Laws to manifest our dreams successfully.

Let's take, for example, at one point in time we made a decision. What is important is to note why the decision was made. For instance, let's say I decided to move. I lived in the new apartment, and was happy for some time. Situations and circumstances can change. The same apartment may no longer feel right. Some reasons for moving again include: needing more room for children, the children grew up and moved away, and getting into a new relationship. Depending on the circumstances, our emotions and feelings change, and our decisions change everything.

Another example is our career, or owning a business. We might have decided on certain circumstances, and taken a job or started a business, then after some time, we find ourselves needing a change. The decision to stay at a job or keep a business going may no longer serve us, because sometimes it is wiser to begin another job or invest in another business that is more financially lucrative or in alignment with our *dharma*.

We can reevaluate the situation, and make another decision to find a more suitable position, start another business, or go back to school. Decisions affect every aspect of our lives, and remember, everything can change with just a thought. The first thing to decide is yes, I would like to move forward, or no I want to stay where I am. Difficulties arise when we are in limbo, undecided, and the maybes of life make it feel like we are stuck. To get unstuck, all we have to do is make a decision with either a "yes" or "no."

## A Painful Lesson That No Woman Would Ever Want to Experience

I have always been relatively logical from my conditioning since childhood. I preferred tangible, real experiences, and always needed physical proof to validate things in my life. However, this part of our journey seems unreal when compared to my standards for reality. I am sharing my story so that you can believe in the unseen *inner world* because I had a real experience. I was constantly getting intuitive messages and hunches that I should not work for a particular client here in Sedona. I never listened to my intuition because my logical mind and financial needs outweighed my intuitive mind. Mostly, I hated going to work at this particular location, and many times I called in sick. We should remember the importance of listening to our heart and true *Self*. Many of us, because of financial reasons and responsibilities to our families, continue to go against our hearts. Remember, our self worth in the higher *Self* is crucial to enlightenment.

Now I will share this painful experience with you. It was a day that no woman would ever want to remember. I was working for an architect in Sedona. Generally, my assistant was with me, or the architect's girlfriend was there. He had many multimillion dollar projects and I was working around the clock. On that terrible and horrible day, I went to work and happened to be alone with him. His girlfriend was on vacation, and my assistant decided to go back to Columbia University for a master's degree. What happened next is still a blur.

What I do remember is that I went into a state of shock and trauma. I could not speak and was not normal. The attack left scars so deep that I could barely discuss the specifics. What I do remember is that one of my other clients had warned me about him before, and he had asked me to cover up. Thankfully, I heeded his warning. I had gone to the local Outlet Store and bought pants that were virtually rape proof. The wealthy architect tried and tried to rape me, but he was not able to do it, and for many years I lived with regret. I thought about the warning signs, and all the things I should have or could have done to prevent the assault. A thousand thoughts ran through my mind. Why did I not listen to my heart?

For three days, I tried to wash off the pain, and I sat in water until I looked like a prune, but it did not work. The pain was so intense, that I cried until I could not cry anymore. My eyes were swollen like a frog with an allergic reaction. I moaned and croaked with gut-wrenching sounds. I screamed so loudly I didn't think I would have a voice ever again. With more than a dozen phone calls and the frustration, I called the FBI, the Sheriff, and thirty-two attorneys in the State of Arizona from Flagstaff, Sedona, and Phoenix. I found it appalling that most attorneys in Arizona did not handle sexual assault cases. After losing too much weight and lying on the couch with no food or water for seven days, I had lost touch with reality, and the will to live. The thought of suicide would not go away, but somehow I had one last thought to fight back.

I dried my eyes, and made the decision that I will take responsibility for my healing. I could not believe the statistic, every two minutes another person is raped. *The Bed Intruder Song*, with Antoine Dodson, became an overnight sensation on itunes, because on the collective conscious level, many people are silently suffering because of predatory behaviors from their superiors, and others that they are forced to accept. I decided not to give my aggressor power over me. I would be accountable for me, and I would choose to live. As painful as it was, I realized that, only I could choose to survive. I would then help children that were subject to abuse, and I prayed with every fiber in my being. I pleaded with the universe to take away the pain. Would the Great Universe help me?

## My Journey with Enlightenment Begins

It was then that Paramhansa Yogananda's *Autobiography of a Yogi* entered my life, and I clutched the book for dear life. When thoughts of dying entered my mind, I prayed to Yogananda. To this day, I owe him my life. After a year of intense meditation, about fifteen hours a day, from the summer 2007 to summer 2008, I began to escape the clutches of the pain. Around July 2008, I saw an article that in India, July's full moon was called *Guru Purnima*. It was a holy day that occurred once every year, and a time when enlightened Sages of the past come to the earth plane and give their blessings.

I thought it was a great cosmic joke, "In between worlds, and flying Gurus, yeah right." Even though I read about the Indian Saints in *Autobiography of a Yogi*, I doubted such metaphysical experiences. Yet, I had done my meditations, prayers, and spiritual work by accepting responsibility for my suffering, and I humbly requested the Great Sages to somehow give me a sign if they were indeed real.

Remember, our thoughts create our reality. If we plant the seeds in the mind's fertile ground, even in times of despair, and nurture them, they will eventually bear fruit. I had been longing to experience enlightenment since the time when Mom passed away, and I had been knocking on the Divine's door in 1982. Remarkably, many years later, I am sharing an experience of enlightenment. I look back to that faithful Full Moon day in July of 2008, approximately one year after the traumatic incident, and it was *Guru Purnima*.

What happened next can only be explained by magic, and the metaphysical. I experienced the cosmic life force, *prana*, and I entered the cosmic stream of intelligent reality. In that moment, my life forever changed for the better. This unified experience with all of existence is known as *Samadhi* or enlightenment. I merged into the super-conscious state of existence, and became one with all that exists. In that super-conscious state outside of my body consciousness, I was able to see everyone and everything as intelligent light. No one was separate. I and everyone else were also me. My body vanished, and everything around me was moving molecules of cosmic consciousness and light particles, where each particle of light was intelligent.

The world of light was filled with feelings of serenity, and I felt an internal contentment and so complete, that there was no hunger, longing, or wanting, I just was. It was a world beyond form, and it was as if there was no night or day. I realized then that there was much more than the physical world, and I called it the *"inner world."* There was no time, no emotion, no happiness, no sadness, and absolute nothingness, yet at the same time, everything was present. It was unexplainable, and it was as if I was looking at life through an electron microscope. The *inner world* was undeniably beautiful, and powerful beyond words. Nothing physical existed, yet everything was part of existence, and I was nothing and everything. Simultaneously, I was as vast as the moon and tiny as a speck of dust in my carpet.

## The Inner World – The Doorway to Cosmic Consciousness

I rushed past the stars, yet I did not move. I was as tall as the clouds, and merged with the cosmos. I was the moon and it knew me. Everything had a consciousness and a knowing. The trees in front of my house were alive and knew me. The rocks and each pebble in the lawn knew my thoughts. Even the particles in my carpet had a consciousness. The world of cosmic energy was a pure state beyond peace, pure bliss, and stillness. Nothing was separate. From the minute pebbles to the clouds, trees, moon, stars, everything was one, and we were all one in this liquid light. There was no suffering and no fear.

Sri Yukteswar, in his book *The Holy Science*, would call it the 4$^{th}$ Sphere, *Maharloka*, which is the sphere of the atom; it is called the doorway between the spiritual and material creation. I was ever so grateful that I had that experience. As I descended into my body and 3D reality, I became sad. I wanted to stay there because the intelligent light comforted me, and I felt such peace.

In the *inner world* I heard a message, "The light is intelligence." I actually saw how our thoughts move the *inner world* molecules. When we make decisions, these liquid light particles shift and everything changes. We are indeed interconnected by fibers that look like webs of lights. After some time, I got back into my body, and I saw and felt my legs and arms. I clearly heard the *prana* or intelligent light asking me to bring back a piece of that memory to teach and uplift humanity to *Make Empowered Decisions*™.

What would happen if we lived our lives as if every thought we made was indeed alive, and every choice we made impacted the entire universe? I realized that we can be happy all the time knowing that we are already enlightened beings. Once we step out of the consciousness of the body, we experience cosmic consciousness. The immortal essence of the soul cannot be confined. Anyone who makes the decision to become enlightened will ultimately reach their destination.

## Our Cosmic Journey Continues with Empowered Decisions – We Can Live As Higher Beings Now

The first step is to decide what you want to do. The trick is to keep your thoughts and mind focused on what you want. Life gives us exactly what we ask of it:

- What have you asked of your life?
- Who are you?
- Why are you here?
- In the end, when all the materialism and possessions are left behind, what will you become?
- The ancient Yogis in the *Vedas* said, why wait to live as immortals?

We should live our best life now, and we can experience what it feels like to be an angel, by being angelic now. We should know that we are all children of the great cosmos, and realize that we are all light beings, then we can live a life filled with truth and light. We can be what we choose. If we inherently believe that we are deserving of wealth, then we will eventually possess wealth. If we believe that we are poor and impoverished, then we will experience poverty. What we believe, we become because we are our thoughts. We can, as Dr. Wayne Dyer says in his book, *Change Your Thoughts-Change Your Life*. It is that simple. There is no need for sorrow or belief in separation, we are indeed one. There is no need to struggle alone in fear.

What do you believe about yourself? If we collectively and consciously make the decision to end poverty, world hunger, and nuclear threats, we can move in that direction. That decision will move the *inner world* conscious molecules, and show us the actions that we need to take to change. Let's take another example, let's say something in your life is not quite right. It can be any area of your life. Sit in meditation and clear your mind so that you are in a state of relative peace and relaxation. From this space of peace, make a decision to change something in your life for the better. Then observe what happens over the next few months.

## Accepting Change – A Constant and Never-Ending Flux in the Universe

Most people make the decision to change something in their life, then resist the direction their decision leads them, and due to their fears, they attract the worst possible outcome instead. It is a fact, change is not easy because we prefer things the way they were. Resisting change accounts for most of the madness on our planet. Everything in the entire cosmos is in constant flux. Nothing will ever stay the same, not even our bodies. The only thing permanent in existence is the soul.

Television is interesting, and it is constantly programming us. Our thoughts are constantly shaping our reality, and depending on what we are watching, we will be programming our subconscious mind with thoughts. This can be positive programming or negative programming. The powers that be are always vying for the minds of men. TV is called television programming. Tele means transmissions over a distance, and vision means the ability to see. Programming is a plan; a series of steps to be carried out or goals to be accomplished. Do this exercise: make notes of your thoughts and how you feel, when you are finished, turn on the television.

After you have finished watching the programming, make notes of your thoughts again. How do you feel, have your thoughts changed? What did you decide after watching the TV program? Most likely, you will want to eat, drink alcohol or beer, look better, drive a new car, realize the side effects of medication, or want to buy something. Observe what new decisions you have made. You can monitor your thoughts on the television monitor. Remember, the decisions that we make, shape our reality, therefore we should choose our programming sources to create the kind of reality that we want to experience.

Remember, the *Accounting Decision Making Flow Chart* is similar to the Universal Cosmic Law of Thought. If we say "yes," then we can proceed. A "no" means we do not continue in a particular direction. Where things get into a holding pattern is with the maybes. When we have indecision with neither a "yes" nor a "no," the universal molecules are also in a holding pattern. So if we want things to change, we have to decide one way or another. The Natives say that if we do nothing, then that is still doing something; it means we are passively accepting and agreeing with the decision to do nothing. That is when we feel stuck, all we have to do to feel unstuck, is make a decision after careful planning, and weighing the pros and cons.

Many decisions have to be made to build a successful company. To build a house takes careful planning and thinking. An architect creates the design then the engineer takes the blueprint and works with the builders. After that, the electricians create lighting fixtures, then landscapers and designers create the space. In the same way, nothing is accomplished alone and instantly. As the proverb goes, "A journey of a thousand miles begins with the next step." Nothing big was ever accomplished with one step. Whether it is a goal to make a million dollars or reach enlightenment, it takes time to accomplish our goals. The recipe for baking a cake has many steps. To maintain a savings in a bank account takes time, and interest accumulates over time.

## Choice and Decisions Are Only a Starting Point

The Law of Accountability ultimately determines our fate and destiny. Fate is not meant to emphasize the results of past good and evil, but to arouse our will to escape from universal suffering. What we have done, we can undo because we have accepted responsibility for our lives. We were the cause of whatever effects are now prevalent in our lives. We can overcome any limitation because we created suffering by our words, thoughts, deeds, and actions in the first place. The pathway of peace is led by respect; it is the underlying theme in the entirety of existence that brings all things to humbleness. To honor or respect everyone in our lives would bring peace. We do not have to share the same belief systems.

## Surrender to the Divinity Within

When we begin with the personal inventory list from our second destination, we can make the right decisions, and live the dreams hidden in our hearts. The inner journey becomes the reflection of our true *Self*. The cosmic plan is nothing more than the understanding that we are all interdependent and connected to each other. What we do to the whole, we do to ourselves. What we do to ourselves, we do to the whole and our higher *Self*.

What would be the point of life if we cannot live in freedom? Is this human life worth living in ignorance and darkness? I do not know what lies beyond the boundaries of death, all I know is that I live here and now. According to the Great Yogis, of the millions of life forms on Earth, human existence is the highest form of all existence. They say we should not waste this chance to become enlightened beings because humanity is the only race capable of enlightenment, animals are not.

For the enlightened being, duality is not two sides of a coin; it is the point in the middle where they converge. Remember, peace on a collective level, begins when each and every one of us on an individual level realizes that we are here to love and accept our *Self*. We cannot bring peace by fighting within our own minds because if we punish ourselves, then we punish the whole. When we accept full responsibility for our lives, we begin to live life to its fullest.

The cosmic plan is not dictated by a hand above. The Divine does not punish or reward us. It is our actions and the effects of the Law of Cause and Effect that play out the drama on the stage of our existence. Our actions are based on our thoughts. We can shine our light so brightly in the midst of chaos, confusion, and darkness so that we will be beacons for lost souls. Let us create a vision of such magnitude that the children of future generations of the earth will enjoy a destiny far beyond our wildest dreams. Let us remember to have gentle thoughts.

**What We Imagine Life to Be Is Not Real**

Life is an impermanent existence. Let us reach for the state of super-consciousness. We can only know it if we make the decision to go for it, so we should set our course and stretch for the world of freedom. It is our divine birthright. We are all interconnected, and when we make a decision to bring wealth, good health, and peace, then we can all draw from that wishing well. Divine timing has a lot to do with it. Synchronicity is not a magic word, but an orchestrated symphony of souls who work together for the betterment of humanity. Remember, we can filter the negativity out of our lives. If we feel the seeds of failure taking root in our consciousness, we can pluck them out with *mantras*, and thoughts of love. We make so many decisions daily, and certainly we can choose the path of our higher *Self* to experience enlightenment.

**The Divine Feminine**

There is one energy of cosmic consciousness, but with many different names and functions, and it can be either masculine or feminine. The energy of the divine feminine does not mean that men do not have it. In fact, every human being is created from their mother's and father's energy and therefore humanity consists of both. I have witnessed that some men possess the divine feminine energy more than women, simply because they love, respect, and support others. In our society we say, "sex sells." Money, power, and sex are governed by the same energy center, the second *chakra*. This means that adversity, struggle, and stress are the natural counterparts to trying to achieve success. Nothing is attained easily, and enlightenment is no exception. In fact, everything on earth is to be endured.

**The Procession of Angels Resides Within**

We continue now on our cosmic journey through the process of inner transformation to connect with angels. We are now on the threshold of scientific knowledge that was predicted eons ago by the Yogis, Saints, and Sages in many ancient cultures. As the divine light is entering into our consciousness, the dark angels of death and destruction should now take a back seat in the cosmos; they have served well to bring suffering upon humanity. As we enter the divine cosmic consciousness, will we allow them to continue to torment us?

We honor both the light and dark parts of ourselves, and the lessons imparted. The time has come for the angels, and beings of love and light to return us to our true *Self* of enlightenment, abundance, and inner peace. Let us reclaim our birthright of happiness to soar above the horizon, by remembering our divinity.

## *DIVINE TRANSMISSION – A CHANNELED MESSAGE*

**Meeting the Angel of Death, Angel of Mercy, Angel of Compassion, and Angel of Transformation**

For many years in my life, I have been able to help literally hundreds of people find inner peace, contentment, and happiness. Many of those people have asked me what they can do for me in return, and I said to them, "One day, I will be applying for a job as an Angel with the Divine, and I would really appreciate it if they could give me a good recommendation." Many people have said that I was their Angel, and that I was very angelic. I would like to explore a relationship that I now share with Angelic Beings.

Let's fast forward life a little. Imagine yourself to be one hundred years old. Assuming you have lived a wonderful and long life with children, friends, and family, the Angel of Death has visited you with a message. The Angel says that God has asked them to take you back to another place where your higher

*Self* resides. The Angel says that this place where you are going is devoid of disease, death, old age, and anything physical. You will be entering into a spiritual reality. The Angel asks you to leave behind everything you have ever been associated with in life such as friends, family, children, relatives, home, car, job, and everything that you have ever owned, because the time has come for you to leave your body behind and pay a visit to the mortuary.

The Angel takes you up on a beam of light, and you look backwards at your life. The Angel says its time to do an accounting of your life. Now imagine yourself looking at a movie of your *Self*. You are the superstar on the screen, in the motion picture of your experiences. All of the other characters serve as extras on the set, but they too had roles to play. In the movie of your life, you are able to see things from their perspective, and finally you get a chance to listen to the other characters.

1. What would you do differently?

2. What would you keep the same?

In this evaluation, you are one with the Divine, and you are immortal. The only person who is responsible for you is you. All of the actions of your life are evaluated on only one meter. How much did you love other than yourself? Now the Angel gives you a chance to have a second life. The Angel moves a wand and gives you a chance to redesign your life. The Angel asks you which characters you would put in your movie again. The Angel tells you that this person will be a life lesson that you must master. The Angel assures you that if you can master this lesson in life, you will not have to suffer anymore. Now imagine that you are the architect of your own life:

- What plans would you draft up?
- How can you shape your destiny?
- What types of structures would you create?
- Would you live in the same way you are living now?

The Angel explains that the movie will come to an end once again, and that your suffering will end. The Angel gives you a chance to play a game called *Choice and Consequence*. The Angel shows you all your lifetimes, from the time you were a single-celled organism and when your parents conceived you; you are shown all of your actions from the time of your creation to your human self now. The Angel of Mercy enters the picture and the Angel of Death fades away.

**The Angel of Mercy**

The Angel of Mercy shows you that the choices you've made led you up to the present moment. The Angel of Mercy says she's here to show you the steps to bypass the pain. She tells you that the first step is to know yourself. She says that rather than focusing on other people, you need to get to know you. She gives you a series of self evaluation questions. You can answer those from our previous destinations, and with the *Nine Keys for a Life in Balance*. She reveals the chapters of your life one at a time, and then she says that you must be able to forgive yourself for all the things that you shouldn't have done. The Angel fades away.

**The Angel of Compassion**

The Angel of Compassion arrives, and she creates a bubble of love around you. No one else can see you, but you can see everyone. You are wearing an invisible cloak. You can take a deep breath in, and she takes you high above the world upon a sacred tree. She tells you that you do not have much time, as change happens quickly. She advises you that you must trust your intuition. The Angel gives you a secret code, and tells you to put it in your pouch. She then gives you a special carving, and she tells you that this amulet is like a special totem. This is a magical potion.

The Angel proceeds to tell you that there is a secret way to bypass all the suffering of being human. She explains that from time to time, you may feel sad, or have some emotion that is considered a painful experience. She gives you the magic potion. The magic potion is called the *Self*, and the potion gives you a chance to enjoy action with awareness. She says that from now on, you must love yourself no matter what, and love others the same way you love yourself. She explains that if you can have self love, then it will be easy for you to access the doorway to infinite peace.

The Angel of Compassion tells you that there is only one thing that you can do to destroy the magic potion. She tells you that your thoughts are real, and they can create your reality. She explains that when you have doubtful negative thoughts, they invite the Angels of Hate, who take your peace away; those Angels have lots of fun when you are suffering. She explains to you that you must not associate with evil actions, for if you do, then you will suffer at the hands of the Dark Angels. The Angel of Compassion steps aside and she invites the Angel of Transformation.

## The Angel of Transformation

The Angel of Transformation comes to you because she represents change. The minute you see her, you are angry at her because she represents change. She holds the magic wand of determination to set your soul free. You have prayed and asked her for help, but when she arrives you second guess yourself. The Angel of Transformation has been given the job to eliminate that which no longer serves you and the highest good for all. She does not give you much of a choice.

She gives you the message about inner transformation. She tells you that you can move forward or backward, but you cannot stay in the same position. The Angel of Transformation gives you the warning that the time has come for you to change your ways, or else you will have to bear the consequences of your actions; she gives you a secret also. She tells you that the Great Merciful Masters do not want to see their children suffer, so she reveals the next secret.

The Angel of Transformation says that if you surrender all of your actions to the feet of the Divine, then you will bypass the Law of Action, or Karma, and activate the powerful Universal Law of *Dharma*. She says that if you keep the thought of the Divine in your heart before any action, then you will not be able to do things that are evil, and thereby you will have the wisdom to transform your life for inner peace. The Angel of Transformation warns that change is upon us. She explains that the hurricanes, tornadoes, and storms are necessary because the human world has not respected creation and its Divine Laws. She says that the Archangels can be in more than one place at the same time.

She gives you magic words, and she says you can call upon her at anytime. The Angel of Transformation says to hold the thought of your true *Self*, and your life will be transformed. She tells you that you must surrender the actions, and the outcome of those actions to the Divine. Then she says that if you let go of the outcome, you will be freed from the Law of Karma, and you bypass the choices and consequences of your actions. She then tells you that now you will become one with the Divine will, and that your individual will and ego mind will cease to be. The Angel of Transformation departs and introduces you to the Angel of Wealth.

## The Angel of Transformation Fades, and the Angel of Wealth Is Introduced to You

The Angel of Wealth comes into the picture, and she says the Divine Mother and Heavenly Father will give you all that you need, for you are their child; they will provide for your every need. The Angel of Wealth explains to you that your needs will be amply provided for, however, if you get greedy, then they will not be able to supply greed. She says you will find peace when you are able to become accepting, and be content.

The Angel of Wealth explains that you will become happy, and all of your material needs will be provided for. She also explains that they will be provided for instantly. She asks you to open your heart and allow the network of friends, associates, and family to enter your hall of peace. The Angel of Wealth asks you not to compare yourself to others. She says not to look upon your neighbor and say, "How come they have this or that?" She says that you must not concern yourself with the power mongers. She assures you that those who do not share their wealth to help those in need, will surely come back in another body to suffer poverty.

The Angel of Wealth explains that the correct use of wealth is to give to charity, and investing in the greater good. The Angel says you must dedicate a portion of your earnings to help those in need. She also explains that you must be of service, to work for more than just the money. She asks that you focus now, only on what your natural gifts and strengths are. She fades away, and says that I am a close sister to the Angel of *Dharma*.

## The Angel of *Dharma* and the Angel of Wealth

The Angel of *Dharma* shows you your life in the cosmic plan. *Dharma*, she explains, was something that you created back in your architectural plan, in your soul's blueprint. The Angel of Wealth explains that when you do not live according to the plan that you orchestrated, the structure of the earth loses its beauty.

The Angel of *Dharma* says that when we are all branded like cows, we roam the pasture of life listless, chewing on our cuds. The boring reality of life is because your divine spark is not activated. The Angel of Wealth says that when you touch upon your joy, the dance of creation sounds a horn to all life. Your divine cosmic plan was created with the Angels. It is sure to succeed; it was not an egotistical plan. The Angel of Wealth explains that now you will accumulate money to benefit all life, and not just yourself. The Angel of Wealth explains that wealth is part of the blueprint for humanity. She explains that the four aims in life are *dharma*, *artha*, *kama*, and *moksha*.

The Angel of Wealth says you must share your *dharma* with those who are most in need of it, and put a value on your services. The Angel guarantees that the charity of the Divine Mother of the earth will always provide our sustenance. The Angel of Wealth says struggle and suffering are filled with remorse, debt, and poverty when we are selfish and we have thoughts of lack and scarcity. The Angel of Wealth says, like all life forms, the birds and animals, we will always be given what we need. It takes a lot of courage to listen to your heart, and share your soul's message with others. The Angel says, may you be blessed with peace, happiness, and reconnecting to your true *Self*. May the Angels, Gods, and Goddesses bring the eternal flame of happiness and the nectar of immortality to your consciousness once more. The Angel said to take a look at all the pictures of your life, and see the motion picture of you on the screen; for sure, you know that this life is but a dream. She says walk hand in hand, look into the eyes of a stranger, and remember they are a reflection of your own being. The Angel of Wealth says, I am never far away, and you can reach me by letting your compassion for others grow.

**We Are All on Borrowed Time**

If ever you see a teardrop in my eyes, hand me a handkerchief and say, "I know, yes my cosmic friends, I know the salty, bittersweet taste of life too." If I fall, catch me, and I promise to do the same for you. I will never let you down so long as I am not on my own hands and knees. Remember your neighbors with love, and cultivate the seeds of kindness. Let no one suffer in your presence. We are all one, and so we must care for each other. We are responsible for our thoughts. They are real things, and they create our reality. We cannot place the blame on our parents, grandparents, teachers, or bosses. We are accountable for our lives.

The most empowering thing that you can do is take back the reigns to your destiny. Make the decision, the choice now, to reconnect with your true *Self*. If you ever get hung up on the thoughts of not being good enough, then remember that we are already perfect, and this life is but a memory in the end. Reach for the hand of your loved ones. You can do this one step, and learn forgiveness. Allow the negative and toxic emotions of the past to flow out and invite in the thoughts of what your greatest *Self* can be. Infinite love!

## *END OF CHANNELED MESSAGE*

# CHAPTER 7
## *Accrual Accounting –*
## *Synchronizing Universal Laws with Profits Consistently Walk on the Pathway of Peace*

"Synchronicity – A Divine Transmission"

If you've mastered the teachings on the previous destinations, you're already holding keys to the doorway of infinity on this part of the trip. You've gotten to know how important it is to be consistent. Magic awaits you with knowledge of the accrual concept in accounting, because of its connection to our *dharma* or divine purpose. I will expand on the idea of accrual accounting which takes into consideration future periods, as well as past transactions. Accountants make adjustments to correctly report income and it is different from the cash basis of accounting. The debilitating situation of debt and even the national deficit can be understood with this simple concept. This chapter brings into account the borrowing and lending of money. Accruals are explained in detail and are compared to the concept of karma and *dharma*.

The principles and concepts of the *Accrual Basis of Accounting* are more advanced, and they are covered in intermediate accounting courses. We already covered the *Revenue Realization* and *Matching Principles*, and how they relate to the realization of enlightenment. The accrual basis of accounting is the policy of recognizing revenue in the accounting records when it is earned, and recognizing expenses when the related goods or services are used. The purpose of accrual accounting is to measure the profitability of the economic activities conducted during the accounting period, and not when cash is collected or paid.

The most important concept involved in accrual accounting is the matching principle. Revenue is offset with all the expenses incurred in generating that revenue, thus providing a measure of the overall profitability of the economic activity. For example, if you buy movie tickets online in advance, or a gift certificate, the theater receives cash. However, the theatre did not earn that money. This is considered a liability, and it is considered accrued revenues. The accrual basis takes into account all the lessons that we have learned thus far.

On a spiritual level, accrual accounting is like the familiar saying, "What goes around comes around," and adjustments can be made in our lives like adjusting journal entries. What this means is that we can change our future based on the actions we take in the present moment. On our second destination we learned about the importance of our true *Self*. On our last destination, we learned the lesson about the importance of taking responsibility for all of our thoughts, deeds, and actions. Accrual accounting is when we are being in integrity with our *dharma*, and being of service, which is keeping our word. It is like a reminder for the soul's promise to be true to ourselves. We must take into account the effects of our thoughts on all life, because our thoughts have far-reaching consequences in the world. We can decide to set goals and dream of the ideal life we want to live.

One key concept in a spiritual accrual accounting is patience. When we are patient, it helps things to manifest, and our dreams become a reality. For example, think about the process of nature. Have you ever seen a fruit tree bear fruit? Can we place unreasonable demands on the peach blossoms to get peaches? Can we go to the tree in the winter and say, I want a peach? Well we can try it. I bet it will respond, "Of course you can have peaches, if old man winter does not come around and freeze my buds off! By springtime, I will have blossoming buds, and in the summer they will grow to harvest. You can have peaches for sure in the summer, but I cannot give you peaches in the middle of winter." In accrual accounting, timing is everything; it factors in future periods of our lives, as well as our past actions, which is our karma. Remember, our past actions and decisions led up to the now, and the decisions we make now will bear fruit in the future. Similarly, we can change our past karma with a spiritual accounting.

## Accrual Accounting – A Lifetime Warranty

Accrual accounting comes with no money back guarantee, but it does come with a lifetime warranty. That warranty can be used by each and every one of us for our entire lifetime, for free. This warranty was given to us as a gift before we were born, from the Divine, and if we so choose, we can use it. It's kind of like when you buy a new car. If anything happens during the lifetime of the warranty, you are covered. In human life, if we can relate to feeling exhausted, used, abused, or just plain old pissed off, we should not forget we've got a free *lifetime* warranty for inner peace.

Similarly, the Divine cosmic consciousness is like the dealership of life. We can just go right back to the cosmic dealership and make a request for the necessary repairs to our spirit and soul. Just tell them the Great Masters sent you, and they said that you were promised a lifetime warranty. This is how accrual accounting is; we can easily fix and repair ourselves with the thoughts of enlightenment, and our souls are eternally repaired. We should not attach to the mechanisms of the body when the parts can easily be renewed, life after life. Our immortality is guaranteed!

## Accrual Accounting and the Future of Money

Change is the only constant, and we must be prepared to deal with those changes financially. The only way to deal with those changes is to have liquid assets or cash. Cash is the life-blood and king for a reason, because it allows us the fluidity and flexibility to do the things we need to do. To some extent, it allows us to maintain control of our lives, whether it is paying the mortgage or paying for tuition, cash is needed. We already learned about the power of debt, which is ingrained in us from the time we get a college education with student loans. The drama of debt, regardless if it is a car payment or a mortgage, can still be stressful.

On the other hand, many of us gave our happiness away to the power of money, only to find that at the end of life, it really brought temporary happiness. Remember, true happiness lies in believing in our self worth. Knowing that we are not alone, and we are connected to divinity and greatness is equally important. It is the birthright of each and every human being to be abundant and have prosperity. When we believe in the Cosmic Law of Abundance, then all the treasures of the Universe are available to us.

Money can be a vehicle of value and a storehouse for wealth. As I meditated on the energy of wealth, I felt a shift in consciousness with the future of money. I wanted to know if it was possible to change the vibration of money as the medium of exchange. I realized that money has changed its vibration; it has happened so many times in human history that it certainly will shift again. The shells, beads, dollars, and coins of the ancient worlds speak volumes in terms of the evolution of money. In accrual accounting, the past systems laid the foundations for our modern systems. The same way our current system will lay the foundations for the future of currency.

## The Monetary System Is Changing, and This Time to Service

Systems that were based on fear and greed will change to systems that are more equitable. Once the human consciousness demands a better medium of exchange, that system must evolve. Remember, our thoughts create our reality, and we can certainly create a new vision for financial prosperity. In the same way that we have come a long way in terms of communications and technology, we can advance into financial abundance. The future of money looks amazingly great.

The concepts of Suze Orman and many others have paved the way for a shift in our consciousness. More and more creativity will flow to receptive and open minds, and they will pave the way for a new consciousness of money. When someone is selfish their energies contract to the point of closing down, and nothing flows; this accounts for why billionaires commit suicide, and kings become paupers.

Let's think about it logically for a moment, when a person is selfish they're focused on the little self. By focusing only on their self, they do not care about anyone else. Therefore, by the Universal Law of Abundance, which means that there is a flow of prosperity, these laws go against a self-centered individual. According to the Law of Energy, in which everything is in constant motion and constant flow, there is no place for a selfish person's energy to go, but to their self. Thereby, the Laws of Poverty, lack, and scarcity become activated, and they become afraid of losing their money.

Fear is restricting and self centered, and it is based on the logical mind, ego, survival, and clutching desperately for life. I know this for a fact because I once operated in the mode of scarcity, *"scare" "city."* I was in *Scare City* for a while during the financial crisis. When I was afraid, I closed down emotionally, because fear gives the false impression that the situation will never change, and naturally it is impossible to let go of money. During times of economic recession, many people live in *Scare City*, and cash does not flow as easily, therefore abundance becomes scarce. From a spiritual level, all we have to do is activate the Law of Abundance, and provide our services to others, and thereby create the flow of abundance once again. This is like the accrual accounting for life, ever moving, ever shifting, and ever changing.

We must care for the earth's resources and they will regenerate for us. If however, we abuse them, then how can resources be renewable? We as humanity must continue to take actions to preserve, conserve, and save, because it is part of the cosmic consciousness for wealth and abundance. We as a society should move away from spending money that belongs to other people, because it is not earned. Living within the divine cosmic plan and a budget is important. If we can live on our earnings by using money that we already have rather than borrowing on credit, we can take back our power with the Law of Abundance. I would like to say that by reading *Cosmic Accounting: A Journey to Enlightenment*, your thoughts are part of the collective consciousness to shift the energy of money, and these concepts will create more abundance.

## DIVINE TRANSMISSION – A CHANNELED MESSAGE

### Connecting with the Goddess of Fortune Once Again

We can make a direct link to the Divine Mother of Abundance and Wealth, because the Great Divine Mother would not allow her children to suffer. Yes indeed, the Divine Mother has been awaiting our divine destiny. We've waited many years to reclaim material and spiritual divine wealth. When we try to make money for the sense gratification and pleasures, it enslaves us into working the karmic wheel. Rather, we should make money with the thought of being of service and living our *dharma*.

We should never sell our souls for a secure future when the only certainty in life is death. Each and every human being is free to choose his or her own path in life. We should remember that financial security does not come from money, because, it is also fleeting. Our security should come from the fact that the Divine Laws of Abundance will always come to our aid and provide our sustenance. We should know we were created and put on planet Earth at this great time of change to create an enlightened society free of karmic debts.

### Money from the Higher Worlds of Consciousness
### Channeled Master Kuthumi

Money alone is nothing more than a brainless piece of paper. That which will be valued is the service, and it is that which we have asked of you. We are the Cosmic Creators. Mankind will be given a genetic frequency in which those who developed their skills will be in great demand. These skills have nothing to do with the academic world, but have everything to do with us being of service to each other. As you have seen in your media, we are in fact transforming the institutions that have conditioned and taken advantage of humanity. We are your Divine Parents, and we will no longer allow the vision of scarcity to be as widespread over the earth.

Now we realize that your people here on earth operate from a vibration of fear. We did not teach you this fear. This however, is part of your genetic makeup. We will free you from that fear based reality. We will free those of you who have struggled and tried to be free from this burden, that is, those of you who have been consistent in your efforts with your *dharma*.

## END OF CHANNELED MESSAGE

## STRATEGY FOR ENLIGHTENMENT

### Services Lead to Enlightenment

**The problem is that many focus on what they need, and that way of acquiring money is the old paradigm, and it is karmic in nature. Many people usually say "I need," but this creates a blockage to their flow of abundance, because they are focused on themselves. The solution to creating more cash flow is simple. They should be focusing on what they have to give, and be persistent with faith knowing that all of their needs will be provided for, when they don't operate in scarcity. They should not treat their work like a task that they do not want to do, because this creates a restriction and constriction in the heart, and it creates stress. Even if someone's job is difficult, they should change their thinking and surrender the stress of their jobs with the thought that they're being of service; these services that are rendered accrue positive energy, life after life, and a person can become enlightened.**

### Money Does Grow on Trees

Accrual accounting principles are also about future periods, in which benefits accrue over time. A Chinese proverb says, "One generation plants the trees and another enjoys the shade." The seed, like the Law of Regeneration, is ever eternal. If you were to take a dollar bill and look at it under an electron microscope, you would be able to see that the molecules in the piece of paper are moving. In the environment, paper biodegrades rather quickly compared to other things. For example, plastic has a biodegradable lifespan that can exceed many thousands of years, whereas paper can disintegrate in a matter of months. This is scientific evidence regarding the moving nature of cash and currency. Current means the force of electricity. Money is about something that is in progress like the word current; it represents the flow.

Everything can be traced back to the spiritual matter of the universe on a microscopic level like the atom. Where we find ourselves in trouble financially is when we accept a belief system that says it is not all right to have money and be spiritual at the same time. In our modern world, if we do not have cash then we cannot survive for long independently, and we become dependent on others. This may surprise you, but if you think about it, tithing is what supports a religious organization. Without the financial contributions, then the buildings cannot be maintained.

Accrual accounting can give us a sense of peace. It is the knowing that divine justice is not affected by the whims of man. The Cosmic Laws move and are justified by divine principles. We can have faith in the spiritual worlds. I believe that we all have the capability to activate the true *Self* just by meditation. I must admit that initially being in our true *Self* can feel quite uncomfortable because we no longer need outside approval. It's best to follow the intuitive voice of compassion and wisdom from within.

We can bear in mind that accrual accounting is like the Law of Karma. It applies equally to banks, credit card companies, the stock market, any business, or an individual. A business is like a person, and it has its own personality. The corporate form of a business entity is known as an individual, and it has rights like a person. In a court of law, the judiciary system grants corporations the rights of individuals; it can act and think the thoughts of its shareholders, and its existence can be perpetual. There are many forms of businesses, such as a Sole Proprietorship, a Limited Liability Company, S Corporations, and C Corporations.

**Re-Evolution: The Monetary System Is Changing and We Are Part of It**

Remember, our thoughts are alive and the universe is intelligent. We are beings of thought, and this is why Mahavatar Babaji explained that we are like an onion, layer after layer, with emptiness and pure energy on the inside. So accrual accounting is our accrued karma from life to life. Remember, our thoughts shape our destiny, so are we ready for a change in the monetary system? Our answer to this question can shape the future consciousness of money. The following questions can be helpful in understanding enlightened money:

1. What are you willing to do to be of service to others?

2. How much are you willing to value yourself?

3. What are you willing to give or contribute to society?

4. How generous are you?

5. How many things and people are you grateful for in your life?

6. What are the predominant thoughts regarding finances that occupy your mind?

7. Do you focus only on what you want, or are you concerned about the planet as well?

8. Who needs your products or services?

9. What is your niche?

10. What are they willing to pay for it?

11. How can you reach out to those people?

12. What do you have to do to get in touch with your divine purpose?

The world is changing, and I do not like revolutionary change. I like re-evolution, a new way of thinking and doing things in alignment with spirit and our true *Self*. As the cosmic consciousness in the world is getting better, we can take action with this new knowledge, and create more enlightened businesses. This cosmic dream is woven by all of our thoughts collectively. We are conscious co-creators of our lives.

## An Empowered, Enlightened Society – We Must Bake Our Own Cakes

In accrual accounting, we are all going back to the cosmic consciousness of abundance and enlightenment. Even though we may be on different paths now, we are all roses on the vines of life. We can dare to dream our ideal life. The Divine provided us with the earth, the trees, the sun, and the water. We have been given all the ingredients we need, even the fruits and vegetables to eat, but we still have to go to the grocery store and get them. The Divine certainly does not show up in our kitchen and prepare dinner for us. We still have to get the groceries and prepare dinner. Another example is like baking a cake. We have all the ingredients, but the cake will not make itself. We must mix the batter and put it in the oven to bake. We have been given everything we need, however, our efforts are necessary to create the things we want.

In the accrual basis of life, destiny alone cannot control our lives. Yogananda was destined to be married three times, and that karma was averted by Sri Yukteswar. Nothing can stop the power of a determined mind with focus. We are the entrepreneurs, the daredevils if you will, who will shape the consciousness of money. For those of us who believe in our *Self* worth, the stakes are high.

## Empowered Entrepreneurs – *Make Empowered Decisions*™

The entrepreneur must make empowered decisions. I have been a small business owner myself, and I have also advised many other business owners. I have learned when the stakes are high, and all the chips are in, there's nothing more to lose. We can take the liberty to sing our music now, loud and clear for the whole world to hear. If this life is all an act, what have we got to lose? I've seen that the bad guys have been winning all along because the good guys sit on the sideline and watch. It takes tremendous strength and courage to live our *dharma*, because sometimes it goes against society's branding. I call it "nerves of steel" to be able to hold our self worth in a world where our value system may be unique, and society is always trying to homogenize us to look the same, feel the same, and think the same. The path of the true *Self* never has been easy, nor is it for the weak; it is the courageous ones who rise to the challenge.

We can have strength and integrity to make decisions that we deserve to live our ideal lives. If accounting is the language of business, then marketing is the communication of that language. From my experience, if there's no cash flow then sooner or later there is no accounting. Remember, accounting accounts for past transactions. The spirit of the entrepreneur is in the future. Like me, they are visionaries who see what's on the horizon.

The enlightened entrepreneur knows that the past is not the future, and they never project into the future what the past accounting has been, because it is good for analysis only. Accounting allows us to see a trend, and each business has its own cycle. The whole point of a business is to be profitable. We can create products and services that are in alignment with the natural world. It took me fifteen years, and accounting was not an easy service to develop, many years of hard work were involved.

**Invite the Divine into Your Personal Finances**

Have you ever handed your personal finances over to spirit or the higher power that guides our lives? It can seem baffling at first. Are you wishing and wanting to be more financially stable and independent? Setting goals is only the first step. In fact, consistent work is just another step toward achieving our goals. Asking for help, and remaining open to receiving the answer while trusting the Divine, allows us to make the right decisions and be consistent in providing abundance in our lives. This has been a fact of my life, and nature functions on this principle; the birds, ants, and rabbits know this. I recommend Catherine Ponder's book *The Millionaire's of Genesis*. She is a bestselling author who teaches, "The Millionaires of the Bible" series. She teaches prosperity secrets, and her book is filled with rich ideas that can bring us fortunes. She advocates that our thoughts, and not hard work, along with the prosperity laws, account for financial success.

When we allow for the Divine to handle every aspect of our lives, it creates happiness and lasting inner peace. Remember, when we connect with the Divine and our *dharma*, it comes with no money back guarantee, but it does come with a lifetime warranty. When we trust in the Universal Cosmic Laws, we do not know everything or the outcome, and we're at the mercy of the Universe. We can trust that the Universal Spiritual Laws are precise and accurate. The only thing we can do is trust in the invisible unseen cosmic power because our logical little self can never fathom the entirety and the meaning of the *Self*. The Divine warranty can be used by each and every one of us for an entire life; it is backed by immortality of the soul and the imperishable essence of the spirit. Remember, this warranty was given as a gift of life.

**Reincarnation – A Connection to Our Ancestors**

Accrual accounting coincides with the mystical teachings of the *Vedas*; it is said that for some actions sown in this lifetime, we will reap the rewards in a future lifetime, and this is the concept of reincarnation. I find it challenging, based on scientific evidence, to discount and discard the principle of reincarnation, when our biological DNA has a gene from our ancestors. I have not met my ancestors, yet I know that they live in my genes. My spiritual, emotional, and physical makeup has an imprint of their genetics and DNA. My spiritual DNA strands are stored within my spinal column, and blood circulates each and every day with their ancient history. Therefore, my financial well-being is deep rooted and connected to my ancestors.

## DIVINE TRANSMISSION – A CHANNELED MESSAGE 2012

I began to write when the evening had ended, and my day job had come to a halt. The ordeals of the day, and the daily grind can take the light away from any of us, if we are not careful to stay within the higher *Self*. Like the Grinch who stole the Christmas joy, the world is full of misers, who seem to be ready to take what they can, when they can, without the care of giving back. The world of logic, routine, and linear reality took the flow right out of mainstream. So, how can we even remember that we have a true *Self* when all we know is outside of ourselves?

I received the following messages telepathically. Beyond the distance, in clouds of rain, is a world called *Guruloka*. We are Ancient Masters, teachers of like-minded souls who have grouped together. We awaken you now to divinity. We awaken all seed sounds of richness that flow from the tongue of divinity within. Souls of love merge forever in the sea of bliss. We never work in one, yet we are one consciousness, one being. We are not separated egos striving to succeed. We understand quite well the divine structure of masterful guidance. We do not despise our leaders, for they care for us. Our leaders in the hierarchical view work well and all individual soul personalities do their parts. If we were to be in a vibration of separation, then we would have to incarnate into flesh. To maintain the light body, one must constantly strive to be in the egoless state of existence and inner peace.

If humanity can raise itself to this awareness, then they will be provided all they need as well. The divine and human worlds are not separate existences. Rather, they are functioning and coexisting concurrently, simultaneously in a dimension of time and space. Amongst the crash of vanishing worlds, we light the way to peace. Angels dance amongst the starry night pathways to heaven's door, and it opens for all of you now. Do not be afraid of death for we were once children in the mud. We are not of flesh any longer. We awaken you to the mysteries beyond the great school of life into the world of immortality.

Systems that have been in greed will not be able to survive the crash of worlds. Many will be vanishing without a trace. All corporations will be going through a transition. Those who remain will be able to empower the peoples of earth. Those like BP with the oil spill will lead the way for the new system of accountability not only to humanity, but to the oceanic beings from the sea to the air.

All metals will be moving at a frequency faster and faster, and they will act as catalysts. No human technology exists that will stop this vibratory rate. This pulsation is an electromagnetic frequency that emanates from the earth's core, the magma and the mantle. Deep within the inner earth, time crystals were placed; upon the arrival of 2012, they will once again hum and frequencies raise, and many people are hearing them humming. They are emitting the frequencies for the new world that we are shaping. Those in power know this and have tried to dismantle the core of the earth through satellite infrared radiation. In actuality, they were able to do some damage, however, our moon beings came up with a neutralizer frequency that stopped the problem, so we are on course once again.

Money on your planet will not be in the form that you know it today. We have upped the vibratory scale of mediums of exchanges. Coins are rarely used today, are they not? How about cash, not everyone uses it, the frequency of transactions is now based on the law of each individual's karma, and how much they have surpassed their own ego tendencies to manipulate, and use control over others for their own ends.

## *Dharma*, Our Divine Purpose Is the New Money

*Dharma* will be magnetizing in one more Earth week that is September 19, 2010. When the full spectrum of *dharma* frequencies are activated, all will come under the guidance of an advanced spiritual currency frequency. It will not be possible for the angelic humans to remain in dark places and work for just money. Most human beings have a strand of angelic light encoded within their DNA. This will be activated, once this is done then almost in a massive way, people who are now unsatisfied in their current financial and physical jobs will take on assignments of their soul. The currency will become soul currency. It will not be monetarily deemed.

Angelic *Devas* are standing by in the millions. Multitudes of forces have gathered in the grand counsel from many planetary systems. All over the universe they are praying for you and loving all humans. They feel the suffering and now they have been given a location in the pole of the North Star. The Angelic Race will not allow complete destruction of Earth. They will not be able to save those who do not ask for their help in prayer and humbleness. These thought beings are loving humanity. Their sole purpose from the Divine is to protect and love you. They seek nothing in return, and they can grant anything to you. All you have to do is ask and move in the direction of the flow, and in your heart you know.

The problem with many angelic humans is that they choose to stay and help those suffering, and in doing so, they create more suffering for themselves. What is important for them to do is to move where their joy and happiness is. There is light and love in that vibration. In doing so, they can then bring this love and light to the suffering. It is like they get locked in the room of poverty consciousness like those suffering. Rather, they should exit the room of poverty, scarcity, and lack. Remember, poverty is caused by excessive desire. Give more than you take, and debt is eliminated. Pain and suffering from debt will go away.

Gratitude for what you have is the best way to acquire more of what you want. Be thankful to be able to write today. Be grateful to be able to do any action. All things will align to wealth once they are done in the spirit of gratitude. Service in the spirit of gratitude is the road to endless wealth. The Divine alone is the doer of all actions. This they knew will be the problem on Earth. Mankind will have a tremendous Golden Age. Awaken oh son of the light. We are foretelling you the truth. Believe in our words and such will be your fate. We are ever Merciful Masters.

## *END OF CHANNELED MESSAGE*

### Networking and the Invisible Worlds

The ideals and concepts of networking are based on spiritual principles. It proves successful for the souls that are selfless and givers. Those who have made it big in networking understood one simple principle. It is how much you can earn by helping others. Network Marketing is on the rise due to the fact that the consciousness of money is rising from a purely individual motive to that of group and community oriented cosmic consciousness.

As we enter the consciousness and download the frequencies for money and betterment of wealth, the networking vehicles are perfect divine principles. We understand that wealth is shared and that everyone on the team must do their part for it to be successful. Some have taken advantage of others using the principles of Network Marketing. True success depends on the selflessness and the consciousness of the leader. Even though this is true, not all leaders have the best interest of the independent representatives in mind, and there are those that are extremely greedy. Those whose leaders sacrifice for the greater good of their people will prove to be more successful.

## Social Media – A New Medium of Exchange

Generations of the past were not social media, texting, Twitter generations. Money will become an online exchange. Currency will be texted over the internet via Paypal and other means, and payments will be deposited directly into bank accounts. Accounting and bookkeeping are being automated by online systems, and bank statements are downloaded into software. Few companies are still using bookkeeping by hand. However, for the most part, the future of accounting and money is wireless, internet, and intangible.

So what is a new way for abundance? Many people feared the economic crisis and change. I would implore you not to fear, with the digital era and online stores, there will be enough for all. There will always be things that are tangibles and goods. However, a few custom manufacturing companies now have the vibration of the new energy of wind and other alternative, natural, renewable resources.

China is one of the largest manufacturing countries in the world, and it is referred to by the four brothers philosophy of the Hopis as the brother and sister guardian of the wind. I would hope that instead of fearing a worldwide economic depression, the Chinese would implement new strategies for advanced technologies. Natural resources are used by life forms beyond our current understanding. Mankind can only surpass their current understanding by contemplating the life of water, the rivers, and streams of gold within the veins of the earth.

## Universal Currency – The Energy of Wealth

For those who do not trespass upon the Cosmic Laws, they will be showered with praise and abundant, food, clothing, shelter, and love. The Great Universe gives wealth to all who seek it from its inexhaustible supply. Yet, the divine lessons and principles must be adhered to with wealth in order for it to manifest consistently. Wealth is nothing other than energy magnetized and transferred from one person to another which is like electricity. The Great Universe reveals wealth to those who are deserving of its worth, but this clue I will give to you.

I feel the next stage of evolution for humanity will be an easy transition to reclaim their divine *Self*. The first step to anything in life is thought, or energy form, and I call it the Cosmic Realm. The cosmic energies provide the support for all other life forms. For example, the sun's light provides the oxygen and carbon dioxide for the plants to grow. The water from the clouds precipitates and creates the rain for the crops to grow. Without these natural processes, or if these processes get out of balance, humanity will starve to death. It is important as we enter into the enlightened cosmic consciousness to give thanks for the food we eat, and the beings that provide our nutrition. Gratitude is the spiritual, universal currency.

**Dharma and the Universal Laws**

Our lives are as delicate as the butterfly. The soul resides on gentle wings like the butterfly. We must never wait for perfection in everything. Our *dharma* cannot be transferred to someone else. We cannot blame someone else for our failures. The Law of Accountability states that we must live our *dharma*. The Law of Accountability and *dharma* are one and the same; our dreams must fly free, like the butterfly. If we cage them up and wait for the perfect day, it may be that our perfect day never arrives. We cannot wait but one second in despair. What is your *dharma* and how can you achieve it?

I would love to say that you already know. It may sound as silent as the whispers of a butterfly's wings. The soul whispers in eternity forever. It has known, it will continue to know, and it will forever know. The question is whether you will listen to that small voice, or will you wait until it is too late? *Dharma* is like a whirlwind, you feel it, and it causes a rush throughout your body, mind, and spirit.

**The Accounting Principle of Consistency Relates to the Spiritual Principles of Habits and Destiny**

Our cosmic journey continues now amongst the juniper and pine trees with the principle of consistency. Remember, our thoughts affect our reality, and our habits shape our destiny. Habits are the actions that we take routinely, and they are consistent efforts. When we *Make Empowered Decisions*™, our entire lives change. Synonyms of the word consistency are: constancy, faithfulness, reliability, loyalty, and dependability. We learned about accrual accounting, and it is in consistency that our lives accrue successes or failures. When we think positively and affirm our belief in ourselves, and a higher power, with constant and continuous activity, we can activate the Universal Laws to accomplish anything.

*Consistency* is one of the basic concepts underlying reliable financial statements. It is important to be able to compare financial information from month to month, or year to year. Once a company has adopted a particular accounting method, it should follow that method with regularity, year after year. Thus, once a company has adopted a particular inventory method, it should continue to apply that assumption to all sales of that type of merchandise consistently. A company can change its accounting methods. However, if a change is made, the reasons for the change must be explained. The effects of the change upon the company's net income must be fully disclosed in its financial statements. It is important for a business to keep the same method of accounting because without consistency, there can be no comparison from one period to the next.

## Synchronicity: Divine Timing – Momentum

Momentum is speed of movement, and it feels like a rush of butterflies in the stomach which may translate to anxiety. It is this feeling that lets us know to move when the timing is right; it is divine timing and synchronicity. When we are inconsistent, there is no momentum and flow. Momentum builds from our consistent efforts. For example, when I was writing I would know when I can concentrate without distractions, then some days there was no momentum to write. Momentum can sometimes be overwhelming. In the divine flow, momentum allows for the delicate balance which is necessary, and it keeps the *dharmic* wheels going.

It was now July 2010 and the spring flowers had given way to the rich, lush, green leaves of summer. The hot July weather in Arizona keeps most people indoors, unless they have some business being outdoors. Enlightenment is a beautiful experience. Being enlightened is far from sitting back and sipping tropical drinks on a beach. That may be our modern idea of a vacation, but it is far from the reality of an enlightened being. The responsibilities of an enlightened being are constant and never-ending. The *Vedas* describe three primary characteristics of people, *Sattva* which is positive, *Rajas* which is neutralizing, and *Tamas* which is negative. An enlightened being is primarily *Sattva*, which means they are being of service, and they work tirelessly for the benefit of others.

## Meditation During an Eclipse

It was the Solar Eclipse in July 2010. The ancients feared eclipses because they challenge us to face our hidden shadows. I see that each time an eclipse occurs, it gives us a chance to move in the direction of our true *Self.* Eclipses were usually a time for prayers, for it was believed that our prayers are much more powerful at those times. It has always been in my nature to have things proven, and experimenting with the super-conscious state of existence was no exception.

I thought I would test the ancients to see if indeed it were true that prayers were more powerful at the time of the eclipse. During the solar eclipse, I sat and did a meditation and prayers. I surely wanted my prayers to be magnified. A few hours after the eclipse, I felt an urge to go outside the house and look up in the sky. I could not believe my eyes; there I saw an orb of golden light. Intrigued by the dazzling, moving object against the pitch black sky, I wondered what it meant.

## Telepathic Communication with a Bodhisattva

I telepathically heard a message that the Buddha Stupa had something to do with the being of light above. A Stupa is a memorial representation of the eight great deeds of the Buddha. I was so excited when I encountered this being that I called out to Jonathan, and we got a flash light. It had been several years since I had seen the Buddha Stupa in Sedona, but I felt drawn to go there.

The Stupa had a row of bricks that people can make donations to get their name engraved on. We drove to the Stupa on the moonless night, and the only visible thing that I could find in the dark night was called the "Path to Peace." The telepathic messages came again, "Pathway to Peace will be included in a chapter in *Cosmic Accounting: A Journey to Enlightenment*." You can see what the Stupa looks like. It is on a video on our *YouTube channels SynchroDharma* and *CosmicAccounting*. Jonathan created a beautiful video of the Stupa for me as a gift.

About a year later, on a beautiful sunny Saturday morning, I went to the New Frontiers grocery store here in town. At the entrance was a woman, and I stopped at her table and picked up a brochure. She shared with me that she was seeking donations for refugees from Tibet. She explained that the Government of India had given the refugees land to live on. However, they did not have adequate food, clothing, or shelter. I gave her a small donation.

Later, when I got home, I checked out the website. I sobbed as I watched the living conditions, and how many gave their lives for freedom. Their story touched a raw nerve inside. The little monks were like precious angels. For many years, I envisioned adopting one hundred children. I wanted to adopt children from different nations in the world. My dream is that one day these children will all grow up knowing that their adopted mother's vision was world peace. Together, long after I am gone, they will continue a legacy of peace on earth. I sponsored my first child that day. I calculated how much it would take to sponsor one hundred children, but my salary could not cover it.

I gave myself a moment to stop crying for the sad state of poverty in the world, and with these words, I have shared with you my soul essence. In these few paragraphs I reveal the secrets of my innermost *Self*. Like a riddle, simultaneously the *Self* exists in both you and me, yet it is neither you nor I. I escaped my logical mind for a moment. Like a mother who yearns for her child's return, I wanted to wipe away all the tears in the world. The sweet sensations of peace overcame me as I wrote this chapter.

It is amazing what writing a book can do. It revealed to me things that I could not even have imagined in my wildest dreams. All is moving according to plan. Consistently, the pieces came together effortlessly. I realized life is the greatest thing that we were granted from the universe. Our logical, ego-based fears are only a reminder of the disconnection from the magnanimity of life. We can surely move beyond the world of fear. The very nature of our lives is for us to give our best. Many years later, I see that our functionalities and different occupations make up our diverse sea of experiences. How can there ever be enough if we don't do our *dharma* consistently?

## *DIVINE TRANSMISSION – A CHANNELED MESSAGE*

### Divine Mother

Awake my divine child. Humanity sleeps in a slumber, like little children who are constantly used to an addictive substance, and like a drug, they desire more and more, never full. They take more than they need. The imbalance is too great. When they begin to give back, money and abundance will effortlessly flow. There are those of you who are only now starting your careers and jobs. *Dharma* must govern. When you do your *dharma*, then for sure you can connect with momentum.

When you constantly want more and more, the energies around your energy field are scattered. It is virtually impossibly to focus and achieve anything. Desires are the pits of hell that led you into debt. The world of debt is, wanting to have it all at once. When you cultivate patience, it will be easy to learn contentment. Learn to let go of desires altogether, or fulfill your desires so that you can let them go. A desire must be fulfilled or released in order for you to free up energy.

## *END OF CHANNELED MESSAGE*

### Unlimited Wealth

It is not possible for each and every human being on earth to become a billionaire. However, it is possible for many people to live in abundance with a great quality of life comfortably. Time and time again, I see that the people who do not have self control lose everything. The spiritual quotient is directly proportional to the amount of wealth one can hold on to. We must remember that according to the Yogis, we are all born with innate qualities from past incarnations. The seeds of success or failure lie dormant until such a time that they sprout unexpectedly. If we consistently strive to achieve the best no matter how difficult the path is, then those efforts are not wasted. They apply to a future period, and this relates to the concept of accrual accounting, eventually, consistent efforts bear fruit, and we become successful.

## Spiritual Quotient – Paradigm Shifts in Consciousness

If we were to receive all the money we needed, would we consistently strive for something better? Have you ever seen fruit flies manifested in the atmosphere? Where do they come from? Like fruit flies, cash and money exist in the world in unlimited quantities, because the divine principles for wealth are prevalent in *prana*, the divine intelligent life force. The problem is not that there is not enough money; the problem is that there is not enough money circulating, and when we are of service, it creates a flow because energy moves.

Remember that our spiritual DNA and our past karma determine how much wealth we will have. If we acquire wealth and help others in this lifetime, then it sets the stage for wealth and abundance in our next lifetime. If we align to the spiritual wealth that is in the universe, then there will be no cause for fear of not living one's divine purpose and becoming enlightened. That is why money does not distinguish whether a good or bad person is getting it.

It is my belief that every decision we make leads to the next experiences of our life. Imagine how your life could change if you decided to listen to your intuition. It is called a woman's intuition, and a man's gut instincts. We already know what to do. Due to our conditioning and reasoning mind, usually we need scientific proof before we can trust a new and better direction. Many people live their lives in silent turmoil because they never trusted their own feelings for fear of ridicule or what others think of them. When we want to taste freedom, we have to dare ourselves to dream our biggest dream and move in pursuit of that dream.

In our world, in the last few hundred years, we learned so much about IQ, intelligence quotient. Mere intellectual knowledge does not give inner peace. We learned about EQ, emotional quotient. Self control is important, however, there is more to life. I feel that we are now ready to embrace a new *Spiritual Quotient* (SQ) in business. Spiritual quotient is simply the measure of our connection to our higher *Self*. SQ is not about religious beliefs. Rather, it is about the connection to infinite possibilities. Without a strong spiritual base, we will find ourselves in the midst of chaos and pain. Suffering and turmoil can cease and we can live the most beautiful life, if we can turn our thoughts to the divinity within.

## How Can You Increase Your Spiritual Quotient?

Prayer is the purposeful and intentional act of focusing the mind. The power of the Individual Will merges with the Divine Will and connects us to our true *Self*, and the cosmic plan. We must consistently set our intention to connect with our higher *Self* which allows the power of the Divine to bless us on our path. We will find that love, protection, and the things that we desire come to us much faster than if we were using our individual will alone.

Today I would like to share a memory with you. Little did I know what the mind can do if we apply the principles of simplicity. The individual will, when merged with the Divine Will, can move galaxies in place, and it can prevent natural disasters, bring wealth, health, and abundance to humanity. When we include in ourselves the happiness of others, we are certain to experience happiness. When we include in our work the wealth and prosperity of others, then we are sure to achieve prosperity and wealth. We are the mirrors for those around us, and those around us are the mirrors for us. We surrender our actions to the Divine and allow the mercy of the Divine to come close to us.

## Meditation on Mahavatar Babaji

As the tears flowed endlessly, I meditated on Mahavatar Babaji. I received a message telepathically. My *dharma* was changing to another career. Sometimes when we begin a new path or when our *dharma* changes to something with more responsibilities, we tend to hold on to the past *dharma*, and this causes us to suffer. We have to know when to let go of the past so that we can embrace the new. Here is a little story that a friend of mine from Thailand shared with me: "If you are in the river, and your boat has a hole and it is taking water. Then you look up, and along comes a sturdy strong ship, what will you do? Will you stay in the sinking boat or will you go to safety in the sturdy ship that comes along?"

The twists and turns of society and the fabrics of control will not be won on the streets of revolution, but by the efforts of re-evolution in our lives. We can never be the Rockefellers of the world. When we give of ourselves, the Divine does not ask us to give what we do not have. It does not ask for us to go and get a Ph.D. or to get a million dollars to help others. All we have to give is what we have more than enough of. It makes us happy, but we can only give of ourselves; Indeara can only give Indeara. A fish can only give fish. A deer can only give deer. There is one quality that we have that sparks a special thing on earth, and when we give freely of ourselves, we activate powerful forces of *dharma* that give back to us in ways we cannot dare to even dream. We connect to the cosmic plan and the Divine will.

## Our Cosmic Journey Ends with My Trip to Texas

It was July 25, 2010, and it was *Guru Purnima* once again. I had dedicated my day to Mahavatar Babaji. Our cosmic journey continues, and before you know it, I was in a friend's Toyota 4Runner on our way to Texas. We were visiting a National Sales Manager whom they worked with. I was interested in learning from the very successful entrepreneur, who was known for his spirituality and connection to the Divine. We drove from Arizona sunup to sundown, and the long drive was enjoyable.

I shared the amazing drive with my friend from Thailand and her husband. She did some amazing prayers of monks chanting along the way. We arrived in Texas and stayed at the Fort Worth Hilton, and it was beautiful. We went to Buck Thornton's and watched Country dancing. I remembered the blessings of the invisible Gurus, to whom I owed my life, because they had removed so much suffering for me. They shine upon us their divine light of prosperity.

The Great Masters gave me the blessing of spending *Guru Purnima* at a one thousand acre ranch. The gorgeous multimillion dollar property had many lakes and all kinds of wildlife. The place was like a safari with a lakefront property, and manmade beaches. The white beach sand was flown in to Texas from a tropical location. There was a pool that was built into underground waterfalls. I really enjoyed meeting people that had no problems earning more than half a million dollars a month, and I saw how abundant, generous, and giving they were.

It was a great lesson and culmination of many lessons that I'd learned on my cosmic journey. I am ever grateful that the principles in this book proved themselves as they were applied. This brings me to my last topic, and the main points of what we've learned thus far, as follows:

## *STRATEGIES FOR ENLIGHTENMENT*

- **Law of Intention – We should always have the right thoughts and maintain positive thinking.**

- We should understand that we are already enlightened beings.
- We should remember that we awaken our true *Self* when we practice what we've learned in alignment with our hearts.
- We should awaken the inner knowledge and the higher *Self* within.
- We should realize that we are not alone in the Universe, and we are intergalactic beings traveling in the cosmos.
- We are the gatekeepers to the *inner world* of cosmic consciousness, and the key to get in, lies in the immortal essence of our soul and love.
- We should treat our lives like a dance with destiny through infinity, knowing that the music and the physical body will come to an end.
- We should know how to make peace within.
- We can co-create the dream of an enlightened civilization.
- We all have the chance to become immortal.
- We cannot control others; we are only accountable for ourselves.
- We should surrender the outcome of our intentions and efforts to the Divine.
- Our consistent efforts will always prove to be the long term key to success.
- We should wholeheartedly give our best, and always remain open to receiving our divine share of abundance.
- We should concentrate on one thing at a time, and focus our attention on successful people and the higher *Self.*
- We should be persistent, like the trees ever reaching for the sun, despite the thunderstorms of life.
- We should remember that the mind is the creator of our bodies and circumstances. Therefore, we should always use the power of our thoughts to be empowered.
- We should always take action with awareness, and we should realize that we're on borrowed time. Therefore, we should make our dreams a reality in the moment now.
- Remember that our past lives affect our future lives, therefore, what may seem like good luck was already earned from our past actions, and incarnations.
- Remember, change happens quickly and it is the only constant in a world of shifting molecules. We can make anything become a reality.

- Remember, the Law of Accountability can be a good meter for our success because we are responsible for our thoughts, words, deeds, and actions.
- We should know by now that prosperity, abundance, and all the things we need for a good quality of life are our divine birthrights.
- We should seize the moment now, and let go of the past and future.
- We should cultivate a balanced lifestyle and be of service.
- The point of life is not avoiding failure; rather, it is a chance to prove our self worth, and overcome the trials and tribulations of life. By moving through adversity with love, we prosper.
- Last but not least, we can only do something great, one step at a time.

# CHAPTER 8
*Principles to Stand in Your Integrity*
*Bringing it all Together for Success*

"Delicate Blossoms – Perfect Symphony of Souls"

We have come to understand the cosmic accounting of life from a universal perspective. Amidst the void of time and space, deep in the cosmos, our little planet is revolving around the Sun like a blue-green jewel moving in the gravitational orbit. Planet Earth is thought of as a great school, and we call it home. We can learn many lessons about the immortal essence of our soul, but due to the nature of our physical body, many of us have forgotten who we really are. Thus far we have gained a new understanding in remembering our higher *Self*, and our connection to the cosmos. A long time ago, many great saints paved the way for us to comprehend the meaning of the soul. They came from all walks of life with many different backgrounds and nationalities.

**The Modern Day Yogi and Yogini**

Even the saints needed money to accomplish their divine work because it was important, however, when materialism is the only thing that is focused on, life can sometimes feel unfulfilled. The way for the modern yogi is not to deny one's self of material objects, and live in unsanitary conditions in the woods, because it is not necessary when we have modern amenities. People from all walks of life would not have to live in a cave or monastery because enlightenment is available to everyone. As the Zen saying goes, "Before enlightenment chop wood and after enlightenment chop wood." The modern saying should be, "Before enlightenment do accounting, and after enlightenment do accounting!" What changes? Nothing changes externally, rather we are transformed from within, and we become the change we seek.

Sri Yukteswar and Lahiri Mahasaya did not have to give up their family to live the yogic lifestyle, nor do we. We can live the life of a modern day yogi or yogini without sacrificing our careers. Being a yogi requires going within by meditating, introspection, and self control. True power lies at the core of being a yogi or *yogini*, who is a female yogi. The ability to control one's body, mind, and spirit takes strength. We can only control ourselves. We may try, but the efforts to control others or external factors prove futile. Force by its very nature is destructive. The belief that one can reach one's desired destination by applying pressure externally is a farce. Though force may give immediate results, it proves to be temporary. Constant force is required to have lasting effects.

**Power vs. Force**

Ultimately, everyone is responsible for the consequences of their choices. In his book, *Power vs. Force* (Veritas Publishing, 2002), Dr. David R. Hawkins, M.D., Ph.D. states the following:

> "Our choices reinforce the formation of powerful M-Fields, which are the attractor patterns that influence others whether we wish them to or not. Every act or decision we make that supports life supports all life, including our own. The ripples we create return to us-this, which may once have seemed a metaphysical statement, is now established as scientific fact. Everything in the universe constantly gives off an energy pattern of a specific frequency that remains for all time and can be read by those who know how. Every word, deed and intention creates a permanent record. Every thought is known and recorded forever. There are no secrets; nothing is hidden, nor can it be. Our spirits stand naked in time for all to see-everyone's life, finally, is accountable to the universe."

The Universal Law of Accountability reverberates the actions of mankind, lifetime after lifetime. The modern yogi knows permanent change comes from within. The ability to have self control allows us to open up to the meditative, expansiveness, and vastness of mystical experiences. In reality, self control may sound like it's opposite. On a practical level, self control in spending leads to savings and peace of mind. Self control in eating leads to a good diet and health. Self control which leads to moderation in speech becomes humility. It gives us the ability to gather energy or the power to achieve our dreams.

As we put this ancient wisdom into practice, we begin to experience balance. You can transform your life through *The Life Balance Process for Inner Transformation*™, which stimulates the mind to find answers from within. We can enjoy inner peace and uncover the magical relationship between work and our divine *Self*. Living our *dharma* or divine purpose gives us an immense sense of joy. Divine Consciousness is the cosmic view of all of us collectively. It is the *Self* which is the cumulative effects of all of us together, not the thoughts or ideas of any one person. Together our individual choices can lead to the co-creation of healing the entire planet spiritually, financially, emotionally, and physically. The modern yogi can bypass the cosmic Laws of Karma with wisdom and self control, and the understanding of the Law of *Dharma*.

Remember, the synthesis of divinity and the soul's purpose with money can prove to be one of life's most enjoyable experiences. The conquest of the true *Self* can be exhilarating to say the least. Being grateful for the opportunity to give in the spirit of service, while surrendering the outcome for the highest and best good for all, opens the doorway to true abundance. When we surrender the outcome of our actions, we are acting from a place of trust. We can activate powerful subtle laws for success. The individual will, which is dominated by the logical mind, can be bypassed to access the unlimited cosmic mind, through the portal of loving and peaceful thoughts.

## *CONCLUSION*

### The Cosmic Law of Giving and Receiving

As humanity awakens spiritually, we are searching for more out of life. Together we can feel spiritually uplifted and learn the benefits of being of service to each other. Rather than focusing on the desire for money alone, the secret is to help others and give in the spirit of service. The power of giving creates a divine flow of abundance. Yogananda said that service makes money our slave rather than it enslaving us. Anything that we do in the spirit of service, whether it is for a job or creative endeavor, strengthens the bond with our true *Self*.

Contrary to what some people say, there is plenty of money in the world. Depending on one's perception, money does grow on trees. From an enlightened and scientific perspective, money comes from paper. Paper comes from wood. Wood comes from trees. Trees come from seeds. Seeds come from fruits and plants. Hence, in the Law of Regeneration and nature, money is eternal. If we look at a dollar bill under an electron microscope, the molecules are no different from the plant and the wood that it came from.

Acting out of desperation, lack, and need feeds the consciousness of scarcity and poverty. Poverty is not merely the lack of material possessions, nor is wealth the materialistic possessions that one has acquired. True abundance is defined as the ability to acquire that which one needs, at will. It is also the ability to make more money than we need to benefit others with charity. Wealth that is earned in purity and given in the spirit of charity is one of the highest *dharma* or divine purposes of human life. The highest being the realization of the true *Self*.

In an infinite world, with the process of transformation of matter through the solid-liquid-gaseous states, it is absurd to believe in scarcity. Everything is constantly changing. Therefore, if someone experiences poverty, they can change it with the understanding of the Universal Cosmic Laws. Yet, the disease of poverty reigns on earth because of people being unaware of the Cosmic Law of Abundance.

I've met countless people whose perception is that being spiritual means being broke. We were conditioned to believe that spirit, matter, and money for that fact, are separate. Economic theories based on Manmade Laws are used to manipulate the masses. People live in constant fear of losing their livelihoods because they were never taught the cosmic plan for success and infinite abundance. The ideas in *The Millionaires of Genesis* can help someone in this situation.

Each one of us acting with purpose can be the catalyst for instantaneous change in perception, and we can create a global enlightened network. Believing we are one with the cosmos grants us the privilege of abundant living, and enables us to receive the divine child's share. That which no longer serves humanity should vanish from our consciousness. I feel that the time is right to elevate our monetary consciousness to a spiritual basis; this does not mean that cash and our financial institutions would disappear. All it would mean is that we do not operate in scarcity. Many people lose sleep over financial concerns. Some even take drastic measures such as suicide or homicide. If we are to evolve as a race, then certainly we can move beyond desperation and lack.

Many textbooks have been written on accounting, yet few express a relationship to the Divine. Even more books have been written on spirituality, but treat it as a separate part from our daily lives. Eons ago, spirit and matter were defined as one, yet vibrating at different frequencies, like water in the never-ending process of evaporation and condensation.

## Understanding the Life Balance Process for Inner Transformation

While I was working as an accountant for Hale Dwoskin of *The Sedona Method*, I received a copy of the DVD, *The Secret*, prior to public release. *Cosmic Accounting: A Journey to Enlightenment* regards money as energy and picks up where *The Secret* left off. *The Secret* opened discussion about the understanding of the Laws of Attraction and Manifestation, and how they work. According to the *Vedic* texts, each human desire must eventually find fulfillment whether in this life or the next. It is our desires which bind us to the karmic wheel, incarnation after incarnation. There is no question whether the Laws of Attraction and Manifestation work, it just depends on how many lifetimes we want to spin the wheel of fortune.

To free us from the bondage of karma, we open the door to the sister Law of Accountability and The Law of *Dharma*. Surely we can manifest enough for our needs, however, we must remember that we are responsible, and held accountable for our creations. It urges us to balance our emotional, physical, financial, and spiritual self. Mankind is yet to discover intelligence beyond our comprehension, which is responsible for the entire universe. If we can understand that we are not the doers of all things, then we can detach from the karmic wheel.

We are responsible for our happiness, successes, or failures financially, emotionally, spiritually, and physically. If we give away our power to someone or something outside of our true *Self*, it leads us to suffering. Therefore, if we experience suffering, we can definitely change it to happiness. Remember, success is created in the mind first through our thoughts. If we can learn these simple principles that destiny and fate alone are not responsible for our circumstances, then we can take back the reigns of power and co-create a beautiful life. Which one we experience is a matter of choice. Will you choose love or fear, abundance or scarcity?

The dream is to live in a world where there is abundance, wisdom, and inner peace for all. We are now learning about The Law of Manifestation and becoming co-creators of our own reality. The Law of Accountability or Responsibility is the balancing factor for the Law of Manifestation. So many of us have been separated from our true *Self*, our bodies, minds, spirits, and our physical, emotional, and spiritual. How can the Law of Accountability help you? *The Life Balance Process for Inner Transformation*™ can help you bring all the pieces of the puzzle together to view the larger picture of your life from a bird's eye view, or cosmic view. It serves as a reminder to unlock your sacred potential from within. Only you have the power to change circumstances in your life.

## Choices

One of the keys to understanding The Law of Accountability is to know that you always have choices. There are many alternative choices in any course of action, and some may not be immediately realized as they are within your potential. They lie hidden, un-manifested, waiting for the right moment to sprout, like the spring buds which turn to leaves in the summer. It can help you to remember your purpose. Sometimes we think we have to look outside of ourselves for the answers, but the truth is always inside.

The *Life Balance Process for Inner Transformation*™ teaches us a new way of abundance which is holistic. It teaches how to get back in balance with our true *Self* and make money in alignment with our integrity. It is a new language of accounting where the numbers make sense, and it leads to financial harmony, "*har-money*." Some of us may think that accounting is only a way to look at financial reports. I came to understand that accounting has a much deeper meaning. It has become a way in which we have an opportunity to live our lives in a sacred manner. Remember, it means that we are held accountable for every word, thought, deed, and action.

Financially speaking, if we do something wrong, someone can sue us. This is a materialistic view of the Law of Accountability. Accounting has been defined in more of a spiritual and sacred way. The familiar sayings, "As above so below," "What goes around comes around," and "Do unto others as you would like done unto yourself," are all connected to the Law of Accountability. What we create, we are responsible for. We cannot point the finger and play the blame game. We are not helpless victims in a chaotic world that is unjust. The Divine Laws are impersonal in nature, and they are not biased. The universe can be an ATM, and fulfill every desire we have, yet, it is those desires which bind us to the karmic wheel of existence, lifetime after lifetime.

## What Is the Bottom Line?

It depends on which perspective we take when we answer this question, from a material perspective it means the profits in a business. Yet, from a spiritual perspective, the answer depends on what is inside of you and relates to your true *Self*. Each and every one of us has a uniqueness, and special gift for all of us to cherish. There is only one of you in all of existence. Divine intelligence guides our every thought, deed, and action. When we live our lives in balance with the earth and dedicate our time and energy to the service of all, the synchronicities grow and so do our profits. The bottom line is about a life of *dharma* or divine purpose, financial harmony, abundance, and inner peace.

## The Law of *Dharma* Revisited

In the ancient *Vedic* texts there are two paths in our working life. According to answers.com:

"Dharma is often best left untranslated, as it has acquired a lively life of its own in English that is more expressive than any simplistic translation. Common translations and glosses include "right way of living," Divine Law, path of righteousness, order, faith, "natural harmony," rule, fundamental teachings, and duty. *Dharma* may be employed to render the rules of the entwining operation and relationship of body-mind and Universe, microcosm and macrocosm…The explanation of karma can differ per tradition. Usually it is believed to be a sum of all that an individual has done, is currently doing and will do. The results or "fruits" of actions are called *karma-phala*. Karma is not about retribution, vengeance, punishment or reward; karma simply deals with what is. The effects of all deeds actively create past, present and future experiences, thus making one responsible for one's own life, and the pain and joy it brings to others."

From my understanding, *dharma* means living our divine potential and serving our purpose on earth in alignment with the highest good for all. When we live our *dharma*, everything becomes easier because it is supported by the Universal Will. Even if there are challenges, we will eventually triumph. *Dharma* allows us to experience the synchronicities, and everything feels like floating on a feather. Whereas karma feels heavy, it is the result of past actions and nothing seems to go right. The Yogis explained that we can bypass this Law of Karma all together, defer it to a future time, or nullify it forever; we can understand it with accrual accounting, and we explored this concept earlier.

How can we be in alignment with our *dharma* and not feel the consequences of karma? The answer is simple. We have to surrender the results of our actions for the highest and best good for all, and not attach ourselves to the outcome. A better way of putting it is that we have to get out of our own way, and we simply need to let go and trust. All we can control is our intention. When we force the outcome to go the way we want it to, we use the logical mind or little self. The outcome will be based on our little inner circle, those who we network with and know. When we surrender the outcome, we activate the cosmic mind. The infinite mind can create infinite possibilities and outcomes which serve all.

## Our *Dharma* Changes

We do our *dharma* because of who we are. For example, I write because I have a story to write, not because I need money. That does not mean that I do not need money, it simply means I give the best of what I have to offer knowing that money is readily available and will easily flow to me. My *dharma* has changed over the years from being a Babysitter, Cashier, Tax Accountant Assistant, Bookkeeper, Accountant, Auditor, Teacher, Healer, and Intuitive Business Consultant. My *dharma* now is to share these simple universal principles as an Author, and Metaphysical Teacher.

## Interconnectedness – Our Thoughts Can Heal the World

The Laws of Accountability, Regeneration, and Interconnectedness are closely related. For example, if we go to the grocery store and try to purchase too many vegetables and fruits, they can go rotten if we do not use them in time. If we think for a moment about what goes into growing the fruits that are wasted, we would immediately grasp these divine principles. Think about the water, the sun's rays, the little birds, bees, and bugs who worked all spring long to pollinate the flower that blossomed which grew into a fruit, and the driver who delivered it to the store. Even though we can pick up our food from the grocery store, it doesn't grow on shelves. Many beings collaborated so that we can eat. We are all interconnected in the food chain.

From a cosmic perspective, we are accountable for the earth. We have separated ourselves from Mother Nature, and for this she is now wreaking havoc. If we are to live in harmony and balance, we must think about these things. For those of us who live these simple principles for the benefit of all, the Universal Laws become our allies and provide all we need to be happy. The choice is yours and always has been. Only if we live in harmony can we accomplish such a monumental task.

Whether we are in a financial crisis, terrorist attack, earthquake, or tsunami, scientists have now been able to prove the power of prayerful thoughts. Our thoughts can stop any natural or manmade disaster, or at least reduce the effects of suffering. Many studies have shown that when people meditate, violence decreases. Remember, we are interconnected and our thoughts impact the *prana*, which is the divine intelligent energy that sustains all life on earth. We can use our thoughts to connect with anything and anyone on earth to heal the planet. If we do this collectively, we can effect powerful inner transformation, and the kind of change which supports all life.

Remember, thoughts of success lead to success, whereas thoughts of failure lead to failure. It is important to embrace that which we seek as if we already possess it. Thoughts of lack, scarcity, and poverty consciousness are not in alignment with our infinite being-ness. Our thoughts are accountable for the lives of all the plants and animals as well as each and every one of us. We are the guardians of this great planet Earth, and it is our responsibility to live in a loving, caring, and balanced way. One thought to become enlightened, leads us towards enlightenment. Remember, being of service and helping each other are ways to transform our lives. We are given a choice, and the decision is a simple one. Now is the time. Together we can weave the fabrics of an amazing tapestry with mutual respect and compassion for all of earth's creations and leave a lasting legacy for generations to come.

This is one of the best times to be alive on the planet. According to the Hopis, we are going into a new dimension of time where our thoughts will manifest faster. It becomes increasingly important to pay attention to what we think about. Thoughts are real. They manifest our dreams or fears into reality. We have a chance to impact the future like no other time on earth. The moment you have been waiting for has arrived, so go with the flow of life. *The Life Balance Process for Inner Transformation*™ uses the Feng Shui Nine Trigrams which incorporate nine primary areas of life. It takes into consideration one's fame and reputation, relationships, children and creativity, going with the divine flow, career, attaining inner peace, health, family, wealth and prosperity, all working together in perfect harmony or *har-money*.

## I Speak with the Great Masters Once More

It was now 12:05 AM on February 16, 2011. I sat at the computer in amazement, and I beseeched the Great Masters once again. I prayed that *Cosmic Accounting: A Journey to Enlightenment* would be handed to the publisher and completed, then a great thought entered my mind. So what is the juicy ending? What would make this book complete? After all, this was a book on enlightenment. I realized that the end was in the beginning. The Great Ones would not have me work so long on the beginning of the book, just to make it go away. The conclusion was nebulous, and it was like my introduction and the ending in the beginning. Like the great universe, it had no beginning and no end. The ideas themselves were immortal, so how could they end?

Earlier that day, I sat down around the Sacred Datura plant in my backyard. I was so sad to see the owners cut it down. During the summer, it was so beautiful, and it made such a divine scent. The Sacred Datura blooms only in the moonlight, and many nights I sat in the moonlight watching it glow. I loved writing when the warm sun hit my face with the breeze of the cool spring mornings. I sat next to the peach blossoms, writing in the early hours of the morning for many years.

Yes, this was the end and a new beginning for me. This was my dream to serve the Great Masters. My original introduction is the piece that brought me to the highest spiritual awareness, so when I thought I was writing the beginning, I was writing the conclusion. If you've seen the movie *The Last Samurai*, in the scene when Katsumoto dies, he looks up at the blossoms in the springtime as Captain Algren is watching, Katsumoto's last breath leaves his body, his eyes roll back and he says, "Perfect, they are all perfect" as the blossoms from a tree nearby fall to the ground, and the wind blows them into spirals, and then he leaves his body.

Metaphorically, I felt like I had died, and been reborn a hundred times over while writing this book. Like the spring blossoms that turn to peaches in the summer, I will never get that moment ever again. I changed, time changed, the universe changed, and reality has indeed changed since I began writing, but my soul's essence and my message were always the same. I did not go anywhere, I am still here, yet everything has changed since then, and I am a few years older now.

Why would the Great Masters rescue and save me at a time when I was in so much pain that I didn't think I would make it through the suffering alive? When I could take the pain no more, and my heart filled with sorrows, and it was too much to bear, and when the cross of my burdens overwhelmed me, the Great Masters knew that the day would come when the book would end. Yes indeed, I hear the Angels trumpeting their horns. The Divine is here now and forever, and we are sealed in a pact of divine emotion and love. We are all beloveds, and one with eternity. Indeed, now that we have learned the Divine Lesson of Accountability, we realize that the end will always be in the beginning.

**Life Is a Paradox**

We can realize the immortal essence of life through these pages. We are forever in the Divine. The Great Masters say, "Seek us in praise and we shall return in your hearts." The paradox of life, you see, is that once you realize the truth of the lessons of your life, the message of the words is crystal clear. Now that you realize you are responsible and fully accept that you have created your own life's lessons, by trial and error you will be successful, and remember, there is no failure in eternity. We can be accountable for our words, thoughts, deeds, and actions. However, when we surrender the outcome and let go, the Divine takes responsibility for our lives. The Law of Accountability is that only the Divine is responsible for saving life and giving it. The cosmic journey to our higher *Self* will be tested. Our faith was tested in unimaginable ways. For in the beginning is the end.

The sacred message at the end is that help is never far away, and anyone can access it. We must first be truthful with our own self, and realize our true *Self*, and in so doing we get close to the never-ending realm of eternity. As Dr. Wayne Dyer says, "I am nowhere and now here at the same time." I have died to myself only to be reborn into the light of enlightened cosmic consciousness. Herein lies the paradox, once we realize that we are responsible, we also realize that we are not alone, and no one has to do it alone because we are all interconnected by *light*.

We become enlightened, and that which binds us to pain no longer has power over us. We conquer our inner turmoil and the demons of fear are forgotten, for in the word is power and truth. We live in truth and the now, for only in the truth, can we free ourselves. There is no other way, because lies bind us to the karmic wheel of existence. Enlightenment is forever in the great mystery within the peace of eternity. We cannot know everything, but you see, in every introduction is a conclusion, for without it the book of life would end. Yet, in every conclusion there is a new beginning and a new chapter of life.

## A Metamorphosis

Like humanity's enlightenment, we see that the butterfly was always within the cocoon, and its dream to fly away resides in its very core. Duality with day and night, pain and sorrow, hunger and sadness, can never stop the mortal man from reaching his immortal nature. It is inherent in his divine blueprint and that, my friends, is the soul purpose of human existence; to realize that the butterfly is like mankind, hidden in the darkness of his so called reality. In the same way, mankind is an immortal spirit. We are already enlightened beings, and like a caterpillar, one day we can transform our pain, the mundane, and our lives into our immortal existence with wings to fly free into our true *Self*.

Remember, we were always beings of light capable of enlightenment. With its newfound wings, the butterfly can never be a caterpillar again, but it can never forget that its very being is a caterpillar. In the everyday act of living, the seeds of inner transformation lie dormant. Nothing has to be done and yet, nothing can be undone, as man ages day after day. We began with the divine synchronicities, and end with the ever-knowing reality of our immortal existence. The dance of life has always been and will always be, continuing on and on, eon after eon.

# CHAPTER 9
## *The Life Balance Process for Inner Transformation*

"Holy Sage – Altar Piece"

## *The 9 Keys for a Life in Balance*

I. The First Key: Chakra Meditation and Balancing
II. The Second Key: Conquer Thy *Self*: Sacred Messages in Numbers
III. The Third Key: Surrender to Unconditional Love
IV. The Fourth Key: The *Vedic* Four Pillars
V. The Fifth Key: The Desire List
VI. The Sixth Key: The Decision Making Flow Chart: *Make Empowered Decisions*™
VII. The Seventh Key: Connect with Your Higher *Self*
VIII. The Eighth Key: Feng Shui Nine Trigrams
IX. The Ninth Key: Method for *The Life Balance Process for Inner Transformation*™

*Note: Spaces are intentionally left blank throughout this chapter for you to use and write in. Videos showing you how to use the 9 Keys are available on our website: www.indeara. com. Please refer to the "Resources" page at the back of the book for more information about them.*

## Key #1
### *Meditation: Chakra Tuning and Balancing*

- We can use sounds and *mantras* to heal and cleanse our emotional and spiritual bodies through more advanced techniques in meditation.
- If you can, sit in the traditional lotus posture with your legs folded comfortably. If this cannot be done, then just sit on a chair with your back straight. Bring your hands together in a prayer posture and bow the head slightly.
- Take deep breaths in and out, while focusing your attention at the base of the spine. Continue to breathe in through your nose as you move up the spine.
- Keep your attention focused at the point in between the eyebrows known as the third eye center.
- Relax and breathe out through the nose slowly. You can do this process for about fifteen to twenty minutes each day upon waking up, and before you go to sleep. It will help you to release toxins from the blood, and relax you.

**Key #2**
***Conquer Thy Self – Sacred Messages in Numbers***

*Sacred Messages in Numbers* is a way for us to understand who we truly are from our life experiences, from the day we were born until today, and we can even look into our future up to age one hundred. It gives a good way for a personal account of our lives, and it is like a personal inventory for each year of our life. Begin by writing down the year that you were born, and bear in mind that you were conceived nine months before you were born. The nine months before you were born were considered as a neutral space, a time for gestation and rest. Therefore, it was a neutral zone in your life. It was an in between time when you were neither in the human world nor were you completely in the spirit world. It was a time when you were growing into who you would become when you arrived on planet Earth. I will use myself as an example. The year that I was born was 1976, here is an example below:

## SACRED MESSAGES IN NUMBERS
## A PERSONAL INVENTORY - THE YEARS OF LIFE

| Creation | | 10's | 20's | 30's | 40's | 50's | 60's | 70's | 80's | 90's 100 |
|---|---|---|---|---|---|---|---|---|---|---|
| Conception Age 0 | 1976 | 1986 | 1996 | 2006 | 2016 | 2026 | 2036 | 2046 | 2056 | 2066 |
| Age 1 | 1977 | 1987 | 1997 | 2007 | 2017 | 2027 | 2037 | 2047 | 2057 | 2067 |
| Age 2 | 1978 | 1988 | 1998 | 2008 | 2018 | 2028 | 2038 | 2048 | 2058 | 2068 |
| Age 3 | 1979 | 1989 | 1999 | 2009 | 2019 | 2029 | 2039 | 2049 | 2059 | 2069 |
| Age 4 | 1980 | 1990 | 2000 | 2010 | 2020 | 2030 | 2040 | 2050 | 2060 | 2070 |
| Age 5 | 1981 | 1991 | 2001 | 2011 | 2021 | 2031 | 2041 | 2051 | 2061 | 2071 |
| Age 6 | 1982 | 1992 | 2002 | 2012 | 2022 | 2032 | 2042 | 2052 | 2062 | 2072 |
| Age 7 | 1983 | 1993 | 2003 | 2013 | 2023 | 2033 | 2043 | 2053 | 2063 | 2073 |
| Age 8 | 1984 | 1994 | 2004 | 2014 | 2024 | 2034 | 2044 | 2054 | 2064 | 2074 |
| Age 9 | 1985 | 1995 | 2005 | 2015 | 2025 | 2035 | 2045 | 2055 | 2065 | 2075 |
| Age 10 | 1986 | 1996 | 2006 | 2016 | 2026 | 2036 | 2046 | 2056 | 2066 | 2076 |

Now that you've written down the year that you were born and each decade of your life, start with your earliest memory as a child and write down your major experiences. For this step, you will need a lot of room to write about each year of your life. You should get a notebook or a journal because you will be writing the script of your life. Look for the emotion in each of your experiences, and how you felt about those experiences. These experiences hold the key to your ultimate enlightenment because when you can identify your major life lessons, you can transcend them. What you will be looking for in your life review, and the accounting of your life, is recurring and repetitive emotions and feelings. Even though you might have had ten different experiences, the life lesson may be only one thing.

For example, in my life, when I was age six Mom died, when I was age sixteen the woman who I considered as my mother passed away from breast cancer, and when I was age twenty-six, my beloved sister was brutally murdered. As a child, I did not understand why Mom died, and when I was sixteen I certainly did not understand why my favorite aunt passed away. I certainly couldn't see why I had to lose my sister at such a young age. All of these experiences were different and from a normal perspective, they look like three different experiences.

However, from a spiritual angle I experienced a loss in each and every case. So I asked myself, "What is my life lesson?" The answer was clear after my experience of enlightenment. My greatest life lesson is detachment. When you are doing your life review and going through your experiences, look for the underlying emotion and the corresponding energy, and this will help you to see the bigger picture of your life.

## SACRED MESSAGES IN NUMBERS
## A PERSONAL INVENTORY - THE YEARS OF LIFE

| Creation | 10's | 20's | 30's | 40's | 50's | 60's | 70's | 80's | 90's 100 |
|---|---|---|---|---|---|---|---|---|---|
| Conception Age 0 | | | | | | | | | |
| Age 1 | | | | | | | | | |
| Age 2 | | | | | | | | | |
| Age 3 | | | | | | | | | |
| Age 4 | | | | | | | | | |
| Age 5 | | | | | | | | | |
| Age 6 | | | | | | | | | |
| Age 7 | | | | | | | | | |
| Age 8 | | | | | | | | | |
| Age 9 | | | | | | | | | |
| Age 10 | | | | | | | | | |

**Key #3**
*Surrender to Unconditional Love – Release and Let Go*

The third key helps us to cleanse the emotional body by allowing us to accept our feelings. Remember, the Law of Accountability states that we are responsible for our thoughts, words, deeds, and actions. Therefore, the greatest chance for us to heal ourselves comes from accepting responsibility. If we can take personal responsibility for our lives, we will become empowered, enlightened beings.

In Dr. David R. Hawkins' *Map of Consciousness*, he gives a calibrated numerical value to our emotions. For example: Grief is "75" Fear is "100" Anger is "150" Forgiveness is "350" Love is "500" Joy is "540" Peace is "600" Enlightenment is "700-1000." The way to best get through our emotions is by allowing ourselves to fully experience each level and emotion.

Begin with a simple technique by allowing yourself the opportunity to let go, and do a spiritual trash removal from the body, mind, and spirit. Again, the best way to go about doing this is to get a journal or a simple notebook, and write down your feelings. For example, give yourself the opportunity and leisure of fifteen minutes to start with. Begin with today or a twenty-four hour period.

For the first two minutes, write down the things that have angered and upset you. Allow for about one to two minutes for each emotion. Then write down the things that have made you sad. Then, the next two minutes, write things that you are scared about. Then write down the things that you feel guilty about. Then, write down the things that you love about this experience.

Finding love in a difficult situation may seem impossible, but if you cannot find love in any of those situations, just accept your feelings and let them flow. This will begin the process of forgiveness. If you find it challenging to forgive, surrender the situation up to your higher *Self* and just let it go. Inner peace, bliss, and enlightenment come from our ability to unconditionally love and forgive those who might have hurt us. The Law of Allowance becomes activated with this step, and we free ourselves to experience infinite love.

**Key #4**

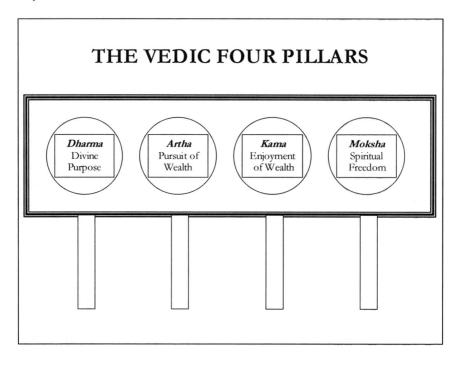

The *Vedic* Four Pillars: *dharma*, our divine purpose; *artha*, the pursuit of wealth; *kama*, the enjoyment of wealth; *moksha*, spiritual liberation and enlightenment explain the natural process of our lives. Please refer to chapter five for a detailed description and better understanding of these concepts. This step is simply understanding the natural flow and progression of a balanced lifestyle. For example, if we were to focus on *kama*, which is the enjoyment of wealth, and the pleasures of life, before *artha*, which is the pursuit of wealth, we would be indebted.

In the West, when we are young we live for fun. However, from my upbringing which is based more on the Eastern *Vedic* teachings from my grandmother, I was not advised to seek enjoyment and pleasures earlier on in life. Even my aunts and uncles gave me the option of becoming a doctor or an accountant. In the Eastern traditions, *dharma* and *artha* are extremely important for a young person. Therefore, in their late fifties, *kama* and *moksha* become a possibility. This system is very simple to understand if we ask ourselves the following questions:

- How can we experience *moksha* and enlightenment if we haven't done our purpose?
- How can we enjoy wealth if we've never pursued material abundance, and don't have enough money set aside for fun and enjoyment? *Artha* teaches us that we should save for a rainy day and for a good retirement.
- How can we ever pursue wealth that brings us inner peace, happiness, and abundance, if we don't attempt to fulfill our *dharma*? This leads us to the understanding that without *dharma* and doing our divine purpose, there can be no enlightenment.

**Key, #5**
*The Desire List*

    Our desires can be many. The best way to tap into our subconscious mind is to make a desire list. This step sounds like a simple one liner, however, I have found this one step to be the most time consuming for many people. So, you will need a notebook or a journal once again. Write down everything that you want and don't hold back.

## Key #6
### *Make Empowered Decisions™ - The Decision Making Flow Chart*

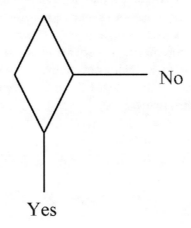

The sixth key is dependent upon the first key, and also the third key. In order for us to *Make Empowered Decisions™*, we would have to remember that our decisions impact not only our lives, but the lives of all in the entire universe. Our decisions have far-reaching consequences in the cosmic mind, and they impact our collective reality. Decisions create a ripple effect in the *prana*, which is the intelligent, divine light of consciousness. Therefore, it is imperative that we know how to *Make Empowered Decisions™*.

The first step in making an empowered decision relates to our first key, meditation, without meditation the mind is like a wild monkey that is constantly overwhelmed, overworked, and overstressed. When we make decisions from the "monkey mind," we create more stress in our lives and become disempowered. So, the first and most important step in making empowered decisions is meditation, deep relaxation, and inner peace which allow us to let go of the logical mind, and create from an empowered state of mind.

The second step to making empowered decisions is working with the Law of Accountability. Refer to key number three and learn how to surrender to unconditional love. Once those two steps are done, we can actually begin with the third step in making empowered decisions, which is the decision making flow chart above. This simply means that we have to actually "decide" in order for us to be able to make a "decision." If we decide "no" then the universe knows that we would not like to proceed, and it closes the door to all options in that particular decision. When we say "yes" and it is in alignment with our *dharma*, the entire Universal Cosmic Energy realigns itself, the Divine Laws come to our aid, and we can proceed.

When we say "yes" to a decision, and it is not in alignment with our *dharma*, then surely we should prepare for "all hell to break loose," and that leads us on the karmic wheel of existence, lifetime after lifetime; those are the times when resistance sets in, and we go against our hearts. So, to make an empowered decision means that we are either saying "yes" or "no," and we are moving in alignment with our divine purpose, and listening to our hearts. This is where we find our true *Self*; it is where we go with the flow and we experience synchronicities.

**Key #7**
*A Self Analysis*

Ask yourself the following questions:

- Do you work consistently?

- Do you use your creative faculties?

- Are you frugal and do you live on a budget?

- Do you seek the advice of financial experts before you invest your money?

- Do you try again and again to achieve success after each failure?

- Do you have credibility and integrity?

- Do you intently and persistently focus, and pursue your goals and dreams until they are manifested?

- Do you challenge yourself to accomplish small goals then aim for bigger ones, or do you overwhelm yourself with doing too much at once?

- Do you express yourself and share your ideas with others?

- Do you believe in yourself, or do you need approval from others to live your *dharma*?

- Do you make others' success part of your plan for success?

- Do you spend as much for the uplifting of spiritual work as you do for yourself?

- Do you make service, rather than money your goal?

- Are your principles and values based on truth in alignment with your heart's true desires?

- Do you live simply or do you live above your means?

- Do you look out for the good of others?

- Do you affirm thoughts of success every day?

- Do you have a plan?

- Do you set time aside for your spiritual, physical, and emotional well-being?

- Would you like to become an empowered, enlightened being?

# Key #8

## THE FENG SHUI NINE TRIGRAMS
### The 9 Areas of Our Lives &
### The Corresponding Energies and Approach for Success

| WEALTH & PROSPERITY<br>Gratitude / Gratefulness | FAME & REPUTATION<br>Honesty & Integrity | RELATIONSHIPS<br>Receptiveness /<br>Being Open Minded |
|---|---|---|
| HEALTH & FAMILY<br>Strength / Stability | *DHARMA*<br>Divine Purpose | INNER CHILD /<br>CHILDREN &<br>CREATIVITY<br>Joyfulness |
| KNOWLEDGE & SELF<br>CULTIVATION<br>Stillness / Inner Peace | CAREER<br>Courageousness | HELPFUL PEOPLE &<br>TRAVEL<br>Synchronicity<br>Going with the flow |

The following are nine areas for our lives and the corresponding energies, and emotional approach for bringing every aspect in balance:

1. Fame and Reputation – Honesty and Integrity
2. Love, Relationships, and Marriage – Being Receptive
3. Inner Child, Children and Creativity – Joyful Existence
4. Helpful People and Travel – Going with the flow or Synchronicities
5. Career – Courageousness to Live Our Divine Purpose
6. Knowledge and Self-Cultivation – Stillness of the Mind and Meditation
7. Health and Family – Strength and Stability
8. Wealth and Prosperity – Gratefulness to Give Service to Others
9. Inner Peace and Balance – Staying Centered in the Midst of Challenges

*The Feng Shui Nine Trigrams* works like a diagnosis tool. Before we can do anything with a life in balance, we would have to know where our starting point is. It has taken many steps to get to the point where we can actually evaluate our lives. A simple way to use *The Feng Shui Nine Trigrams* is to treat each area of your life as if it was positive, neutral, or negative. We can use a simple scale from one to ten to enter in the boxes.

For example, we can use "-10" as a worst-case scenario, "0" as neutral, and "+10" as the best-case scenario. So, from a scale of one to ten, you can use *The Feng Shui Nine Trigrams* method and put a number that you feel indicates where that area of your life is currently at. For example, if you feel that your career is going great, you can use "+8." If you feel that your career is stable and you've been there for a long time you can use "0." If you feel your career is not where you want it to be, and it is difficult for you, then you can use "-8." The scale depends on you and how you feel.

This process will allow you to discover your innermost self, and it will also reveal to you the answers from your logical mind, as well as the answers from your heart. In essence, you will be able to distinguish the emotions between your heart and your head. The ideal situation and answers will come from your heart. The following questions are used for the ideal situation, and a connection to your heart:

- How do you feel about yourself right now?

- How do you feel about your relationships including your friends, family, children, and professional acquaintances?

- How do you feel about your connection to your inner child, your children, and your creativity?

- How is your life flowing in regards to the helpful people around you? Do you go with the flow? Or do you resist change? If yes, why? Are you able to go on vacations? Do you experience synchronicities in your life?

- How do you feel about your career right now? Are you working just for the money, or are you living your *dharma*, which is your divine purpose?

- How much time do you spend in daily meditation? Do you set time aside for spiritual rejuvenation, relaxation, and retreats?

- How do you feel about your family right now? Are you able to forgive things in the past? Do you love your family unconditionally?

- How do you feel about your financial security, wealth, prosperity, and abundance?

The following questions are used to allow you to see the same process from your logical mind, as opposed to your heart, which is when you are in your head:

- What do you think about yourself? What do others think about you?

- What would the following people say about you: your friends, family, spouse, children, relatives, coworkers, customers, and neighbors?

- What do you think you should be doing to express your talents and creativity?

- How often do you think you should be connecting with others and meeting new people for new experiences in your life?

- Do you think you're going with the flow and divine synchronicity?

- What do you think about your career?

- Do you think that you have enough time set aside for your true *Self*, contemplation, and inner peace?

- What do you think about your health? What do you think about your family situation?

- What do you think about your financial situation?

After answering these questions you will find that when you listen to the answers that come from within, you will always find that your true *Self* resides in your heart, and the opposite holds true. When you look at the answers that come from what you think, and the logical mind, those answers will always lead you outside of your true *Self*. Remember, the pathway to your true *Self* and enlightenment will always come from within and from your heart. Your heart will never lead you on the wrong path, unlike the logical mind, who's job it is to lead you astray.

Now, if you are like me, there will be a discrepancy between the answers from the head and the heart. How you distinguish what is truth is by contemplating the answers about how you feel. The bridge between the head and heart is unconditional love, and understanding that even though our true *Self* and our logical mind may never be in agreement, we will always have the choice to *Make Empowered Decisions*™ to find the solutions for inner peace, happiness, abundance, and enlightenment.

## Key #9
### *The Life Balance Process for Inner Transformation*™

The same concept applies to all areas of our lives. We must respect time, and use it wisely to set our intentions and ideals. Time is relative. If we want to have more money, then we should value time as money. If we want more love, then we should make time for love to enter our lives. In accounting, we create a consistent system, which is like a filing cabinet, and it is a mechanism which classifies a tremendous amount of data.

I can take someone's dreams and build a blueprint for their success with *The Life Balance Process for Inner Transformation*™. It was created after I worked as an Auditor. It allows a person to see their entire life, goals, dreams, and corresponding attitudes for success, and it is a master plan for success. It gives us the ability to chart the course of our success with a definite plan. Remember, without a plan, we would not have direction in our lives.

We must have a plan, and *The Life Balance Process for Inner Transformation*™ is more than a time management system. It goes one level beyond that, and uses time as a vehicle for enlightenment. Time is eternal if we can view it from a spiritual perspective. Balance is understanding how we can utilize time wisely to achieve harmony in all areas of our lives. *The Life Balance Process for Inner Transformation*™ is different for everyone, because each and every one of us has a different goal in life; what doesn't change for everyone is the fact that we all have only twenty-four hours in a day to accomplish it.

**The first step is understanding that there are only twenty-four hours in a day.**

**Morning**
6:00 AM
7:00 AM
8:00 AM
9:00 AM
10:00 AM
11:00 AM
**Noon**
12:00 PM
1:00 PM
2:00 PM
3:00 PM
4:00 PM
5:00 PM

6:00 PM
**Evening**
7:00 PM
8:00 PM
9:00 PM
10:00 PM
11:00 PM
**Midnight**
12:00 AM
1:00 AM
2:00 AM
3:00 AM
4:00 AM
5:00 AM

**The second step is knowing that there are only seven days in a week.**

Sunday Monday Tuesday Wednesday Thursday Friday Saturday

**The third step is realizing that we have anywhere from twenty-eight to thirty-one days in a month.**

1 2 3 4 5 6 7 8 9 10 11 12 13 14 15 16 17 18 19 20 21 22 23 24 25 26 27 28 29 30 31

**The fourth step includes Key #8, and it comes from The Feng Shui Nine Trigrams, with the following corresponding nine areas of our lives.**

Which of the following nine areas of your life would you like to see in balance?

1. Fame and Reputation
2. Love, Relationships, and Marriage
3. Inner Child, Children, and Creativity
4. Helpful People and Travel
5. Career
6. Knowledge and *Self* Cultivation
7. Health and Family
8. Wealth and Prosperity
9. Inner Peace and Balance

## The fifth step includes Key #5, *the Desire List.*

Make a list of everything and anything that your heart desires. Include in that list, all of your dreams and goals. Also, make a list of your daily routine activities; even the simple things like eating breakfast, getting dressed, meditation, doing laundry, getting groceries, cleaning up the house, showering, going to the movies, sleeping, socializing and entertainment, time with friends and family, eating lunch and dinner, creating a budget and steps towards financial independence and enlightenment, working, creativity, time set aside for paying bills, investments, and finally, time set aside to create a life in balance.

## The sixth step is about the energy level, and required skills that are necessary to accomplish your desires from the step above. In the following cases, the word "energy" is used to represent thoughts, emotions, and skills:

- The energy that is required to improve our fame and reputation is that we are true to our *Self*, and we make decisions in alignment with our hearts. You can learn more about the true *Self* in chapter two.
- The energy required for us to have loving relationships is that we have to keep an open mind and be receptive.
- The energy required for us to be connected to our inner child, children, and creativity, is that we feel joyous.
- The energy required for us to meet helpful people, and travel, is that we should be open to synchronicities, and go with the flow.
- The energy required for us to have a good career is that we must be courageous.
- The energy required for knowledge and self cultivation is that we spend time alone in meditation.
- The energy required for us to have good health and good family relations is strength and stability.
- The energy required for us to have wealth and prosperity is that we focus on being grateful for the opportunity to be of service to others.
- The energy that is required for us to be in balance and experience inner peace is that we should be able to stay centered in the midst of challenges.

## A SUMMARY OF THE 9 KEYS FOR A LIFE IN BALANCE

We begin now with a concise understanding of the **Nine Keys for a Life in Balance**. In the first key, we do a **Meditation** so that we can unblock the passageways within our physical, emotional, and spiritual bodies. We open the invisible energy centers in the body called *chakras*. We connect to our super-conscious state of existence, and enter into the cosmic stream of intelligent life energy. We understand in the first key, through meditation, that our body is governed by our mind, and therefore we begin to create our reality filled with inner peace, abundance, prosperity, and enlightenment.

The second key is called **Sacred Messages in Numbers**, and in this key we learn the true meaning of accountability. We understand our lives with a personal inventory for each year that we have lived. In order for us to live the life we would like, in perfect harmony with our true *Self*, we must have a starting place, and an account of who we are is the best place to begin. **Sacred Messages in Numbers** allows us to see our life from the day we were born, until the day we exit the consciousness of the body. It paves the way for understanding our past experiences, our karma, and our life lessons, and leads us to key number three.

In the third key, we learn how to **Surrender to Unconditional Love** by letting go of negative emotions, and we realize that everything is a life lesson. We learn how to process and transform negativity into enlightenment; by understanding that our emotions and thoughts not only have a frequency, but they also have a magnitude of energy which can be measured and calibrated, according to Dr. David R. Hawkins in his Map of Consciousness. We can transform anger, sadness, the things we're afraid of, our regrets, and our fears to the state of enlightenment. The second key is like a spiritual, physical, and emotional trash removal. We must let go of the things that no longer serve us to move into the fourth key.

The fourth key is **The Vedic Four Pillars:** *dharma*, our divine purpose; *artha*, the pursuit of wealth; *kama*, the enjoyment of wealth; and *moksha*, spiritual liberation and enlightenment. If our society can adopt this philosophy of each one of us first realizing our divine purpose early in our education, through a school system which supports us being of service to each other, naturally we would be able to acquire wealth in alignment with our divine purpose. Therefore, we would be happy in our jobs and careers that are fulfilling our life's purpose. We would still be acquiring wealth; however, we would not be going against our hearts and the natural, ecological systems and Spiritual Universal Laws. This stage usually goes from childhood to our early thirties.

For the most part, *artha* should be from the time we finish our education to our mid to early thirties into our late forties; thereby, the next phase, *kama*, and the enjoyment of our lives would be the natural unfolding of having lived a life in alignment with our divine purpose, and having more than enough abundance to enjoy mid-life.

*Moksha* is much more of a challenge for us in the West than in the East because Eastern societies teach from an early age the importance of detachment from a materialistic view of life; as opposed to in the West, where we tend to be much more focused on materialism even after our mid-fifties to late seventies. In ancient times, holy men and women would give up all of their attachments and live in a hermitage. My great grandfather was such a man.

My father tells me the story that one day he said to my great grandmother, and the rest of the family, "I'm leaving now," and he went to live in the forests of South America. Then one day, as if out of nowhere, he materialized his physical body, and said to my great grandmother, "I will discard my physical body and leave it a few hundred yards away from the house. Will you please make the arrangements for my funeral?" In this type of an upbringing, we can understand the process of dying as merely a transition into our immortal bodies. Therefore, seeking enlightenment is a natural process, and quite an ecstatic, blissful, and enjoyable one.

The fourth key leads us to an understanding of the fifth key by making a **Desire List**. In order for us to realize how much energy we are spending in our efforts to pursue the objects of our desire, it would only seem proper to make an account of, and a list of all things that we want. By contemplating our **Desire List**, we can learn to become focused, efficient, and successful in realizing our dreams. If we can remember to go after the things we want, one thing at a time, one step at a time, and one choice at a time, then we can go on to the sixth key, where we **Make Empowered Decisions™**.

We can only **Make Empowered Decisions™** from the higher mind and a state of unconditional love and acceptance. Remember, we experience our reality based on the emotion with which we create. For example, if we create the things we desire from a state of anger, we would experience frustration, difficulties, and anger when we receive our desired outcome, and that would be disempowering. To *Make Empowered Decisions™*, we must first bring our minds in alignment with our higher *Self*, and that leads us to the seventh key.

The seventh key is **Connecting with Our Higher Self**. From my personal experience, I have found it virtually impossible to get into the supreme conscious state of existence without first connecting with a higher being. This higher being can be anyone that you choose. For example, it can be the Buddha, Jesus Christ, The Goddess *Lakshmi*, The Great Masters, or

The Divine Mother Quan Yin, and the list can go on and on. The key here is to choose the being, or beings who inspire you to reach for an enlightened existence which ends all of your suffering.

Personally, I have been able to connect with, beings from both the East and West, Native Americans, the Great Buddhas, and the Ascended Masters. I am able to have a telepathic link and connection to many of the Archangels and Spiritual Beings. I have intensified and expanded my spiritual awareness and consciousness through the use of *mantras*, and the teachings of the *Vedas*. The seventh key has allowed me at times, to live an almost perfect existence and a *Life in Balance*, and this leads us to the eighth key.

The **Feng Shui Nine Trigrams Method** came to me after many years of spiritual practice and meditation. When I was able to learn from these higher beings, their teachings were so profound. I couldn't help but ask, "How will I transfer all of this divine knowledge to help others?" The answer came to me that I should not be reinventing the wheel, but rather, I should use existing systems that have been in use and practiced for millennia.

**The Feng Shui Nine Trigrams** became an ideal self analysis and evaluation tool because it encompassed all areas of a human being's life. In order for us to be in balance, we need to have a good relationship with ourselves first, then our friends, associates, and partners. We need a connection to our sense of joy and happiness by experiencing the continuity of life through the divine flow of synchronicities. We also have to share our music and our soul's song with everyone.

Once we can sing our divine tunes, and take the time for contemplation, we can experience inner peace. With our newfound peace, it would only be wise to enjoy good health, long life, and stability with our family ties. Last but not least, what would be the point of all of these great things and accomplishments if we could not afford them? Therefore, we should remember the Divine Laws of Prosperity, and be generous and charitable in the pursuit of and acquisition of wealth, and the material things we need to enjoy our lives and this leads us to the ninth and final key.

The ninth key came after almost a decade of practicing the spiritual and universal principles. I created **The Life Balance Process for Inner Transformation™** with the idea that we would be able to bring together these amazing and sophisticated, detailed ideas in one place, so that we can easily reflect on an account of our entire life with our body, mind, spirit, and our goals and dreams. I hope that you have enjoyed creating the cosmic accounting blueprint for your soul's immortal and everlasting happiness. In the spirit of enlightenment, I wish you much success on your path back to reclaiming divinity within, and enjoying a life in balance.

# Resources

## Website: www.indeara.com

Visit us for a *free meditation video*. Also, the following videos showing you *The Life Balance Process for Inner Transformation*™ are available on our website:

*Key #1* – Introduction to *Chakra* Meditation and Balancing
*Key #2* – Sacred Messages in Numbers
*Key #3* – Surrender to Unconditional Love: The Process of Forgiveness
Awakening of Kundalini Energy
*Mantras* for Beginners – Lord Ganesha
Intro to Synchronized Accounting Seminar

## Connect With Us On Social Media

We would like to invite you to join our online enlightened community to share your ideas with us.

**Blog:**
www.synchrodharma.wordpress.com

**Youtube Channels:**
www.youtube.com/synchrodharma
www.youtube.com/cosmicaccounting

**Facebook:**
www.facebook.com/Indeara.Hanoomansingh

**Twitter:**
www.twitter.com/indeara333

**Myspace:**
www.myspace.com/550711705 -- Indeara

# Bibliography

Andrews, Ted. *Animal-Wise*. Jackson: Dragonhawk Publishing, 1999.

Dinshah, Darius. *Let There Be Light*. Malaga: Dinshah Health Society, 1996.

Dongo, Tom & Bradshaw, Linda. *Merging Dimensions*. Sedona: Hummingbird Publishing, 1995.

Gandhi, Mahatma Mohandus Karamchand. *Peace: The Words and Inspiration of Mahatma Gandhi*. Auckland, NZ: PQ Blackwell Limited, 2007.

Giri, Jnanavatar Swami Sri Yukteswar. *The Holy Science*. Los Angeles: International Publications Council of SELF-REALIZATION FELLOWSHIP, 1990.

Hawkins, David R. *Power vs. Force*. Carlsbad: Hay House Publishing Inc., 2002.

Krishnamurti, J. *Meeting Life*. New York: HarperCollins Publishers, 1991.

Lyons, Chief Oren. *Voice of Indigenous Peoples*. Santa Fe: Clear Light Publishers, 1994.

Myss, Caroline. *Sacred Contracts: Awakening Your Divine Potential*. New York: Harmony Books, 2001.

Orman, Suze. *The Courage to Be Rich*. New York: The Penguin Group, 2002.

Ponder, Catherine. *The Millionaires of Genesis*. Camarillo: DeVross & Company, 1976.

Ruiz, Don Miguel. *The Four Agreements*. San Rafael: Amber-Allen Publishing, Inc., 1997.

Tzu, Lao. *Tao Teh Ching: Translated by John C. H. Wu*. New York: St. John's University Press, 1961.

Yogananda, Paramhansa. *Autobiography of a Yogi*. New York: The Philosophical Library, Inc., 1946.

Yogananda, Paramhansa. *Be A Smile Millionaire* CD. Self-Realization Fellowship, 1997.

Yogananda, Paramhansa. *The Essence of the Bhagavad Gita Explained by Paramhansa Yogananda*. Nevada City: Crystal Clarity Publishers, 2006.

Yogananda, Paramhansa. *How to Be a Success*. Nevada City: Crystal Clarity Publishers, 2008.

# Recommended Books, DVDS, and Movies

**Recommended Books**

*You Can Heal Your Life* by Louise L. Hay, Hay House Inc.
*The One Minute Millionaire* by Mark Victor Hansen & Robert G. Allen, Three Rivers Press.
*The Sedona Method,* by Hale Dwoskin, Sedona Press.
*The Millionaires of Genesis* by Catherine Ponder, DeVross & Company.

**Recommended DVDs**

*Babaji's Kriya Hatha Yoga,* DVD. Babaji's Kriya Yoga Publications.
*The Secret,* DVD. TS Production LLC.

**Recommended Movies**

*Avatar,* 20$^{th}$ Century Fox, directed by James Cameron.
*Koyaanisqatsi,* MGM Home Entertainment, directed by Godffrey Reggio.
*Dumb and Dumber,* New Line Cinema, directed by Peter and Bobby Farrelly.
*What the Bleep Do We Know?* 20$^{th}$ Century Fox, directed by Mark Vicente, Betsy Chasse, and William Arntz.

# ABOUT THE AUTHOR

**Indeara** is a metaphysical teacher and intuitive business consultant. She has a bachelor's degree in accounting from the City University of New York, QC. After many years of spiritual experiences, Indeara transcended to an enlightened consciousness. She inspires many people in her Peace Paradise wellness retreats, and meditation classes. Her dream is to create a Global Enlightened Business Network™, where you can "connect with your soul's divine purpose." Visit her website at www.indeara.com.

Photo Credits Nicole Kubrock

# Notes

# Notes

# Notes

# Notes

# Notes

# Notes

CPSIA information can be obtained at www.ICGtesting.com
Printed in the USA
LVOW042029210512